ENGLISH FURNITURE

1660-1714
From Charles II to Queen Anne

Pair of chairs (1705-15), black and gold japanned frames with later cut velvet upholstery. From a large suite made for the Duke of Leeds and originally installed at Kiveton Park, Yorkshire (completed 1704).

ENGLISH FURNITURE

1660-1714
From Charles II to Queen Anne

Adam Bowett

ANTIQUE COLLECTORS' CLUB

ISBN 1 85149 399 9

British Library Cataloguing-in-Publication Data
A catalogue record for this book is available from the British Library

Origination by Antique Collectors' Club, Woodbridge, England
Printed and bound in Italy

THE ANTIQUE COLLECTORS' CLUB

The Antique Collectors' Club was formed in 1966 and quickly grew to a five figure membership spread throughout the world. It publishes the only independently run monthly antiques magazine, *Antique Collecting*, which caters for those collectors who are interested in widening their knowledge of antiques, both by greater awareness of quality and by discussion of the factors which influence the price that is likely to be asked. The Antique Collectors' Club pioneered the provision of information on prices for collectors and the magazine still leads in the provision of detailed articles on a variety of subjects.

It was in response to the enormous demand for information on 'what to pay' that the price guide series was introduced in 1968 with the first edition of *The Price Guide to Antique Furniture* (completely revised 1978 and 1989), a book which broke new ground by illustrating the more common types of antique furniture, the sort that collectors could buy in shops and at auctions rather than the rare museum pieces which had previously been used (and still to a large extent are used) to make up the limited amount of illustrations in books published by commercial publishers. Many other price guides have followed, all copiously illustrated, and greatly appreciated by collectors for the valuable information they contain, quite apart from prices. The Price Guide Series heralded the publication of many standard works of reference on art and antiques. *The Dictionary of British Art* (now in six volumes), *The Pictorial Dictionary of British 19th Century Furniture Design, Oak Furniture* and *Early English Clocks* were followed by many deeply researched reference works such as *The Directory of Gold and Silversmiths,* providing new information. Many of these books are now accepted as the standard work of reference on their subject.

The Antique Collectors' Club has widened its list to include books on gardens and architecture. All the Club's publications are available through bookshops world wide and a full catalogue of all these titles is available free of charge from the addresses below.

Club membership, open to all collectors, costs little. Members receive free of charge *Antique Collecting*, the Club's magazine (published ten times a year), which contains well-illustrated articles dealing with the practical aspects of collecting not normally dealt with by magazines. Prices, features of value, investment potential, fakes and forgeries are all given prominence in the magazine.

Among other facilities available to members are private buying and selling facilities and the opportunity to meet other collectors at their local antique collectors' clubs. There are over eighty in Britain and more than a dozen overseas. Members may also buy the Club's publications at special pre-publication prices.

As its motto implies, the Club is an organisation designed to help collectors get the most out of their hobby: it is informal and friendly and gives enormous enjoyment to all concerned.

For Collectors — By Collectors — About Collecting

ANTIQUE COLLECTORS' CLUB
Sandy Lane, Old Martlesham,
Woodbridge, Suffolk IP12 4SD, UK
Tel: 01394 389950 Fax: 01394 389999
Email: sales@antique-acc.com
Website: www.antique-acc.com
or
Market Street Industrial Park
Wappingers' Falls, NY 12590, USA
Tel: 845 297 0003 Fax: 845 297 0068
Email: info@antiquecc.com
Website: www.antiquecc.com

CONTENTS

For my mother and father

ACKNOWLEDGEMENTS

My biggest single debt of gratitude is to the staff at the many houses, museums and galleries whose furniture forms the core of this book. I have everywhere met with forbearance and interest despite the inevitable nuisance caused by my visits. Similarly, documentary research would have been impossible without the help of many conscientious men and women employed by the British Library, the Corporation of London Record Office, the Guildhall Library, Public Record Office and local record offices. These collections and their staff are a resource beyond price, whose value is reaffirmed with every unique and irreplaceable document they entrust to our hands. I am also particularly indebted to those scholars and administrators responsible for the care of our major national furniture collections – Sebastian Edwards for Historic Royal Palaces, Simon Jervis for The National Trust, Dr. Tessa Murdoch for the Victoria and Albert Museum, Hugh Roberts for the Royal Collection and Anthony Wells-Cole for Leeds City Art Galleries. One cannot write a book such as this without seeing and handling the objects one writes about, and it has been a great privilege to be allowed to examine the historic furniture held in these collections.

Other individuals who in their various ways and respective capacities have helped me enormously include; Bruce Bailey, Robert Bradley, Peter Brown, Clare Browne, The Duke of Buccleuch, Roger Carr-Whitworth, Frances Collard, Lucinda Compton, Edward Clive, Jon Culverhouse, Peter Day, Viscount De Lisle, David Dewing, Simon Feingold, Maria Flemington, Ian Fraser, Kate Hay, Peter Holmes, Eleanor John, Polly Legg, Laurie Lindey, James Lomax, Rupert McBain, Daniel Morris, Margaret Mullardie, Tim Phelps, James Rothwell, Christopher Claxton Stevens, William Vincent, Christopher Wilk, Robin Harcourt-Williams and James Yorke. In this context I would particularly like to mention Michael Legg, whose unrivalled understanding of historic cabinetmaking has taught me an entirely new way of looking at furniture. Without his generous help this book would be greatly impoverished. Finally, I cannot forget the late and much missed Christopher Gilbert, who suggested I write the book, and the late John Steel, who was rash enough to commission it. I have been supported throughout by the confidence of my publisher, Diana Steel, and by the patience and forbearance of my editor, Primrose Elliott.

Notwithstanding all the foregoing, I should emphasise that the opinions expressed in this book are my own, unless otherwise stated, and any errors of fact or omission are mine alone.

Chapter One
THE RESTORATION

Plate 1:1. Charles II. State
portrait by John Michael Wright
(1617-1700). This painting emphasises
the huge symbolic and financial
importance of fabrics in the late 17th
century. Joinery and cabinet-work, by
contrast, were relatively cheap.

WINDSOR CASTLE.
THE ROYAL COLLECTION, ©2002,
HER MAJESTY QUEEN ELIZABETH II

1. Macaulay (1849, edn., 1953), p. 125.
2. Macquoid (1905), pp. 4-5, cites the
inventory of the Countess of Warwick, which
described apartments replete with satin, silk
and velvet, as evidence of luxurious living
under the Commonwealth.
3. Beard (1996), p. 83.
4. These are filed under two classes LC 5 (Lord
Chamberlain's warrants) and LC 9
(Tradesmen's bills).

The court style of Charles II

The year 1660 has long been regarded as marking the beginning of modern English furniture making. Like most generalisations this sweeping idea greatly oversimplifies a complex subject, but it has more than a kernel of truth at its heart. The Restoration of Charles II to the English and Scottish thrones was not only a momentous political event, but also represented a decisive cultural shift whose ramifications extended to all the fine and applied arts, including furniture making (1:1). This was the moment when England turned its back on Puritan republicanism, which had left it politically and culturally isolated for two decades, and re-entered the mainstream of European artistic intercourse.

In the past, the contrast between England before and after 1660 has perhaps been overplayed by furniture historians. Oft-quoted extracts from the diaries of courtiers such as John Evelyn dwell on the public euphoria that accompanied the king's return and contrast it with the supposedly joyless Commonwealth that preceded it. Popular interpretations also lean towards a didactic view of history, which contrasts grim, thin-lipped Puritans ('the sad coloured dress, the sour look, the straight hair, the nasal whine')[1] with loyal, brave, devil-may-care Cavaliers. In the same vein, 'Cromwellian' furniture is characterised as heavy, utilitarian and uncomfortable – leather-seated chairs, 'monks' benches' and crudely made oak chests – whereas Carolean furniture is gay, colourful and modern. These are mere caricatures and one finds little evidence to bear them out in surviving inventories of the period.[2]

On the other hand, we should not minimise the very real impact of the king's return on England's decorative arts. The power of the Royal purse, exercised through the Lord Chamberlain's office, to stimulate every branch of furniture making was enormous. In January 1662 the King's Upholsterer, Robert Morris, submitted a petition claiming to have supplied His Majesty's Wardrobe with nearly ten thousand pounds' worth of goods, and this all since May 1660.[3] The rebuilding and furnishing of the Royal Palaces continued wholesale for most of Charles' reign, employing thousands of craftsmen and women and filling the purses of suppliers of every commodity from rich Oriental silks to writing paper and close-stools. The Lord Chamberlain's accounts, which were meticulously kept and survive almost complete in the Public Record Office, record the manufacture and delivery of dozens of State Beds, hundreds of looking glasses, tables and pairs of stands, scores of chests and dining tables, and literally thousands of chairs, stools and couches.[4]

As the king set new standards in conspicuous consumption, he also redefined the taste of the English court and nobility. At heart he was always a Francophile, both by personal inclination and political conviction. His mother, Henrietta Maria, was French, and this filial bond was greatly strengthened during a decade of exile in France following his father's execution in 1649. In the French king, Louis XIV, Charles beheld the exemplar of a modern monarch, and if Parliament would not allow him the same untramelled political power enjoyed by Louis, he could at least

Plate 1:2. State bed (c.1673), upholstered in gold silk embellished with gold and silver thread and originally lined with cherry coloured satin. This is probably French and might be one of the six beds brought to England in 1672-3 by Jean Peyrard, upholsterer to Louis XIV. The overall shape is slightly less severe than most 'French' beds of the period. Note how the low, shaped headboard follows the shape of contemporary mirror crestings. The carved 'lyons feet' for the posts are referred to in numerous bills of the period. KNOLE, NATIONAL TRUST PHOTOGRAPHIC LIBRARY/ANDREAS VON EINSIEDEL

Plate 1:3. 'French' chair (1665-1675). Walnut frame with later needlework upholstery. The characteristic boxy shape of the typical 'French' chair is well illustrated in this frontal view. In this case the chair is probably French rather than English. It has a high fore-rail and no rear stretcher, and the arms are straight with blocked and turned terminals. The feet have been replaced.
TENNANTS

emulate the appearance of it through the furnishing and decoration of his court. Thus France, the dominant political and cultural power in Europe, set the style of the English court, and this is evident from the very first years of Charles' reign. It is significant that, despite the presence of Englishmen such as John Baker and Robert Morris in official positions (the former as 'Upholsterer' to the king until his death in 1663, the latter as Royal Upholsterer Extraordinary in 1660-1), it was Frenchmen who virtually monopolised upholstery work for the Royal Palaces from 1660 onwards.

First among these was John Casbert, who, together with his son, succeeded John Baker as royal upholsterer in 1663. Casbert was almost certainly a French emigré; even before his official appointment Casbert was working almost exclusively for the crown, and among the very first of his bills is one for altering a bed 'bought by his Matie of a Frenchman' (1661).[5] The 'French' bed was a type adopted throughout Europe and remained popular until the end of the seventeenth century.[6] Its severe, box-like shape, relieved only by a plumed finial or 'cup' at each corner, was offset by the extreme luxury of the fabrics used for its curtains, valances and counterpane. 'French bedsteads' feature prominently in bills for furnishings ordered during the 1660s and early 1670s and as well as these Charles bought no less than six State beds directly from France, all supplied by Jean Peyrard, upholsterer to Louis XIV.[7] One of these, made for the king's brother James, Duke of York, survives at Knole in Kent (1:2).

As the centrepiece of every suite of royal apartments, the French State bed set the tone for the whole. It was almost always supplied with chairs and stools *en suite,* and bills for 'French' chairs and stools also feature prominently in the Lord Chamberlain's accounts. During the 1660s these, like the beds, combine a severe, rectilinear form with rich upholstery of silk damask or velvet (1:3), but from c.1670 onwards new, more curvaceous forms were introduced, with dished backs and downcurved arms (see the elbow chair on the left-hand side of 1:2). The stylistic development of English chairs will be discussed in more detail in subsequent chapters, but it is worth making a general point here. Although almost every stylistic innovation in upholstered seat furniture originated in Paris, it rarely made the transition to England without modification. This was partly due to the pragmatic traditions of English joinery, which ensured, for instance, that almost all English chairs retained a rear stretcher even when Parisian fashion dictated otherwise. But it also reflects singular prejudices in interpreting new forms. Thus the English 'horsebone' and the French 'os de mouton' leg probably derive from the same source (see Chapter Three), but the English version is unmistakably different from the French.

Another French innovation which few fashionable apartments lacked was the ensemble of a table and pair of candlestands, often with a mirror *en suite,* which modern scholars have coined the 'triad'. If the Lord Chamberlain's accounts are an accurate reflection of the general trend, then the 'triad' was the most numerous single product of the cabinet-maker's workshop, but few matched the magnificence of that shown in 1:4. Most were modest affairs in walnut or olivewood, but their presence in so many domestic inventories demonstrates their extraordinary popularity at many social and economic levels. The most important new introduction, in terms of its long-term impact on English furniture-making, was undoubtedly the cabinet and its writing variant, the fall-front *scriptor* (escritoire). As we shall see in the following chapter, English cabinets were based initially on French models and most of the decorative techniques, such as floral marquetry, also emanated from France. But English cabinet-makers soon developed distinctly English forms which conform to a uniquely English typology. The techniques employed in the making of cabinets also

---

5. Beard and Gilbert (1986), p. 149; Beard (1996), p. 83.
6. Thornton (1978), pp. 160-166.7. Beard (1996), p. 91, figs 49-50.
7. Beard (1996), p. 91.

Plate 1:4. 'Triad' (c.1670-05). This splendid suite was supplied to Hopetoun House, near Edinburgh, and is tentatively attributed to the Huguenot émigré John Guilbaud. It is carved, gilt and japanned, although the floral decoration is European rather than Oriental in style.

HOPETOUN HOUSE

Plate 1:5. Ham House, Middlesex, south front. The new range built by the Duke and Duchess of Lauderdale between 1672 and 1674 fills the space between the projecting bays of c.1610. It created two suites of rooms on the ground floor, extending in enfilade from the centre in the French manner, and another suite of apartments on the floor above. Note the new style sash windows.

HAM HOUSE, NATIONAL TRUST PHOTO-GRAPHIC LIBRARY/WILLIAM R. DAVIS

Plate 1: 6. Ham House, Middlesex, plan of the ground floor in the early 1670s showing the two almost symmetrical apartments made for the Duke and Duchess. 1 – Marble Dining Room; 2 – dressing room (right), withdrawing chamber (left); 3 – bedchamber; 4 – closet.

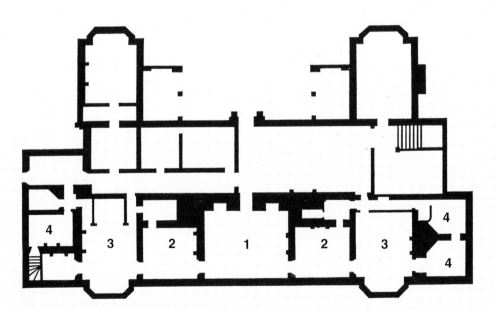

extended to the manufacture of numerous other furniture forms, such as chests of drawers, candlestands, mirror frames and tables. Thus, although the demand for cabinets was primarily an expression of fashionable taste, and ownership of them was restricted to relatively few people, the changes in methods and materials it entailed had repercussions for the whole furniture-making industry.

The king's taste set the tone for the Restoration court as a whole and rampant Francophilia is evident from John Evelyn's description of the Duchess of Portsmouth's apartments in 1683:

> …that which ingag'd my curiositie, was the rich and splendid furniture of this woman's Appartment, now twice or thrice puld downe, and rebuilt… Here I saw the new fabrique of French Tapissry, for design, tendernesse of work and incomparable imitation of the best paintings, beyond any thing, I had ever beheld: some pieces had Versailles, St Germans and other Palaces of the French King with Huntings, figures and Landscips, Exotique fowle and all to the life rarely don: Then for Japon Cabinets, Skreenes, Pendule Clocks, huge Vasas of wrought plate, Tables, Stands, Chimney furniture, Sconces… Surfeiting of this I went home to my poore, but quiet Villa.[8]

The extent to which the court's lead was taken up by the wider nobility naturally varied according to circumstances and personal inclination, but the luxurious French style was particularly favoured among the small group of nobles who formed Charles' inner circle of government. Here is John Evelyn again, commenting on a visit to the Countess of Arlington in 1673:

> She carried us up into her new dressing room at Goring House, where was a bed, two glasses, silver jars, and vases, cabinets, and other so rich furniture as I had seldom seen; to this excess of superfluity were we now arrived, and that not only at Court, but almost universally, even to wantonness and profusion.[9]

Plate 1:7. Boughton House, Northamptonshire. The 'English Versailles', built around a medieval core by Ralph Montagu in the late 1680s and 1690s. The design of the main block is taken directly from French architectural engravings.
BOUGHTON HOUSE
THE DUKE OF BUCCLEUCH

8. Evelyn, *Diary,* 4 October 1683.
9. Evelyn, *Diary,* 17 October 1673.

Plate 1:8. Belton House, Lincolnshire (1684-88). Built by Sir John Brownlow between 1684 and 1688, this is more typical of the English style and follows on from the sort of houses built by John Webb and Sir Roger Pratt in the 1650s. The design lent itself much more easily to a domestic scale of living.

Plate 1:9. Belton House, plan of the *piano nobile* or principal floor. The compact arrangement, having suites of rooms grouped around the saloon and hall, is typical of the period and persisted into the 18th century. 1 – Marble Hall; 2 – Saloon; 3 – Drawing Room; 4 – Ante Room; 5 – Chapel; 6 – Bedchamber; 7 – Dining Room; 8 – Kitchen(?).

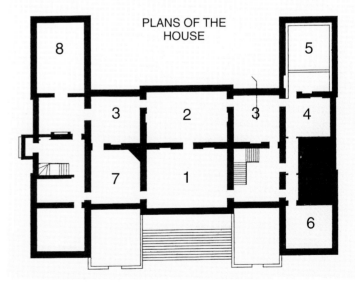

PLANS OF THE HOUSE

The Countess was the wife of Henry Bennet, Earl of Arlington and one of Charles' closest political allies. He was a member of the notorious 'Cabal', a handful of powerful nobles who dominated Charles' government from 1667 to 1674. He was strongly pro-French, an instigator of the disastrous policy which took England into alliance with France in 1670 and war against Holland in 1672.

A similarly extravagant taste was evident in the apartments of another Cabal member, the Duke of Lauderdale. Lauderdale acquired Ham House in Middlesex by marrying Elizabeth, Countess Dysart, in 1672. After their marriage the Lauderdales set about modernising Ham in grand style (1:5 and 1:6). They added an entire range of rooms along the back of the house, creating twin suites for the Duke and Duchess arranged in enfilade in the French manner, either side of a central reception room. Above was another range of State Apartments intended for the use of the Queen, should she ever favour the Lauderdales with a visit. The inventories of Ham, taken in 1677, 1679 and 1683, are among the fullest to survive and together constitute one of the most important primary sources used for this book.[10] They describe in wonderful detail a Carolean house furnished almost in regal style.

The most striking feature of the furnishings at Ham, apart from their quantity, was the range and quality of materials used. The fabrics were rich and many were imported – silk damask, velvet, satin, morella, sarsnet and 'Indian silk'.[11] The wooden furniture was veneered with walnut, ebony, olive, cedar, princeswood and tortoiseshell. Much of it was inlaid with marquetry and some was 'garnished' with silver. The few non-upholstered chairs were either caned or japanned and the walls were either hung with rich cloths or painted to simulate marble and exotic woods. Some floors were inlaid, the chimneypieces were carved wood or marble. The sheer richness of colour, texture and form is something which it is very difficult for the modern reader to appreciate and, even though many of Ham's rooms survive in a remarkable state of preservation, the intervening years have taken their toll. The muted colours, time-worn fabrics and patinated furniture are like a sloughed skin, complete, ostensibly unchanged, but bereft of their vital spark.

Some courtiers had their own social, commercial and political connections with the Continent and so had opportunities to acquaint themselves directly with the latest stylistic developments in Paris and elsewhere. One such was Ralph Montagu, who on several occasions acted as Charles II's envoy to Louis XIV. Montagu was thoroughly imbued with and, indeed, captivated by French style. His houses at Bloomsbury (London) and Boughton (Northamptonshire) were built in the French manner and furnished almost entirely in the French taste, in large measure by French craftsmen (1:7).[12]

However, the fact that much scholarly attention has recently been devoted to prodigy houses like Ham and Boughton has tended to highlight the influence of France, but such undiluted Francophilia, though notable as an expression of political and artistic sympathy at the highest level, was perhaps less common in the country at large. More typical of the landowning classes was a house like Belton in Lincolnshire, built for Sir John Brownlow in the English classical tradition of John Webb and Sir Roger Pratt (1:8). It had a compact plan, eschewing the long, French-style enfilade of Ham, Boughton and Petworth in favour of suites of rooms grouped around a central hall and saloon (1:9). When the house was completed in 1688, an inventory of its contents was taken, which shows us the house as it was newly furnished. Sir John was a rich man, whose advantageous marriage in 1676 had netted him some £6,000 per annum. His furnishing style was naturally modern, rich and comfortable, but nothing like so rich as Ham. The entrance hall, hung with twenty-eight paintings of royalty, contained no movable furniture other than twelve rush-seated 'Dutch' armchairs.[13] In the saloon or Great Parlour were 'two very large seeing glasses', probably on the window piers, and certainly the most expensive items of furniture in the room. Beneath each glass was a japanned table, with three crimson sarsnet curtains to the windows themselves. The walls were panelled in plain, bolection-moulded oak and hung with paintings. In each side-wall was a marble fireplace with a carved wooden overmantel and flanking these were architectural doorcases, the doors providing access to and from adjoining rooms. One can see that once the windows, doors and fireplaces are accounted for, there was very little wall space left for furniture and, with the exception of the japanned pier tables, this was occupied by eighteen rush-seated chairs.

10. Thornton and Tomlin (1980).
11. Damask – a silk cloth with a figured surface; velvet – a silk cloth with raised pile; satin – a silk cloth with a smooth, shiny surface; sarsnet – a thin, diaphanous silk; morella – a type of mohair, produced from the hair of the Angora goat.
12. Jackson-Stops (1992), pp. 57-65.
13. Lincoln Record Office, Belton Inventory, 8 November 1688.

The rather static arrangement of the hall and saloon at Belton is very typical and reflects the formality of the 'public' or 'parade' areas in fashionable houses. As one progressed into the more private areas, the furnishing became both more comfortable and more intimate. Thus the drawing rooms to either side of the saloon were furnished in silk and velvet, as were the bedchambers beyond them. As one might expect in a newly built house, most of the furnishings were of the latest type – longcase clocks, looking-glasses, gilt and japanned tables, and the ubiquitous 'triads'. On the other hand, the sheer princely luxury of Ham – inlaid marble, princeswood cabinets and lacquer screens – is absent.

Whereas Belton was newly built, Lyme Park in Cheshire was an Elizabethan mansion, partially refurbished by its owner Richard Legh in the 1670s. The inventory taken on Legh's death in 1687 reveals a rather rambling house, comfortably appointed with a mixture of fashionable and traditional furnishings. Few rooms were without a 'Glasse, Tables & Stands'. There were also japanned cabinets and screens, caned chairs, 'folding' dining tables of cedar, and quite a number of silk and velvet upholstered chairs. On the other hand there were curtains of 'Kederminster' (Kidderminster wool), 'dimity' (a stout cotton cloth) and 'paragon' (a woollen cloth), while Richard Legh himself slept in an old-fashioned 'worked' (embroidered) bed, perhaps of what is now called crewel-work.[14] Legh had close contacts with the house of Stuart, particularly with the Duke of York (later James II), but he was a landowner, not a politician. His extensive estates lay mainly in Cheshire and Lancashire and one gets the impression that this was where his true allegiances remained. Even if he could afford it, the princely style of Ham or Boughton was not for him.

Across the Pennines a modern but sparse interior is recorded in the 1688 inventory of New Lodge, Beverley, near Hull, the country seat of Michael Warton. On the walls of the entrance hall were '12 Ceaser heads in gilt frames' and a landscape painting over the fireplace. The only furniture was '12 oake chairs painted blue'. The drawing room contained ten caned chairs, two pieces of tapestry on the walls, a landscape painting over the fire and an iron fireback. Another drawing room, perhaps more frequently used, was more fully furnished, with eighteen caned chairs, a table and stands of cedar wood with a looking glass over, a leather screen, two tapestry hangings and white curtains at the windows. Michael Warton was not a poor man, far from it; he had the reputation of being 'the richest man, for to be a gentleman only, that was in all England, for he was worth fifteen thousand a year'.[15] But the furnishing style is curiously reticent, with nothing conspicuous or showy about it. The impression is similar to the well-ordered interiors depicted in contemporary Dutch paintings, very different from the courtier's apartments described by John Evelyn, and different again from the comfortable, rich style of Belton or Lyme.

This handful of inventories, all rich in content but varied in geographical location and social class, illustrates an important point, which is that the Restoration style is not necessarily a homogenous entity. Even among the wealthiest ten or fifteen per cent of people, Restoration interiors were as varied as money, class, political and religious affiliations and personal taste could make them. Hence the 'Restoration style' is identified not so much by a unified textbook approach to interior décor as by the presence of specific 'marker goods' which characterise the period – cabinets and scriptors, tables, stands and looking-glasses, lacquer and japanned ware, caned chairs. Later in this chapter we shall see how these 'marker goods' can be found percolating down the social scale, so that even relatively humble households manifested at least some elements of high-style Restoration taste.

The influence of the Orient

Apart from the French tapestries, the thing that struck John Evelyn most forcibly about the Duchess of Portsmouth's apartments was the profusion of Oriental lacquerware, 'Japon' cabinets and screens in particular (1:10). Although lacquerware crops up occasionally in English inventories from 1600 onwards, it was not until after the Restoration that it became common. This was partly due to the general increase in seaborne trade from 1660 onwards, but there is no doubt that the Bullion Act of 1663 also had a significant impact. Prior to this Act the East India Company was not allowed to ship bullion to the Far East, so that it could only buy Oriental goods to the value of

14. Chethams Library, Raines Mss., Vol. 38, 'An Inventory of all the Goods etc. of Richard Legh of Lime…' (1687).
15. Hall, ed. (1986), p. 4.
16. 15 Charles II, cap. 7.
17. BL, A True Relation of the Rise and Progress of the East India Company; see also Polloxfen (1697), p. 98.
18. Polloxfen (1697), p. 99.

Plate 1:10. Chinese lacquer cabinet,
late 17th century. This was perhaps the
definitive status symbol of the age.
Lacquer cabinets were hugely
expensive, costing between £20 and
£50 (a good longcase clock could be
bought for £10). They appear commonly in aristocratic inventories from
c.1670 onwards but were generally
beyond the reach of the middle classes.
This example retains its original feet,
on which it stood on the floor in a
Chinese house. These are sometimes
removed to facilitate placing on a
European stand. The example shown
here is English c.1700-10.

whatever it could export. Since European goods were of limited appeal to the Indians and Chinese,
their return cargoes were correspondingly small. In 1663 the Company successfully lobbied Parliament to amend the laws controlling the export of bullion, giving it much greater purchasing
power thereafter.[16] The effect of the 1663 Act was highlighted in the famous pamphlet *A True
Relation of the Rise and Progress of the East India Company* (1697): '...till then, little Silver or Gold
was Exported. After that Law was made, began the great Exportation of Bullion to *India*'.[17] The
subsequent increase in importations inaugurated a craze for all things Oriental which was one of
the most extraordinary aspects of Restoration style. The degree to which it affected even quite
modest households is evident from the remarks of contemporary commentators, of whom John
Polloxfen was amongst the most outspoken:

> As ill Weeds grow apace, so these Manufactured Goods from India met with such a
> kind reception, that from the greatest Gallants to the meanest Cook-Maids. Nothing
> was thought so fit to adorn their persons as the fabric of India; nor for the ornament of
> Chambers like India-Skreens, Cabinets, Beds and Hangings; nor for Closets, like
> China and Lacquered Ware...[18]

Plate 1:11. Caned chair, c.1675. This is probably the most widely recognised form of Restoration seating. The rise of the caned chair manufactory was one of the great success stories of English furniture making.
DRAYTON HOUSE, PRIVATE COLLECTION

Genuine Oriental lacquerware was never cheap, even as it became more plentiful, so that it was usually found only in the houses of the wealthy. But just as Chinese porcelain was copied by the potters of Delft and elsewhere, so the widespread use of simulated lacquer or 'japanning' allowed the middle classes to acquire Oriental-style goods of all descriptions. Moreover, because demand always outstripped supply, and because the range of Oriental furniture suited to English houses was limited, japanned furniture was made even for the richest patrons, from the king downwards. In 1675 the warehouse of Edward Traherne, one of the foremost cabinet-makers of his day, contained 'Japan' tables and mirror frames alongside cabinets of princeswood and ebony garnished with silver.[19] More than any other class of furniture, japanned ware narrowed the gulf between the super-rich and the merely well-off, for how many people could reliably tell the difference between true lacquer and good japanning?

A similar across-the-board appeal attached to that most typical of all Restoration seating forms, the caned chair (1:11). This was a genuine innovation, unknown in Europe except for a very few Chinese imports, and one which for once owed nothing to France. Although inspired by Chinese prototypes, English caned chairs immediately established a stylistic and structural vocabulary of their own and, indeed, became a distinctively English product which achieved European renown. The rise of the caned chair manufactory was one of the most significant developments in the furniture industry of Restoration England. Although caned chairs were made predominantly in London, they could be found in noble and gentry houses all over the country, and even in a student's lodgings at Oxford.[20]

Even ephemeral consumer goods from the Orient had an effect on furniture design. The demand for tea tables arose directly from the fashion for tea drinking, and it was thought appropriate that the tables should be lacquered or japanned. The lacquer table at Ham House, which stood in the Duchess's Private Closet, was probably a tea table and had a set of japanned chairs made to go with it (1:12). A similar table at Dyrham Park was described in inventories as a 'large black Japan Tea Table'.[21] Tables of this sort were once common; a Joiners' Company petition of 1701 records that in the previous four years 6,582 tea tables were imported.[22] English cabinet-makers soon developed their own versions, of which the most successful was the half-round fold-over tea table which became a standard English type from about 1700 onwards.

The popularity of blue and white porcelain, which reached such extraordinary heights under Queen Mary (1689-94) and Queen Anne (1702-14) was already growing apace in the 1670s, and this brought its own furnishing requirements in the form of display shelves and china cabinets. Many of the former were improvised, so that porcelain stood on chimneybreasts and mantel shelves, atop cabinets or beneath tables, but very occasionally one sees purpose-made examples

Plate 1:12. Lacquer table (c.1675-80). This tea table stood in the Duchess of Lauderdale's private closet. The twist-turned lower stage is English and was presumably added to raise the table to a height more suitable for European usage.

HAM HOUSE, THE NATIONAL TRUST

19. CLRO Orphans Court Record, Roll 1177, Box 15, Co. Ser. Book 2, f. 405.
20. Symonds (March 1951), p. 10.
21. Walton (1986), p. 44.
22. BL., 'THE CASE OF THE JOYNERS COMPANY, AGAINST the Importation of Manufactured CABINET-WORK from the EAST INDIES.

Plate 1:13. Hanging shelves (c.1725). These extremely rare shelves were probably made to carry porcelain or glass. They bear the cipher and lozenge of Lady Betty Germaine (widowed 1718) and were made to match an existing set of shelves dating from the 1670s. Very few shelves of this type survive, although they are known from contemporary Dutch paintings.

DRAYTON HOUSE, PRIVATE COLLECTION

23. Earle (1989), pp. 291-2.
24. CLRO, Orphans Court Inventory, Vol. 4, Roll 1697.
25. Ibid., Vol. 4, Roll 1783.
26. Brears (1972), p. 141.
27. Ibid., (1972), pp. 156-60.
28. Sleep (1996).
29. Ibid., Vol. I, p.87.
30. Ibid., pp. 124 and 131.
31. Ibid., p. 168.

(1:13). Some glazed cabinets have survived from this period and one supposes they might have been used for displaying China ware, but references to China cabinets *per se* are very scarce.

Town and country

It is apparent from the great quantity of late seventeenth century furniture which survives, much of it of modest quality, that the changes wrought in the top echelons of furniture making percolated down to relatively humble levels. The degree to which fashions established at court were taken up in the country at large was very variable and was influenced by many factors, of which money was just one. Geography or location was certainly important, but this was not simply a matter of the distance from London. Noble and wealthy families travelled frequently between their London and country homes and furnished both houses in fashionable style, no matter how geographically remote. More significant than mere distance was the social and economic milieu in which people led their lives, and particularly whether their sphere was essentially urban or rural.

Probate inventories of the 'middling sort' of people in London – merchants, members of the professions and successful tradesmen – reveal that their houses were comfortably furnished with fashionable goods. Almost invariably most money was lavished on the best bedchamber, which in London houses tended to be on the second floor above the parlour or dining room. At this time the bedchamber was still a semi-public room, used not merely for sleeping but also for entertaining, so such expenditure was well merited.[23] The parlour and dining room were next in importance, but quite some way behind. When Francis Chaplin, an alderman and clothworker, died in 1680, the contents of his best bedchamber were valued at over £139. These included a velvet bed and twelve velvet chairs together with another twelve caned ones, a Japan cabinet and a triad.[24] The contents of his parlour, furnished with twelve Turkey-work chairs, an olivewood triad and six glass sconces, were valued at £13, and the contents of his dining room or little parlour at £15. In total, his worldly goods amounted to nearly £1,400, which made Francis Chaplin a rich man.

Robert Ashton, a merchant tailor whose furniture was worth only £187 in 1681, had a dining room furnished with eight Turkey-work chairs and a fashionable oval table with a Turkey carpet to go on it, total value £3.10s.0d.[25] The contents of his best bedroom were worth £19.12s.0d., of which the bed alone accounted for £14. Both these houses also had their share of the smaller items which make up the clutter of everyday living – candlesticks, fire irons, pewter and brass vessels, pictures, pots, beakers and jars.

Inventories from provincial towns reveal that middle- and upper-class houses contained many of the same fashionable artefacts found in their London counterparts. The possession of 'marker goods' such as looking glasses, pendulum clocks, upholstered and caned chairs, oval tables and walnut or olivewood furniture suggests both surplus income and a fashion-conscious society. Among the furniture of John Webster, an alderman of Doncaster who died in 1674, were a number of items which reveal social aspirations. In the best chamber were a bed, four 'stuff' (upholstered) chairs and four stools, together with a chest of drawers, a cabinet, and the fashionable triad of table, stands and looking glass.[26] The value of Webster's estate was only £548.18s.2d., which placed him very firmly among the 'middling sort' of people. It is interesting to note, however, the difference between the furnishings of townsmen like Webster and that of rural men of equal or greater wealth. Thus John Ryall, yeoman, of Halifax in Yorkshire, died worth £2,782.5s.3d. in land, livestock and money, but his furniture was both scant and very traditional – no looking glass, no chest of drawers, no table and stands, but old-fashioned buffet stools, the odd chair and panelled chests for storage.[27]

The same discrepancy between urban and rural furnishings is apparent in other areas of the country. Recent research into Norfolk inventories has revealed significant differences between the furnishings of town and country houses there.[28] In Norwich, a prosperous city of about 30,000 people, with a buoyant cloth manufactory and a fast growing population, fashionable consumer goods appear not only in the houses of the gentry and professional classes, but also in those of tradesmen. But in the countryside, the houses of farmers and country tradesmen of equivalent means were furnished quite differently. For instance, inventories taken between 1650 and 1674 reveal that over 62 per cent of Norwich tradesmen had at least one looking glass in their house, compared with only 12.5 per cent of farmers.[29] Similar patterns emerge for other fashionable goods such as upholstered couches and chests of drawers. In both cases these became markedly more popular in Norwich from the 1670s onwards, but took several decades to catch on in the countryside.[30] This phenomenon is partly explained by the much greater and more frequent access to consumer goods enjoyed by urban dwellers, but it goes deeper than that: 'Such huge lags between town and country... could only have come about because the two societies... were genuinely different in their preferences and maintained those differences wilfully over long stretches of time'.[31] Country dwellers, whose lives and livelihoods depended primarily on the land, tended to be conservative in outlook and cautious with money. If they had cash to spare, land and stock took precedence over consumer goods, and utility, not fashion, was the highest virtue, whether in tools, clothes or furniture. Hence archaic furniture types such as settles, or boarded chests, or press cupboards persisted in rural areas decades, even centuries, after they had lapsed from use in towns. Nor should we forget the subtle but powerful forces of social conformity, for nobody wants to stand out too far from their neighbours. Hence the same pressures that induced a townsman to buy a set of caned chairs for his parlour might have the reverse effect on a countryman. For him and his peers continuity and stability were far more desirable than change. Many late seventeenth century rural inventories offer absolutely no indication that the fashionable world of Restoration London made the slightest impact on rural lives.

Ultimately, however, change was inevitable. The halting interaction between fashionable and vernacular culture produced an extraordinarily rich and varied furniture, which is usually described

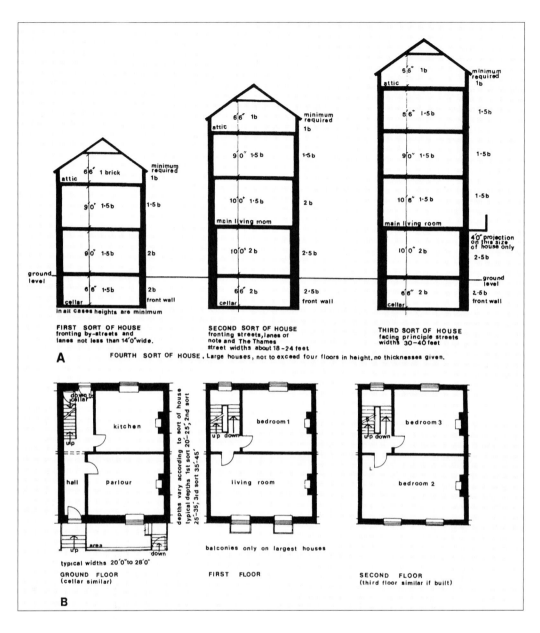

Plate 1:14. The Rebuilding Act of 1667, showing the several sorts of houses permitted by the Act. This Act standardized house building in the capital and established typical plans and elevations which were adopted throughout England in the 18th century.

as 'country'. This is an inadequate and often pejorative term for a vast range of furniture which is only just beginning to be codified and understood. This book has no aspirations in that direction, and most of the furniture discussed in the ensuing pages would have been familiar only to the wealthiest ten or fifteen per cent of the English population. It was to this relatively small number of people that the furniture trades of London and the larger provincial towns owed their livings. It was they who created the demand and they who determined the style which future generations have called Restoration.

The 'commercial revolution'

The conspicuous consumption that is such a notable feature of fashionable society during the Restoration had its roots in what some scholars have termed the 'commercial revolution' of late seventeenth century England.[32] In the immediate aftermath of the Restoration few observers could have predicted the extent of England's commercial and industrial growth, for the 1660s were years of both demographic and economic stagnation. Modern estimates suggest that the population of England and Wales (around 5.5 million in 1660) was actually in decline from the 1650s to the late 1680s.[33] The reasons for this are manifold, but one significant factor was the high incidence of disease, most famously the Great Plague of 1665, during which 68,000 deaths were recorded in

32. Holmes (1993), pp. 58-68.
33. Ibid., pp. 44-6.
34. Ibid., p. 47.
35. Pepys, *Diary*, 31 December 1666.
36. Holmes (1993), p. 66.

London alone. Another factor was emigration, primarily to North America and the Caribbean, which reached new heights during the Civil War and Commonwealth, and continued at a high level for the rest of the century.[34]

The economy as a whole had naturally suffered during the Civil War and, despite a partial resurgence under Cromwell, underwent a serious recession between 1658 and 1663. The nation's political and economic fortunes reached their nadir between 1665 and 1667, when London endured the Plague (1665), the Great Fire (1666) and a second Anglo-Dutch war (1665-7). At the end of this sequence of catastrophes the heady optimism of 1660 was thoroughly quashed, and on New Year's Eve 1666 Samuel Pepys saw little prospect of improvement:

> Thus ends a year of public wonder and mischief to this nation… Public matters in a
> most sad condition. Seamen discouraged for want of pay, and are become not to be
> governed. Nor, as matters are now, can our fleet go out next year. Our enemies, French
> and Dutch, great, and grow more by our poverty, The Parliament backward in raising,
> because jealous of the spending, of the money. The City less and less likely to be built
> again, everybody settling elsewhere, and nobody encouraged to trade. A sad, vicious,
> negligent Court, and all sober men there fearful of the ruin of the whole Kingdom this
> next year – from which, good God deliver us.[35]

Yet from 1667 onwards there began a remarkable recovery, developing into an economic boom which lasted, with some interruptions, into the 1690s. Part of this boom was home-grown. England's woollen cloth manufacturers, jointly the nation's largest industry and single greatest foreign currency earners, rose successfully to the challenge of cheaper, lightweight foreign competition. The English 'New Draperies' found new markets both at home and abroad, particularly in the Mediterranean and the Levant. But remarkable though their performance was, the clothier's share of the nation's total export trade was actually falling, so that by 1700 cloth accounted for less than 50 per cent by value for the first time.[36] The reason for this was the even more remarkable expansion in the re-export trade, as goods from Asia, Africa and the Americas

Plate 1:15. 'The manner of Building after the Burning', from William Morgan, *Survey of London,* 1682. This engraving shows houses 'of the third sort' built after the 1667 Act. This size of house was permitted on principal streets 30-40ft. in width. The first floor balcony indicates the position of the principal reception room. On the ground floor are shops full of wares for sale. Note that the windows are still casements rather than sashes.

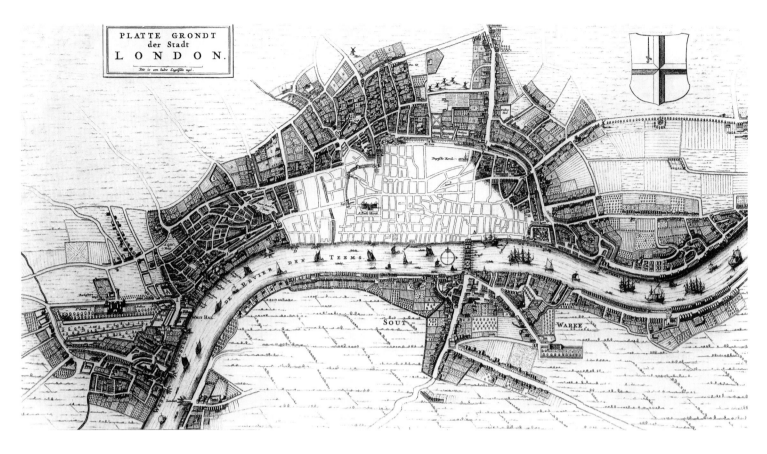

Plate 1:16. Map of London, by
Marcus Willemsz Doornick, 1666.
This map shows the areas devastated
by the Great Fire, comprising 80% of
the area within the City walls.
GUILDHALL LIBRARY,
CORPORATION OF LONDON

Plate 1:17. Map of London, by John
Oliver, c.1700. By this date the area
destroyed by fire had been completely
rebuilt; the city had expanded rapidly
in all directions, but particularly to the
north and west. GUILDHALL LIBRARY,
CORPORATION OF LONDON

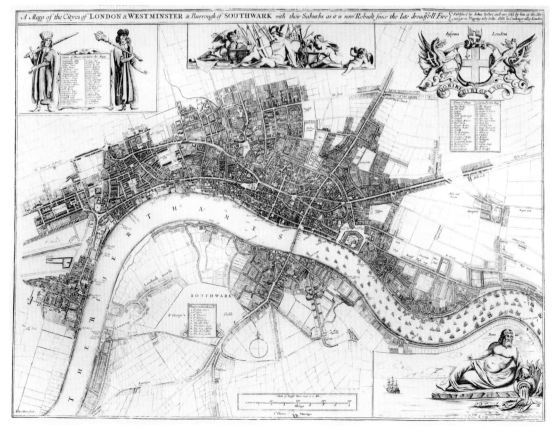

flooded into London and were carried thence to all parts of Europe and the Mediterranean.

The key to this great maritime bonanza was the political control of English seaborne commerce created under the Commonwealth, in the form of the Navigation Ordinance of 1651. This Act excluded all foreign ships from the carrying trade between England and its overseas possessions, and excluded all but English ships, or ships of the producing nation, from trade between England and other countries. The object of the Act was to eliminate the Dutch, who hitherto had dominated the seaborne carrying trades both around Europe and between Europe and the Americas, from competition with English shippers. The Act sparked off a long-running struggle for naval supremacy between England and Holland which, after three hard-fought wars (1652-4, 1665-7, 1672-4), established England in sole control of its overseas trade. Significantly, the Navigation Ordinance was one of the first of Cromwell's policies to be renewed and reinforced by Charles II, and the Acts of Navigation, as they became known, formed the basis of English mercantile policy for the next one hundred and fifty years.

From the 1670s onwards seaborne trade was the primary engine of commercial growth, employing hundreds of ships and thousands of seamen. Some measure of the scale and direction of this growth can be gained from a few statistics. The total tonnage of the English merchant fleet increased from 126,000 tons in 1663 to 190,000 in 1686.[37] Of this by far the most significant increase was in shipping to North America and the West Indies. In 1664, 88 merchant ships cleared the Port of London bound for the Americas; by 1686 this had increased to 247 ships, or by nearly 300 per cent. On the outward voyage they carried English and European manufactures, provisions for the plantations and, if going via West Africa, slaves. On their return they brought sugar, molasses, rum, dyewoods, tobacco, cotton, indigo, furs and countless other commodities from the West Indies and North America, of which the majority was destined for re-export.

One of the most important provisions of the Navigation Acts was that commodities from English plantations in America, or from Africa and the East Indies, could not be shipped to Europe except via England. Conversely, the Staple Act of 1663 decreed that European manufactures could not be imported into the English plantations and colonies except via England. Thus London, and to a lesser extent the provincial ports of Bristol, Liverpool and Lancaster, became entrepôts to rival and even surpass Amsterdam. The great engine of seaborne trade now did for England what it had earlier done for Holland, transforming a small nation into a world power in the space of a few decades.

Some indication of the buoyancy of the economy is shown by the very rapid recovery of London after the Great Fire of 1666. True, it took over twenty years completely to eradicate its scars, and the new St Paul's cathedral was not opened until 1697, but the bulk of the rebuilding was accomplished with remarkable speed. At its heart was the Rebuilding Act of 1667, which specified exactly how London should be rebuilt and of which materials (1:14 and 1:15).[38] By the end of 1671 nearly 7,000 houses had been built to the new specifications, replacing the 13,000 assorted dwellings consumed in the fire (the discrepancy in numbers is largely explained by the fact that the rebuilt houses were on the whole larger, and the streets wider, than before the fire). In addition to these, there was extensive building outside the city, particularly to the west, where the streets and squares which now comprise London's fashionable West End were first established (1:16 and 1:17). Vast quantities of materials were consumed, giving work to brickmakers, tilemakers, glaziers and timber merchants. Most of the timber was Norwegian fir and deal – Norwegian timber importations into London increased by 150 per cent between 1663 and 1669.[39] To work this timber many hundreds of carpenters, joiners, turners and carvers were needed, so many, indeed, that the Rebuilding Act obliged London's Livery Companies to lift their restrictions against 'foreign' workmen. Finally, once these houses had been built, they had to be furnished. Here was an extraordinary opportunity for London's furniture makers, for such a wholesale refurnishing of the nation's capital had never happened before or since. As a consequence the pace of stylistic and technical change was greatly accelerated, leading to what might justifiably be termed a revolution in English furniture making. The new style was neater and lighter, literally so because of the greater window area specified by the 1667 Rebuilding Act. Mirror glass was cheaper and more

37. Davis (1972), p. 17.
38. 19 Charles II, cap. III.
39. Davis (1972), p. 18.

widely available, enhancing and multiplying the available daylight and candlelight. Halls and stairways of set widths discouraged bulky and traditional joined furniture, favouring instead furniture built on a smaller, neater scale. Regulation room sizes, pier widths and ceiling heights encouraged standardisation of type, size and form, and this in turn encouraged efficiency, specialisation, and sub-division of labour. London inventories from the 1670s onwards reveal a remarkable consistency in the layout and furnishings of the new houses,[40] and this is still apparent today, with the survival of so many standard furniture types – caned chairs, chests of drawers, cabinets, scriptors, tables, stands and looking glasses.

London's prosperity was shared, to a less dramatic extent, by most regions of England, particularly in the larger towns. The rise in real incomes after 1660 was a nationwide phenomenon, and the nation's increasing disposable income was matched by the increased opportunity to spend it, as goods from all over the world flooded into the country. The sheer volume and variety of imported goods available to the average late Stuart householder would have astonished their forebears.

This was also a time of falling prices, so that commodities which a generation earlier had been luxuries – sugar, tea, coffee or tobacco – were now staples. The same was true of many of the raw materials of furniture making. The average price of Norway deals halved between the 1580s and the 1660s, and this accounts for the greatly increased use of deals for floorboards, panelling and cabinet-work.[41] Snakewood from Surinam, once highly prized and valued at up to £40 per ton, had fallen by 1660 to just over £8.[42] Jamaica ebony, or cocus wood, cost £18 the ton (very much cheaper than the genuine Asian ebony at £40). Olivewood furniture, scarcely known in England before 1660, was commonplace after 1670. The wood itself cost between £10 and £12 the ton which, when cut into veneers, amounted to a great deal of furniture. Cedarwood furniture was also common in upper-class houses and the wood was also used for flooring and panelling. The only important exception to this deflationary trend was the high quality imported oak known as 'wainscot'. Between 1582 and 1660 the price of this timber more than doubled, from £4 to £10 per hundred boards. Consequently, the use of quarter-sawn wainscot is always an indicator of quality in late seventeenth century furniture (as a general rule, the price of wainscot was four times that of deal, typically 4d. per superficial foot, compared to 1-1½d. for Norway deal).

The Joiners' Company

We know very little about the size or organisation of the English furniture trade before 1660, except that it made hardly any impact on the world at large. Compared with the great workshops of Augsburg, Antwerp and Paris, London apparently had little to offer, and certainly produced nothing of international renown. The documentary record is fragmentary, but isolated snapshots that survive suggest a parochial, inward-looking industry frequently riven by internecine disputes. Within the City of London and its immediate environs, furniture production was divided between a number of separate trades – carpenters, joiners, carvers, turners and upholsterers – each with its own tools, methods and jealously defended prerogatives. Each trade was represented by a Livery Company whose role was to regulate its practices, support its members and protect their livelihoods. From the surviving minute books and Company Ordinances one might easily think that the Livery Companies' sole preoccupation was to protect their monopolies from infringement by other trades, such is the time and effort given over to complaints and accusations between one Company and another. Probably the most significant dispute was that between the Joiners and Carpenters, which came to a head in 1632. It ended with a historic arbitration by the London Court of Aldermen, which firmly established the Joiners' ascendancy in the hierarchy of woodworking trades (1:18).[43]

With hindsight, it seems possible that the 1632 arbitration was a turning point in the history of English furniture making, since it provided the foundation for the Joiners' dominant role in London's furniture industry from the middle of the seventeenth century onwards. But in 1632 one would have needed extraordinary foresight to predict the extent of the transformation of London's furniture trade between 1660 and 1714. True, the internecine disputes continued, and the

40. Earle (1989), pp. 205-212, 290-301.
41. Books of Rates (1582); 12 Charles II, cap. 4 (1660).
42. Bowett (1998), p. 217.
43. Chinnery (1979), pp.42-3.
44. CLRO, Minutes of the Joiners' Company, 1661-97.45. B.L. *The Case of the Cane-Chair Makers of England* (1690) quoted in Symonds (March 1951).
46. BL, *For the Encouragement of the Consumption of the Woollen Manufacture of the Kingdom* (1689).
47. *The Case of the Cane-Chair Makers of England.*
48. BL, *For the Encouragement of the Consumption of the Woollen Manufacture of the Kingdom* (1698).
49. Houghton (1683)
50. Ibid..

preoccupation with interlopers was as strong as ever, but growth, productivity and diversification were the dominant themes. Several entirely new trades emerged – cabinet-making, caned chair making and japanning – and since all of them were offshoots of the Joiners' Company, that Company's dominant position was further strengthened. From these new trades came new forms, styles and techniques of furniture making, greatly expanding the range and output of the furniture industry as a whole. All this required skilled labour and, although it is impossible for us to calculate how many furniture makers were employed in the London trades, we can get some idea of the scale of the industry by looking at the number of apprentices and freemen recorded in the Joiners' Company minutes. From the 1660s to the 1690s the number of apprentices taken on each year ranged from fifty to over one hundred, with an average of about eighty.[44] Since a master was in theory limited to two apprentices at any one time (and many presumably had only one or none), this means that a minimum of forty master joiners took on apprentices each year. The seven year cycle of apprenticeship therefore gives us a minimum figure of 280 master joiners working in London. As each apprentice finished his training, so he was admitted as a freeman of the Company, and so the number of admissions approximately balanced the number of apprenticeships – around eighty per annum. Even allowing for the natural wastage of death, bankruptcy and emigration, this was a formidable body of skilled manpower. We cannot say how many of these men were furniture makers, since many joiners worked more or less exclusively for the building trades, but the number must have been large. In 1689 the Joiners' Company calculated that there were one hundred and thirty joiners in London solely employed in making the frames for upholstered chairs, without considering those making caned and other chairs.[45]

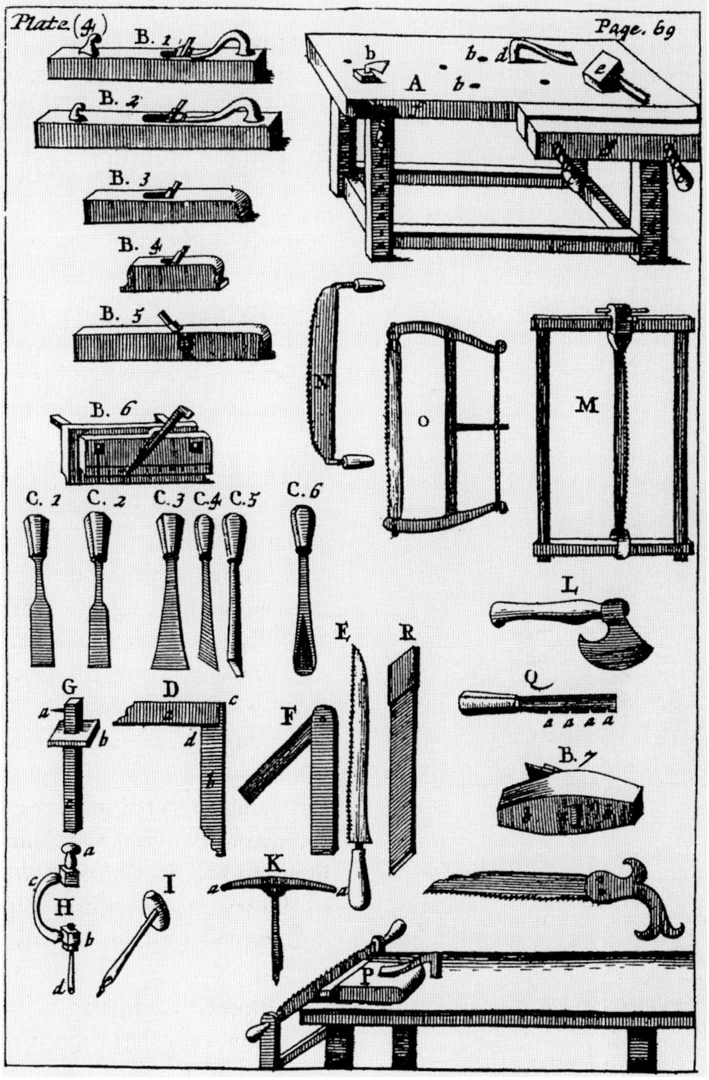

The output of these men was astonishing. In 1689 the Upholsterers' Company reckoned that its members produced 192,000 chairs per annum, upholstered in either woollen cloth or leather (and not including those chairs upholstered in silk and other imported fabrics).[46] In the same year the Joiners' Company estimated its own production of caned chairs at 72,000 per annum, of which a third was exported.[47] By 1699 the upholsterers had revised their estimates upwards, to an astonishing 300,000 chairs per annum.[48]

Some corroboration of the high levels of furniture production achieved after the Restoration comes from a brief compilation of export figures published by one John Houghton, which shows that in January and February 1683 1,754 chairs were exported from London. Other furniture exported during the same two months included 2 cabinets, 10 scriptors, 13 clock cases, 21 chests of drawers, 31 sets of tables and stands and 196 looking glasses.[49] Importations of raw materials for the woodworking trades were commensurately high. In January 1683 there were imported 5,656 oak wainscots, 34,255 deal boards, 15 tons of olivewood, 35¾ tons of cedar, and 5½ tons of *granadilla* or cocus wood.[50]

Many accounts of the Joiners' Company dwell on the frequent complaints against 'foreign' workmen, but these can be misleading. In the first place, a 'foreigner' did not necessarily come from abroad – he was merely someone who was not a member of a Livery Company. This is why the majority of foreigners recorded in the Company's Minute books had English names. Secondly, reading the Minute books alone gives one a very skewed impression of the Company's activities,

Plate 1:18. Joiners' tools, from Joseph Moxon, *Mechanick Exercises* (1678). The design of most of these tools changed very little between the 17th and early 20th centuries. A – the work bench; B – planes of various sorts; C – chisels; D – a square; E – compass saw; F – bevel; G – marking gauge; H – piercer; I – gimlet; K – auger; L – hatchet; M – pitsaw; N – whip saw; O – bow saw; P – whetstone; Q – saw set; R – mitre square.

since dealing with infringements of Company Ordinances took up a disproportionate amount of the Company's administration. In fact the Joiners' Company had a long history of assimilating immigrant artisans into its ranks, seeking both to gain from their expertise and to protect their own craft monopoly. The ordinances of the Joiners' Company adopted in 1571 made specific provision for 'Denizens and Forraines',[51] allowing them to work under the Company's auspices so long as they paid their fees and observed a number of restrictions. One of the most important of these was that immigrant craftsmen were obliged to take only English apprentices. Conversely, members of the Company wishing to employ immigrant artisans could do so, but only by binding them as apprentices. Both these provisions ensured that imported techniques and skills were rapidly assimilated into the mainstream of London furniture making.

The most restrictive Ordinance against 'foreigners' stated that no one who was not a member of the Joiners' Company could undertake work except for a member of the Joiners' Company – in other words he could not act as a principal or deal directly with a client – but this was routinely ignored. None of the immigrant furniture makers who came to prominence after the Restoration – John Casbert, Francis Lapiere, Jean Poitevin, Philip Guibert, Jean, René and Thomas Pelletier, to name but a few – seemed to have been bothered by this restriction, nor were the penalties for infringement particularly severe. In 1680/1 Thomas Pistor, a longstanding and senior member of the Company, was found to be employing 'two foreigners... contrary to the ordinances of this Company'. His punishment was to be called before the Court of the Company where he 'received a check and [was] ordered to reform for the future'.[52]

The immigrants' real difficulty lay in their ineligibility for the benefits of Company membership, so that they were denied the mutual support and succour that the Company provided to its English members.[53] This was perhaps one of the reasons why immigrant craftsmen tended to group together in areas like Southwark, where they could operate in a mutually supportive enclave. For its part, the Joiners' Company was able both to regulate and benefit from the activities of foreign craftsmen while at the same time offering them little in return. Occasionally 'foreigners' were allowed to become members of the Company by redemption, i.e., by paying a fee, but the number of men so admitted was relatively few.[54]

The restrictions on immigrant artisans were clearly not sufficient to discourage the active pursuit of their trades. Figures for the Restoration period have yet to be compiled, but between 1511 and 1625 over four hundred foreign-born furniture makers were recorded in London and its immediate environs. Of these a large concentration was recorded in the several parishes of Southwark, but many were also working in London itself, and all these were obliged to take English apprentices.[55] After seven years' training, each apprentice was permitted to work as a journeyman and, after a further two years, could apply to become a master and then take apprentices himself. Skills learned in one workshop were thus rapidly transmitted to another and, given the right economic conditions, a numerous and skilled workforce could be built up within a few decades. This systematic dissemination of skills and techniques goes a long way towards explaining the remarkable consistency of style and construction which characterises London furniture in the second half of the seventeenth century. At the same time, the danger of stagnation was prevented by the constant infusion of new talent from the English provinces and, of course, from Continental Europe. These infusions became a flood when, in the aftermath of the Great Fire of 1666, the restrictions on 'foreign' workmen were lifted. The 1667 Rebuilding Act gave those craftsmen that assisted in London's rebuilding liberty to work in the city for seven years as if they were freemen of their respective trades.[56] At the end of this term they were allowed to enjoy the same liberty to work as freemen 'for and during their natural lives', provided they paid the necessary dues to their Companies. Thus they effectively became freemen by redemption. According to a Joiners' Company petition of 1694, 'a very great number' of 'foreign' joiners and carvers gained their freedom in this way, and continued to ply their trades thereafter with very little regulation by the Company.[57] The implications of this are far reaching, because it suggests that, as well as those joiners whose apprenticeships and freedoms are recorded in the archives of the Joiners' Company, there was a substantial group who were nominally under the cognisance of the Company,

51. A 'denizen' was foreign-born immigrant naturalised by royal letters patent. A 'foreigner' was any artisan from outside London who was not a member of the Joiners' Company

52. G.L. Minutes of the Joiners' Company, 2nd March 1680.

53. Forman (1971), p. 97.

54. Ibid., p. 97.

55. Ibid., Appendix I.

56. 19 Charles II, cap. III.

57. G.L. Minutes of the Joiners' Company, 5 June 1694.

58. Holmes (1993), p. 54.

59. Camden Society, 82 (1862), pp. 29 *et seq.*

60. Scouloudi (1987); Murdoch (1982).

61. Murdoch (182), p. 238; Beard and Gilbert (1986), pp. 16-17.

62. Jackson-Stops (1987), p. 113.

63. Roseveare (1987), pp. 74-75.

64. Tait (1987), pp. 98-99.

65. Murdoch (1982), p.131.

66. Jackson-Stops (1987), pp. 115-118; Beard and Westman (1993), p. 515.

but whose presence is not recorded in any official documents. Consequently, calculations of the number of joiners working in London based solely on the Joiners' Company records are likely to underestimate the true number.

The upshot of all this is that London's furniture makers constituted a highly productive and fast growing industry. They had an effective and well-funded Livery Company to protect their livelihoods against threats from other Companies or from interlopers. They were protected from price wars and undercutting by the Company's ability to confiscate and destroy shoddy goods, which at the same time ensured that the quality and reputation of London-made furniture was maintained. They benefited from a continual influx of new talent, acquiring technical and artistic skills from home and abroad which, once acquired, were rapidly disseminated throughout the industry. The city in which they worked was growing faster than any other in the Western world and the exponential growth of English commerce to all corners of the known world opened markets of seemingly limitless opportunity.

The Huguenot question

Modern authorities estimate that over 50,000 Continental immigrants entered England between 1660 and 1689.[58] Of these, the largest single contingent comprised Huguenots, French Protestants forced out of France by the increasingly intolerant policies of Louis XIV's Catholic government. An Order in Council of 28 July 1681 offered Royal protection to the 'poore distressed protestants' of France and allowed them, having been granted Denization, 'all rights, privileges and immunities as other free Denizens do'.[59] Their contribution to England's intellectual, commercial and artistic culture has been extensively documented by numerous authors, of whom the late Gervase Jackson-Stops was perhaps their most constant champion.[60] It is nevertheless extremely difficult to measure or quantify the impact of Huguenots in the field of furniture making. Some individuals stand out, but how representative were these of the whole? Nineteen Huguenot cabinet-makers are named in the records of the Huguenot churches in England between 1660 and 1714, of whom only one, Philip Arbuthnot (or Arbunot), gained sufficient prominence in his trade to have left his name in the accounts of the Lord Chamberlain.[61] Of the others little or nothing is known, and one may question how much influence nineteen men can have had on a trade that employed hundreds in London alone.

One may also question the notion of the Huguenots as a distinct and coherent artistic force, characterised by Jackson-Stops as 'a whole web of Huguenot craftsmen'.[62] The fact that these people had a common language and religion and attended the same few Huguenot churches in London must certainly have tended towards close social ties, but how can we gauge the effect of these on their professional life? Many Huguenots who sought professional advancement clearly felt the need to move beyond past allegiances into the mainstream of London commercial life. This was why Charles Maresco, a successful Huguenot merchant, secured his naturalisation in 1658 and became a freeman of the Clothworkers' Company in 1662.[63] Similarly Peter Harache, the most prominent Huguenot goldsmith of his generation, applied to become free of the Goldsmiths' Company in 1682.[64] The cabinet-maker John Guilbaud, who worked in Long Acre between 1693 and 1712, was almost certainly a Huguenot, but he anglicised his name from Jean to John and worshipped in his local parish church at St Martin in the Fields. Guilbaud's work is further discussed in Chapter Seven, but it is worth making the point here that the only known piece of cabinet-work bearing Guilbaud's label is thoroughly English in its style, materials and construction.

One of the difficulties in assessing the true impact of Huguenot craftsmen on English furniture making is that historians have been too ready to assume that every Frenchman working in England was a Huguenot, and to attribute every baroque State bed or finely-made cabinet to Huguenot workmen. The upholsterer Francis Lapiere is a case in point. His work is extensively documented and he was clearly a major force in English upholstery from the 1680s until his death in 1714 (6:18). As recently as the 1980s Lapiere was regarded by furniture historians as 'the leading Huguenot upholsterer of the day',[65] but we now know that he was a Catholic.[66] Of the other leading French upholsterers working in England – John Casbert, Jean Poitevin, Philip Guibert, Etienne Penson – none is known to have been a Huguenot.

Religious persecution was not the only reason why foreigners emigrated to England. London was a fast expanding city, awash with money and, as the Rebuilding Act of 1667 revealed, short of skilled labour. Notwithstanding the apparent difficulties facing immigrant artisans, many made their fortunes and died rich; money, rather than religious freedom, was their driving force. When he visited the city in 1669, Duke Cosimo III of Tuscany observed: 'the French make fortunes in London, for being more attentive to their business, they sell their manufactures at a lower price than the English'.[67] The Great Wardrobe in particular was a refuge for workmen of talent, whether English or immigrant, who succeeded in obtaining the favour of the Keeper. Within its precincts 'any artificer or tradesman native or foreign... [was] exempted from paying all taxes and duties'.[68]

Because so few of the French craftsmen working in London's furniture trades are known to have been Huguenots we must conclude that the majority were either Catholics or atheists. But does it matter? The important point is not that particular craftsmen were Huguenots or Catholics, but that they were French. Thus the contribution of outstanding Huguenot artisans such as the Pelletiers (a family of carvers, whose careers are discussed in more detail in Part II) ought to be seen in a wider context, in which France and French arts were of the utmost importance in influencing arts and design in late seventeenth century England.

We should also bear in mind that the French were by no means the only nation to make their contribution to the resurgence of English arts after 1660. In the field of cabinet-making one man stands out as the exemplar of this phenomenon. Gerrit Jensen, whose name was frequently anglicised to Garret or Garrard Johnson, first appears on the London scene in 1667, when he became free of the Joiners' Company by redemption (in other words, he bought his way in). He was almost certainly a Dutchman or of Dutch descent. It is possible that he was a descendant of Garret Johnson, a Dutch stone carver working in Southwark in the 1580s,[69] but the fact that he gained his freedom by redemption, rather than by servitude or patrimony, suggests that he was not apprenticed in London. The date of his freedom could be significant, since 1667 was the year when England signalled its need for skilled workmen in the Rebuilding Act. Jensen could well have arrived directly from Antwerp or Amsterdam, lured by the prospect of wealth and advancement as London rose, phoenix-like, from the ashes of the Great Fire. If so, his subsequent career is an admirable demonstration of the way in which the Joiners' Company was able to assimilate new talent into the mainstream of English furniture making. He was clearly ambitious because, rather than take advantage of the licence allowed by the 1667 Act and work on the semi-official fringes of the trade, he went straight to the heart of the matter and joined the Joiners' Company. By the early 1670s his business was sufficiently advanced to employ at least three apprentices[70] and in 1675 we find him as one of three assessors of the estate of Edward Traherne, one of London's most prominent cabinet-makers.[71] In 1685 he became a Liveryman of the Joiners' Company and in 1689 was appointed Cabinet-Maker in Ordinary to William III. By the time he died in December 1715, Jensen had become a rich man, owning several properties in London and Kent and a country house in Hammersmith.[72]

67. Jackson-Stops (1987), p. 114.
68. Ibid., p. 114. The Great Wardrobe was the government department responsible for supplying all furnishings to the royal palaces.
69. Beard and Gilbert (1986), p. 485.
70. Joiners could apply for licence to take a third 'supernumerary' apprentice on payment of a small fee, usually ten shillings.
71. G.L. Minutes of the Joiners' Company, 1 September 1685; Beard and Gilbert (1986), pp. 485-87.
72. Beard and Gilbert (1986), p. 486.

Plate 1:19. French bed 1660-1700. This bed, although heavily reconstructed, is a good example of the ubiquitous, box-like enclosed beds which were popular throughout Europe in the second half of the 17th century. This is but one example of the cultural and artistic dominance of France under Louis XIV.   COTHELE, THE NATIONAL TRUST

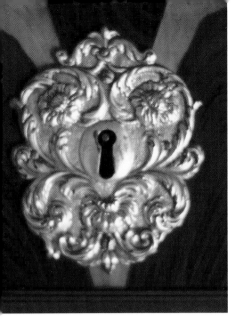

Chapter Two

CASE FURNITURE
1660–1689

he origins of English cabinet-making

The rapid proliferation of veneered carcase construction after 1660 is one of the most notable features of post-Restoration furniture making. This development is often portrayed as a direct result of the influx of skilled foreign cabinet-makers in the wake of the king's return, but such radical advances do not happen overnight. The techniques of true cabinet-making – the manufacture of dovetailed carcases combined with the use of decorative veneers – had been known and practised in England since at least the beginning of the seventeenth century and the origins of these practices go back further still. Dovetailed seamen's chests have been recovered from the wreck of the *Mary Rose* (1545) and it is clear from the London Aldermen's arbitration of 1632 that dovetailed construction was a statutory part of the joiner's technical repertoire by this date (2:1 and 2:2).[1]

Because of their inherent rigidity and stability, dovetailed carcases were ideally suited to the application of veneers and marquetry of the sort found on the many late sixteenth and early seventeenth century 'Nonsuch' chests which survive in English collections (2:3). The name 'Nonsuch' is a nineteenth century invention, arising from a fancied resemblance between the marquetry townscapes which decorate these chests and Henry VIII's long-vanished palace of Nonsuch.[2] The example shown here bears the initials GT, probably for George Talbot, 6th Earl of Shrewsbury (d.1590). There is a longstanding debate about where these chests were made, since similar marquetry work occurs in South Germany and the Low Countries, but it is now thought that many were made in England, and specifically at Southwark, opposite London on the south bank of the Thames.

> At St Olaves in Southwark, you shall learn, among the Joyners what Inlayes and
> Marquetrie meane. Inlaye (as the word imports) is the laying of colour'd wood in their
> Wainscot works, Bedsteads, Cupboards, Chayres and the like.
>
> Edmund Maria Bolton, *Elements of Armories* (1610)[3]

1. Chinnery (1979), p. 119-20.
2. The site of the palace, Nonsuch Park, is in Cheam, south-west London.
3. Quoted in Forman (1971), p. 103.
4. Forman (1971) pp. 99-103; Chinnery (1979), pp. 120-121.

The Southwark joiners were mostly immigrant Protestants, who had fled the onslaught of Spanish troops in Holland, Flanders and the lower Rhine during the 1560s and 1570s. They settled in Southwark because there they were outside the overcrowded City of London but close to its

Plate 2:1. Chest (first half 17th century). Solid walnut, with figured walnut veneers and carved mouldings. Chests of this type are frequently described as 'Italian', from their resemblance to Italian cassoni, but there is no reason why this example should not be English. The feet are not original. NUNNINGTON HALL, THE NATIONAL TRUST

teeming markets and wealthy clientele. They brought with them an advanced style of furniture-making learned in the workshops of Cologne, the Rhineland and the Low Countries.[4] 'Nonsuch' chests are true cabinet-work in the modern sense, having a carcase of boards dovetailed together, overlaid with marquetry veneers. Pilasters, arches, mouldings and other quasi-architectural details were applied to the carcase but were not integral to the structure. The drawer construction used in these chests is often highly sophisticated, and would not look out of place on joiner-made furniture of a century later (2:4).

Plate 2:2 . Detail of 2:1. This rear view shows the dovetailed construction of the carcase, on to which the mouldings are glued.

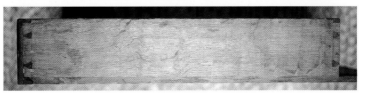

Plate 2:3. 'Nonsuch' chest (c.1560-90). Oak carcase overlaid with various woods. Probably made for George Talbot, 6th Earl of Shrewsbury, and possibly the 'great Inlayde Chest' recorded in Bess's Withdrawing Chamber in the Hardwick inventory of 1601.
HARDWICK HALL, THE NATIONAL TRUST

Plate 2:4. Detail of 2:3. Drawer from the Hardwick chest, showing the dovetailed construction. This type of sophisticated construction is typical of 'Nonsuch'-type chests, but was not common in England before the middle of the 17th century. Note the nailed up bottom, whose boards extend backwards to act as a drawer stop.

Plate 2:5. **Cabinet, Paris** (c.1654-55). Attributed to Pierre Gole. Ebony veneers on an oak and deal carcase. This is a fine example; the rippled geometric mouldings and delicately incised decoration on every surface is typical of Parisian cabinets of this date.
RIJKSMUSEUM, AMSTERDAM

Although the immigrant joiners formed a close-knit and discrete community, it is unlikely that they retained a monopoly of their skills for long. At Southwark they were still within the jurisdiction of the London Livery Companies and we have seen how the regulations governing immigrant artisans tended to encourage assimilation. Moreover, in the competitive environment of England's capital city, commercial pressures must have driven furniture makers to acquire new skills, materials and techniques by fair means or foul. Sooner or later the specialised skills of the Southwark joiners will have entered the mainstream of London furniture making.

By the second quarter of the seventeenth century the 'Nonsuch' style of chest was obsolete, but the skills employed in its construction gained a wider currency with the increasing popularity of the cabinet. The cabinet was originally 'a small piece of furniture, more or less portable, with or without feet, placed either on a buffet, a chair, or table, but always rectangular and having behind its door an infinity of small drawers'.[5] At the beginning of the seventeenth century portable cabinets of this type were relatively common in noble houses in England, almost always enriched with silver, ivory, ebony and other precious materials. Many of these were undoubtedly imported but some, perhaps, were English made. The craftsmen who worked with these materials needed skills of a high order and thus formed an élite group among furniture makers in many European countries.

In the first decades of the seventeenth century the cabinet began its transition from an essentially personal, portable item to an imposing showpiece for public rooms – *un meuble de parade et d'apparat*. Cabinets from Augsburg, Antwerp and Paris acquired particular renown and examples of these can be seen in many English collections (2:5 and 2:6).[6] The point at which English joiners

5. Edwards (1954) I, p. 160, quoted from a French source of 1560. For further discussion of the origins of the cabinet in all its forms, see Riccardi-Cubitt (1992).

6. For further information on these European cabinet-making centres see Riccardi-Cubitt (1992), pp. 39 *et seq.*; Baarsen (2000).

7. PRO LC/3 333. The term cabinet-maker also occurs specifically in connection with veneered furniture in Evelyn's *Silva* (1664). See page 53.

8. Beard and Gilbert (1986), p. 133.

9. Brodstock's bills occur several times in the Lord Chamberlain's accounts, beginning in 1667. Several bills from Thomas Malin, survive, dating from 1661-3. Traherne appears in the Lord Chamberlain's accounts in 1669, when he supplied 'a pair of stands of Jamaica wood for the Kings Closset in the Newe Lodgeings at Whitehall... £1.15.0'. [PRO LC 9/271, f. 140].

10. CLRO, Orphans Court Records, Roll 1177, Box 15, Co. Ser. Book 2, Fol. 405. I am grateful to Laurie Lindey for her detailed transcription of this important inventory.

11. Thornton and Tomlin (1980).

12. It should be remembered that many joiners were not furniture makers, but confined themselves to the interior joinery of buildings – floors, panelling, doors, window frames, etc.

13. Beard and Gilbert (1986), p. 485.

14. B.L., *THE CASE OF THE JOINERS' COMPANY AGAINST the Importation of Manufactured CABINET-WORK from the EAST-INDIES* (1700-01)'.

began to recognise some of their number specifically as 'cabinet-makers' is unclear. One of the earliest uses of the term occurs in a document of 1660, when Adrian Bolte, cabinet-maker to Charles I (1625-1649), applied to be reinstated to his post.[7] During the 1660s the term cabinet-maker was used with increasing frequency and we know the names of at least four London joiners who described themselves as such – John Burroughs, William Brodstock, Thomas Malin and Edward Traherne. John Burroughs was a prominent member of the Joiners' Company who supplied a cabinet worth £56, a huge sum at the time, to Robert Clayton, a future Lord Mayor of London, in 1662.[8] William Brodstock, Thomas Malin and Edward Traherne all supplied furniture to Charles II,[9] and Traherne was certainly a member of the Joiners' Company. His probate inventory, drawn up in 1675, reveals him as a maker of the first rank, whose stock-in-trade included large quantities of looking glasses, together with cabinets, scriptors (*escritoires* – writing cabinets) and chests of drawers in walnut, olivewood, ebony and marquetry. His debtors and creditors included the Queen, two future queens (Mary and Anne), several members of the government, including the Duke of Buckingham, numerous other nobles and two of the King's mistresses, Nell Gwynne and Barbara Villiers, Duchess of Cleveland.[10]

By the 1660s, then, we have a select body of men working within the London Joiners' Company who were recognised as cabinet-makers. The rapid increase in their numbers thereafter, and the adoption of cabinet-making techniques by furniture makers throughout the country, is accounted for by two concurrent developments. The first is the great increase in demand for luxury furniture, which was a consequence of England's booming economy. The second is the popularity of the cabinet as an emblem of wealth and status. Once the cabinet had become an essential and highly visible attribute of the fashionable apartment, demand inevitably escalated. At Ham House in 1677 there were no less than seventeen cabinets and scriptors, and of the nine principal rooms on the ground floor only three were without cabinets. In 1654, by contrast, there had been only one 'blak ebonie cabinet' in the entire house.[11]

As with many luxury goods, what were originally costly extravagances for the super-rich soon became a common feature of most upper-class and even middle-class houses. Most were relatively modest pieces, built to a standard design with readily available materials – oak, deal, walnut, and olivewood. Among London furniture makers any meaningful distinction between cabinet-maker and joiner had effectively vanished by the 1680s.[12] Thomas Pistor, one of the most prominent members of the Joiners' Company who served in several of its offices in the 1680s and 1690s, was also a cabinet-maker. Gerrit Jensen, who became free of the Company in 1667, was eventually appointed 'Cabinet Maker in ordinary' to William III in 1689.[13] By the end of the seventeenth century cabinet-work was assumed to be part of the ordinary repertoire of London joiners. According to the petition submitted to Parliament by the Joiners' Company in 1701, its members were 'bred up in the said Art or Mystery of making Cabinets, Scrutoirs, tables, chests and all other sorts of Cabinet Work. They have arrived at so great a perfection as exceeds all Europe'.[14]

Plate 2:6. Cabinet, Antwerp (c.1680-90). Veneered with ebony, tortoiseshell, rosewood and olivewood on an oak and deal carcase. The drawers are inset with marble panels painted with Old Testament scenes. This is a late example of a typical Antwerp type, heavily influenced by Spanish taste; Spain was one of the most important export markets for this type of cabinet.
RIJKSMUSEUM, AMSTERDAM

Plate 2:7. Cabinet, London (?)
(c.1660-69). Cocus wood veneers and
silver mounts on an oak carcase. One of
a pair made for Henrietta Maria,
widow of Charles I and mother of
Charles II. These *tours de force* of
cabinet-making are unmatched by any
other surviving examples in England.
They are sometimes attributed to
immigrant craftsmen, but there seems
no compelling reason to doubt their
English manufacture.

WINDSOR CASTLE,
THE ROYAL COLLECTION, © 2002
HER MAJESTY QUEEN ELIZABETH II

Plate 2:8. Detail of 2:7, showing the side of one of the cabinet drawers. Fine, straight-grained oak is used throughout and the dovetailing is neat and accurate. The rectangular slots close to the lower edge reveal where cut steel pins were used to hold the drawer sides and bottom together until the glue set.

Plate 2.9. Detail of 2:7; underside of the same drawer, showing the finely mitred corner at the junction of the side and front (bottom right of picture). This is a feature which is common to most early cocus wood cabinets.

Early Restoration cabinets

Although we know that English cabinet-makers were working in London in the 1660s, there are only two surviving cabinets which can unequivocally be assigned to this period. These are the cabinets made for Henrietta Maria, wife of Charles I and mother of Charles II (2:7-9). They probably formed part of the furnishings of Somerset House, which the dowager Queen occupied after the Restoration until her death in 1669.[15]

These cabinets are outstanding in every respect. Each carcase is of fine, straight-grained wainscot, veneered with cocus wood oysters. It is embellished with repoussé silver mounts, bearing the Queen's monogram on the central door and on the shaped apron below (see detail). The cabinet-work is exemplary throughout and every aspect of construction suggests the work of first-class craftsmen (2:8).

Detail of 2:7, showing the silver cipher of Henrietta Maria from the central door of the cabinet.

In stylistic terms the cabinet owes a great deal to France, particularly in the shaping of the stand with its three silver aprons. The use of raised mouldings on the central door and on the edges of the drawers is a vestige of the Mannerist style which characterises French ebony cabinets of the 1640s and 1650s.[16] The drawer construction is also typically French in its use of mitred joints around the drawer base (2:9). This type of construction, although not unique to France, is particularly characteristic of contemporary Parisian cabinets, including those attributed to Louis XIV's cabinetmakers, Pierre Gole (c.1620-1684) and André-Charles Boulle (1642-1732). The purpose of the mitre is to provide a neat finish to the drawer base, with no exposed end grain (2:15).

The use of cocus wood and, to a lesser extent, princeswood, is common to a large group of similar but more modest cabinets which survive in English collections. The example in 2:10-14 is representative of the genre. The cabinet doors are veneered inside and out with geometrically arranged oyster-cut veneers of cocus. The small exterior mouldings are solid cocus wood and run along the grain, as are the edge mouldings to the drawers. The waved figuring of the veneers on the drawer fronts is also very typical, and on some cabinets the inclusion of sapwood makes the figure even more dramatic.

The stylistic and technical attributes of this numerous class of cabinets suggest a fashionable life at the tail-end of English Mannerism. The use of edge mouldings to the drawers and the geometric arrangement of the veneers are vestigial reminders of an earlier style, and it is significant that most cabinets have either ball-turned or tapered pillar supports to the stands, rather than the twist-turned style introduced in the 1670s.[17] Few are likely to have been made after 1675 and most perhaps date from between 1660 and 1670. One of their most telling technical details, the mitred bases to the drawers, was soon dropped and is not often found on English work after c.1680.

15. Edwards (1954), I, pp. 163-4.
16. Peter Thornton has published two engravings of 1688, showing the Cabinet of Curiosities in the Library of the monastery of Sainte-Geneviève in Paris, which depict no less than six cabinets of this form. [Thornton (1978), figs. 291 and 292.]
17. There is a cocus wood cabinet on twist-turned stand at Ham House, which may conceivably be one of the two cabinets described as 'princes wood' in the 1677 inventory. [Thornton and Tomlin (1980), pp. 104 and 113, fig. 98.]

Plate 2:10. Cabinet (c.1660-75).
Cocus wood veneers on a deal carcase.
There are quite a few cabinets of this
type extant, all sharing the same basic
form and materials. This has been
restored and the escutcheons and
hinges are not original.

POWIS CASTLE, NATIONAL TRUST
PHOTOGRAPHIC LIBRARY/
ANDREAS VON EINSIEDEL

The similarities in form and construction between most of these cabinets are sufficient to
suggest, if not a common source, then some common values of design, materials and workmanship.
It could be argued that the entire group is indeed French, but there are a number of reasons to
believe that they were made in England. First, the interior layout of drawers and cupboards is
different from French examples and similar to that routinely used on later English cabinets.
Second, cocus wood was not commonly used on Parisian cabinets (nor indeed on Dutch or Flemish
ones), and oak drawer linings are suggestive of English work rather than French (high-class
Parisian cabinets of this date tend to use walnut or imported tropical woods for their linings).
Third, the handles, locks and other fittings appear to be English rather than French. It is worth

Plate 2:13. Detail of 2:12. The drawer front is deal, the sides oak. Note how the edge moulding is glued on top of the veneer, indicating that it is there not to hide the dovetails but to conform to stylistic convention. The angled cut below the last dovetail betrays the presence of a mitred joint common to most cabinets of this type.

Plate 2:11. Interior of 2:10. Note the much richer colour, unfaded by exposure to light. The layout of the drawers and cupboard is typical of these early pieces. On later cabinets it was usual to enclose the upper and lower drawers within the doors.
POWIS CASTLE, NATIONAL TRUST PHOTOGRAPHIC LIBRARY/ANDREAS VON EINSIEDEL

Plate 2:14. Detail of 2:12. Finely cut dovetails at the rear of the drawer, again showing the angled cut below the last dovetail.

Plate 2:12. Interior drawer. Note the careful arrangement of veneers for decorative effect, and the drawer edge moulding. The handle appears to be original but has been regilt.

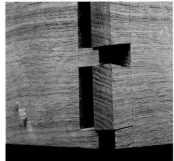

Plate 2:15. Mitred joint, exploded view, showing how the mitre avoids exposing end grain on the vulnerable bottom corners of the joint.
IAN FRASER

noting that most of these cabinets have lock escutcheons placed towards the top of the drawer in the English manner, rather than centrally, as was customary in France.

These differences are sufficient to suggest that, despite their debt to contemporary Parisian work, these cabinets were probably made in England. We know that English cabinet makers like John Burroughs were making expensive cabinets in London in the 1660s, while cabinets 'garnished with silver', and presumably of a similar quality to the pair made for Henrietta Maria, were recorded among the stock-in-trade in Edward Traherne's warehouse in 1675. Given his links with other members of the Royal family, it is possible that the dowager Queen was also one of his clients.

Plate 2:16. Longcase clock (1663). Ebony veneers and mouldings on an oak carcase. The movement, by Ahasuerus Fromanteel, is not the original, but the case-maker, Joseph Clifton, left his token dated 1663 hidden in the trunk. Although the case appears to be of framed and panelled construction, the panelling is sham, created by gluing additional wood to the boarded trunk and door.
PRIVATE COLLECTION

The first pendulum clock cases

The early date proposed for the cabinets discussed above is supported by stylistic analogies between these and early pendulum clock cases.[18] The invention of the pendulum clock in or about 1657 created a revolution in timekeeping and introduced an entirely new article of furniture into English houses. It is often argued that the chronology of pendulum clock case design is not analogous to that of case furniture, because clock cases lagged behind in stylistic development.[19] The reasoning behind this argument has never been adequately explained and it seems both illogical and unfounded. Clock cases were intended to stand alongside cabinets, scriptors and other fashionable furniture. It makes no sense to suggest that the owners of longcase clocks, having bought an expensive and technically advanced movement, should house it in a case which, when placed alongside their other furniture, would appear outmoded. A letter of 1675 from Sir Richard Legh, of Lyme Park, Cheshire, to his wife, throws an interesting light on the choosing and buying of a longcase clock:

> I went to the famous Pendulum makers Knibb, and have agreed for one, he having none ready but one dull stager which was 19L; for 5L more, I have agreed for one finer than my Father's, and it is to be better finish'd with carved capitalls gold, and gold pedestals with figures of boyes and cherubimes all brass gilt. I wold have itt Olive Wood, (the Case I mean), but gold does not agree with that colour, so took their advice to have it Black Ebony which suits your Cabinett better than Walnutt tree wood, of which they are mostly made. Lett me have thy advice herein by the next.[20]

At a time when a good walnut scriptor cost £10, a 'dull stager' of a clock was no mean investment at £19. Interestingly, Sir Richard says nothing of the movement, but is keen to make sure that the case is not only impressive but compatible with other furnishings. Unsure of his judgement in this novel purchase, Sir Richard allowed Knibb to steer him away from an unfashionable combination of olivewood and gold in favour of the sombre luxury of ebony. Sir Richard's wife Sarah certainly approved of his choice; 'My dearest Soule: as for the Pandelome Case, I think Blacke suits anything'.

For furniture historians, the importance of clock cases lies in the fact that they can usually be closely dated. Although the case makers are mostly unknown, the makers of the movements are well recorded and their dates known. Because of the rapid technical development of clock movements, many can be dated to within a few years and this allows the cases, *where original,* to be similarly dated.

On cases of the 1660s and early 1670s, veneers of ebony, cocus wood and princeswood predominate (2:16-18). As with contemporary cabinets, oyster veneers are generally laid in a geometric fashion. The trunks appear to be panelled, but this is a sham construction, created by gluing additional thicknesses of wood to the boards of the trunk. This is very telling, since it demonstrates that the panelled appearance results not from structural necessity but from stylistic convention. The same conventions applied to cabinet furniture, such as the Ham House library

18. The development of English pendulum clocks and their cases has been comprehensively covered by Dawson *et al.* (1982) and Robinson (1981).

19. For instance, Symonds (1929), p. 61: 'The different varieties of marquetry continued to be used by the case-maker for a number of years after they had gone out of fashion with the cabinet-maker. Floral marquetry is found on clocks belonging to the reign of Queen Anne, and arabesque marquetry on clocks as late as 1720'.

20. Quoted in Edwards (1954), II, p. 84.

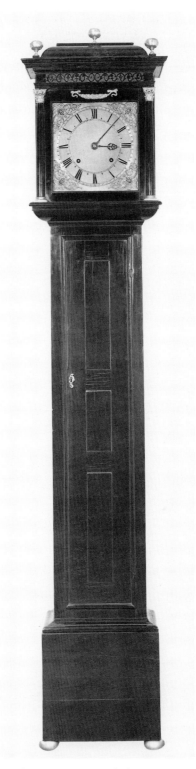

Plate 2:17. Longcase clock (c.1670), by Edward East. Cocus wood veneers on an ebony case. PRIVATE COLLECTION

Plate 2:18. Longcase clock (c.1668-70). The movement is by Samuel Knibb, who died in 1670. The case is of oak, veneered with princeswood. A stunning example of case making at the highest level. PRIVATE COLLECTION

Plate 2:19. Longcase clock (c.1675), with movement by John Knibb. Ebony veneered on an oak case and garnished with silver mounts. By this date the panelled door and trunk were slightly old-fashioned, being superseded by flush veneered cases.

PARTRIDGE FINE ART

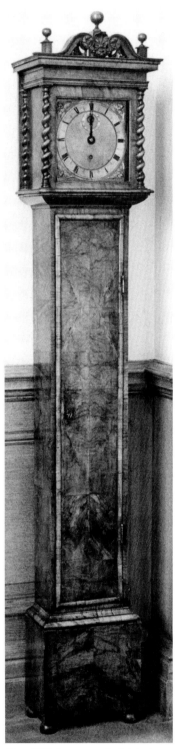

Plate 2:20. **Longcase clock** (1673).
Figured walnut veneers on an oak
carcase. One of a pair supplied to St
Andrews University in 1673 by Joseph
Knibb. This is the first documented
English longcase clock to have twist-
turned pillars in the hood and a
half-round edge moulding on the door.
UNIVERSITY OF ST ANDREWS

scriptor discussed in the next section. Similarly, the treatment of the moulding around the door is analogous to the use of drawer edge mouldings on contemporary cabinets.

Despite their outward similarities, the construction of pendulum clock cases differs significantly from that of veneered case furniture. Clock cases have few, if any, proper joints. The boards for the trunk are butted and nailed together, and the hoods either nailed or glued in a similar fashion. The cleated ends of the doors are not tenoned but simply 'shot' (glued). The crudity of construction belies the often superb and finely wrought mouldings on the hood and the high quality of the materials used, and also seems at odds with the great cost of the movements. These differences in construction might suggest that clock case makers and cabinet-makers were two different trades, but on the other hand it is highly unlikely that the output of pendulum clocks in the 1660s was sufficient to support an independent trade of case-makers.[21] Dawson *et al.* suggest that Ahasuerus Fromanteel's early cases were the work of one very skilled and experienced man.[22] If so, he cannot have gained this experience by making pendulum clock cases, since the type was entirely new. The probability is that he was already an established joiner or cabinet-maker. Since clock cases were intended to be static, there was no need for a strong but expensive dovetailed carcase, and this is the most plausible explanation for the rudimentary method of construction. English furniture makers rarely wasted effort where it was not needed. In time it might have been possible for some cabinet-makers to abandon routine cabinet-work to concentrate on clock cases exclusively. On the other hand, there was nothing to prevent any cabinet-maker or joiner trying his hand at clock cases, and this must have been the case in most provincial cities and towns.

The clock in 2:19 is probably similar to that bought by Sir Richard Legh in 1675. The movement is by John Knibb and the case is veneered with ebony, enriched with silvered metal mounts. By 1675, however, the panelled trunk was declining in fashion, being superseded by flush-veneered cases of the sort shown in 2:20. This clock is one of a pair supplied by Joseph Knibb to the University of St Andrews in 1673. Its significance here is threefold, since it is: (i) the earliest documented flush-veneered walnut clock case; (ii) the earliest documented appearance of the half-round door edge moulding; (iii) the first documented appearance of twist-turned columns on the hood. All these features also first appear on case furniture in the early 1670s.

Two scriptors at Ham House

Among the furniture recorded in the 1677 inventory of Ham House are two scriptors which are worth discussing in some detail. The first is built into the fittings of the library which were installed between 1672 and 1674 by the joiner Henry Harlow (2:21).[23] It is of cedarwood veneered on an oak carcase. The fall and external drawers are fitted with edge mouldings and the fronts have raised fields created by an additional thickness of veneer. As with contemporary clock cases, the panelled appearance is therefore sham, and dictated not by structural necessity but stylistic convention. The main exterior drawers are through-dovetailed, the fronts being finished with edge mouldings in the usual joiner's fashion. The drawer bottoms are rebated well above the base of the drawer and a running strip is added on all four sides (2:22). This unusual arrangement prevents the base of the drawer rubbing on the dustboards, an expedient possibly necessitated by the rather coarse, fast grown oak used for the drawer linings.[24]

Thus far the scriptor is conventional joiner's work, albeit of a high order. The interior, however, is rather more sophisticated (2:23). The small interior drawers are flush-bottomed, and the through-dovetails are hidden by cedarwood veneer (2:24). There are no edge mouldings to the drawers; instead, half-round mouldings are applied to the rails and drawer dividers, the first time this feature occurs on a piece of documented English case furniture.

21. The *Dictionary of English Furniture* discusses the question of whether clock case makers and cabinet-makers were the same and suggests that the former might have been French Huguenots, but offers no evidence to support this hypothesis. [Edwards (1954), II, p. 91.]

22. Dawson *et al.* (1982), p. 150.
23. Thornton and Tomlin (1980), pp. 152-4. Curiously, the Ham inventories consistently describe this piece as a 'cabinet'. although it has a fall-front in the manner of a scriptor.
24. It might be significant that at the time this

was constructed England and Holland were at war (third Dutch War, March 1672-February 1674). The consequent cessation of the trade in Dutch wainscots could well have obliged Henry Harlow to use home-grown timber.

Plate 2:21. Cabinet or scriptor (1672-4). Cedar veneers on an oak and pine carcase. This was installed in the Duke's Library at Ham House, probably by Henry Harlow. The piece is in superb condition, and retains all its original metalware. HAM HOUSE, THE NATIONAL TRUST

Plate 2:22. Drawer from the scriptor, showing the rebated bottom framed all round by running strips. This is an unusual method of construction, but it does occur from time to time on high quality furniture.

Plate 2:24. Interior drawer, showing through-dovetails veneered over. The three-dovetail joint, with a rebate cut into the lowest pin to accept the drawer bottom, is the most commonly found version on London work of this period. The fact that the rebate is visible means the corners are no longer mitred. The bruising on the wood around the third dovetail indicates that the joiner has 'bishoped' the dovetail – i.e., hammered it to get a snug fit – but without much success. Note the rather fast-grown oak used, very different from the much finer, slow grown imported wainscot usually found on London work.

Plate 2:23. Interior of the scriptor, showing the drawers without edge mouldings. Instead, a half-round moulding is applied to the leading edge of the rails and dividers.

Plate 2:25. **Scriptor** (c.1670-75). Burr-elm veneers, inlaid with ebony, on an oak carcase. Made for the Duke of Lauderdale's private closet at Ham House. The legs of the stand were silvered, but are now tarnished. Note the black line painted on the hollow of the spiral. HAM HOUSE, THE NATIONAL TRUST

Plate 2:26. **Interior** of the scriptor. The layout used here remained essentially unchanged well into the 18th century.

Plate 2:27. **Interior drawer**, with oak front and walnut linings. This has the by now usual three-dovetail system. The sides are square-topped and level with the drawer front, which has a very slight bevel on it to make a snug fit. The rectangular cut-out in the lowest dovetail shows where the drawer front is rebated to accept the bottom boards. The mitred corners are no longer used.

Plate 2:28. **Drawer** from the stand. Oak front and linings. The cutting of the pins and dovetails is clearly different from the drawers above.

Directly below the library at Ham is the Duke's closet, a small, snug room refurbished for the Duke of Lauderdale's private use between 1672 and 1674. The room was fully furnished in 1677, when the scriptor 'done with silver' shown in 2:25-28 was described *in situ*.[25] This beautiful piece of furniture inaugurates a new era of English cabinet-work, establishing many stylistic and structural conventions which held good for the next thirty years. In its combination of simplicity of form, richness of surface and restrained detail it is typically English, quite different from the ponderous tortoiseshell cabinets of Antwerp or the slab-sided cupboards of northern Holland. In some respects it is closest to French models but the workmanship is characteristically English.

The primary veneer is burr elm, stained a golden yellow, probably by using *aqua fortis* (nitric acid) in the fashion described by Stalker and Parker,[26] and inlaid with ebony. The main carcase is of oak, with walnut backboards and interior divisions. The forward edges of the latter are faced with half-round mouldings running along the grain. The cabinet drawers are through-dovetailed and flush-bottomed, with oak fronts and walnut linings.

The stand is of elm and ebony veneered on a deal carcase, and the quality of work here is palpably inferior, suggesting a different hand at work. The construction of the frieze drawer reveals different dovetailing from the cabinet drawers, with linings of oak rather than walnut. The legs have a single bine turning with richly carved capitals and bases. The original silvered finish has tarnished badly, and a faintly perceptible black line is painted in the hollow of the spiral. The bun feet are probably replacements.[27]

'First phase' cabinet construction

In its extreme simplicity of exterior form the Duke's scriptor resembles an oriental lacquered cabinet and in this respect it differs from most English cabinets and scriptors, which have projecting cornice and base mouldings. On the other hand, its construction might be regarded as a benchmark for an entire generation of English cabinet-work. Whereas earlier cabinets owed much to the Continent in terms of workmanship and design, the 1670s saw the emergence of a definitive English style. For the next thirty years the form, construction and materials of London-made cabinets varied very little, and this remarkable degree of uniformity is testament to the consistency of training and production among London's cabinet-makers. Although anomalies are inevitably encountered, particularly in provincial work, the degree of standardisation is sufficient to allow case furniture of this period to be characterised as true 'first phase' English cabinet-work.

Summary of typical 'first-phase' cabinet construction.

Carcase: wainscot or deal boards, from ⅞ to 1¼in. (22mm to 32mm) thick, butt-jointed and glued to create the necessary width. The backboards, either oak or deal, run vertically and are nailed into a rebate in the back edges of the carcase.

Interior: horizontal divisions of wainscot or deal boards, ½in. (12.5mm) thick or less, housed in grooves ploughed into the carcase walls. On the most sophisticated examples the interior fittings are made as a separate unit which is then fitted into the main carcase.

The interior arrangement was determined by function. Scriptors usually had a central cupboard flanked by drawers. Below was an open shelf to receive papers, and above was a row of pigeon holes, often with 'secret' compartments behind. For cabinets, both the open shelf below the cupboard and the pigeon holes above were replaced by drawers. Conversions from scriptor to cabinet can usually be identified by the unaltered interior arrangement.

Drawers: of wainscot, deal or, on high quality pieces, walnut. The most common arrangement was to have a deal front with oak sides and bottom. Through-dovetails all round, the sides square-topped and flush with the top of the drawer front. The bottom boards run front to back and are rebated in all round, giving a flush bottom.

Mouldings: made of short, cross-grained sections, usually of the same wood as the primary veneer. Half-round mouldings were of solid wood glued on to the leading edge of the interior divisions. Cornice and surbase mouldings were backed on a deal core.

The usual cornice profile was based loosely on the Tuscan order, but there was considerable variation in its detail. Below that, the convex or pulvinated frieze with 'secret' drawer was almost universal. The surbase moulding was of ogee or reverse-ogee section with a flat fascia below. This moulding was applied partly to the main carcase and partly to a deal strip fixed around three sides of the carcase bottom.

Stand: this was made in an identical fashion to contemporary side tables, the only difference being that the top was veneered only up to the edge of the surbase moulding of the upper carcase. The edge moulding had an ovolo (quarter-round) section, as on other tables.

25. Thornton and Tomlin (1980), pp. 61-67. Subsequent inventories describe the scriptor as 'garnished with silver'.
26. 'To stain a fine yellow', Stalker and Parker (1688), pp. 82-3.
27. In 1731 George Nix was paid £1.10s. 'for mending an old cabinet with Silver corners and other Ornaments & mending the frame, and 4 new black Balls and lining the inside with cloth'. I am grateful to Dr Tessa Murdoch for drawing this bill to my attention.

The Carolean chest of drawers

The techniques developed for the manufacture of high-status cabinets inevitably percolated down to less sophisticated furniture, of which the most obvious example is the common chest of drawers. There is a striking contrast between the heavy, mannered, joiner-made chests of the 1650s and 1660s and the light, cabinet-made versions which superseded them (2:29 and 2:30).[28] Indeed, no other article of furniture better illustrates the revolution in design and form brought about by the advent of modern cabinet-making. Inventory evidence reveals that chests of drawers become common in 'middling' houses from the 1670s, although they are rarely described in sufficient detail to identify the type and style.[29] By contrast, they occur infrequently in the inventories of noble houses at this date (there were only two in Ham House) and it is possible that the chest of drawers was initially a middle-class urban artefact which only gradually made its way into noble houses. Its small size and neat appearance were undoubtedly an advantage in the new type of London houses built after the 1667 Act.

Plate 2:29. Chest of drawers (1650-60). Oak carcase with facings and inlays of ebony, snakewood and ivory or bone. This type of heavily moulded chest embellished with exotic materials represented the ultimate fashionable development of the joiner-made chest of drawers. The introduction of the new, cabinet-made version made this type of chest both stylistically and technically obsolete.
TOWNELEY HALL MUSEUM AND
ART GALLERY, BURNLEY

28. Chinnery (1979) illustrates numerous examples of joiner-made chests of drawers. For a discussion of the sophisticated London-made versions with exotic veneers see Bowett (1998).
29. Sleep (1996), I, pp. 89 and 124.

Plate 2:30. Chest of drawers (c.1670-1700). Olivewood veneers on a deal carcase. The handles and escutcheons are replacements, but are of the appropriate style for the period. The use of a light-coloured holly banding around the drawers is very typical.
PARTRIDGE FINE ART

The carcases of 'first phase' chests of drawers are made in a similar way to those of contemporary cabinets, beginning with an open box made of butt-jointed deal boards joined at the corner by through-dovetails. Lateral bracing is provided by the dustboards, each of which is composed of two or more half-inch (12.5 mm) deal boards, butt-jointed together and housed in grooves cut into the carcase sides. The boards often stop short of the back of the carcase by two or three inches (50 to 75mm). The back is constructed from vertical boards nailed into a rebate on three sides. At the bottom, the backboards overlap the bottom boards and are nailed into them. Occasionally one finds carcases of wainscot rather than deal, but the dustboards are invariably of deal.

The term dustboard is sometimes considered a misnomer. The late R.W. Symonds stated that the primary purpose of dustboards was to prevent theft, by making it impossible to get at the contents of a drawer by removing the one above it. This makes little sense, since if a thief were able to open one drawer he could presumably open the rest. The purpose of the dustboard (apart from adding structural strength to the carcase) was to protect the contents of each drawer from dust created by the friction of the drawer above, and hence the name is perfectly apt.

Drawers were made either of wainscot or of deal or a combination of the two. The most common arrangement in good quality work was to make the drawer front of deal and the sides, back and bottom of wainscot. Although the drawers were larger than those found in cabinets, the construction was essentially the same, with through-dovetails all round and rebated flush bottoms

Plate 2:31. **Drawer bottom** (c.1670-75). This a cabinet-made drawer with a flush bottom, rebated into the sides and front, with no runners. The front of the drawer is on the left. Note the slots left by the pins used while gluing.

Plate 2:32. **Drawer** (c.1670-75). A joiner-made drawer with two large dovetails concealed by edge mouldings. The bottom is not rebated but glued up to the sides.

PRIVATE COLLECTION

(2:31). The drawer sides were squared at the top, and finished level with the top of the drawer front. Almost invariably there is a slight bevel on the top edge of the drawer front to ensure a snug fit in the carcase. Some pieces have drawers with nailed-up bottoms rather than rebated (2:32). This is a joiner's rather than a cabinet-maker's technique and is unlikely to be found on high quality veneered work.

The introduction of banding and crossbanding for drawer and carcase edges was a significant innovation which had both decorative and functional roles. Its decorative purpose was to define areas or panels with borders of contrasting colour or grain. Its other function was to act as a sacrificial veneer, so that chipping or tearing of vulnerable edges was limited to the crossband and did not extend to the main veneer. Damaged sections were easily replaced without disturbing adjacent areas. The banding on early cabinets and chests (perhaps 1670-90) were often of a plain light wood such as holly or sycamore, laid along the grain and forming a strong contrast with the main veneer. Crossbanding in walnut or olive was also common, but featherbanding seems to have been a later introduction, perhaps from about 1690 (see Chapter Seven).

The half-round or D-section rail moulding served a number of purposes. It formed a robust

Plate 2:33. **Base moulding and foot** (1670-1720), showing the usual construction. The mouldings are composite, of olive wood veneers backed on to a deal core, and the turned foot is simply dowelled into its block. The back board overlaps the base of the carcase and is secured by a hand-made nail.

embellishment for the leading edge of the dustboards, where a flat veneer might chip or tear. It added visual interest to the carcase and made the cabinet-maker's task easier, since any slight misalignment of the drawer fronts, which would be obvious if the whole surface were flush, was disguised when broken up by mouldings into a number of separate planes. Finally, by creating a strong shade on its flanks, the half-round moulding served to hide any slackness in the fit of the drawers. As we have seen, on some early cabinets the mouldings were made in long grain strips. Increasingly, however, they were composed of short, cross-grain sections. This method made the most of figured woods such as walnut and olive.

Mouldings were also applied to the top and bottom of the carcase. These served both to cover the joints at the corners of the carcase and to enhance the chest's quasi-architectural form. The upper moulding was usually an ovolo section, identical to that used on tables, and was made by backing a thick, cross-grained facing on to a deal core. The lower moulding was most commonly of an ogee or reverse-ogee section with a flat fascia below. It was attached partly to the carcase and partly to a deal batten running around three sides of the carcase bottom (2:33). Finally, the feet were fixed by dowelling either into the base of the carcase or into a block glued to the carcase bottom. In some cases the dowels were originally threaded into their sockets.

Many chests have an ogee or reverse-ogee top moulding rather than the

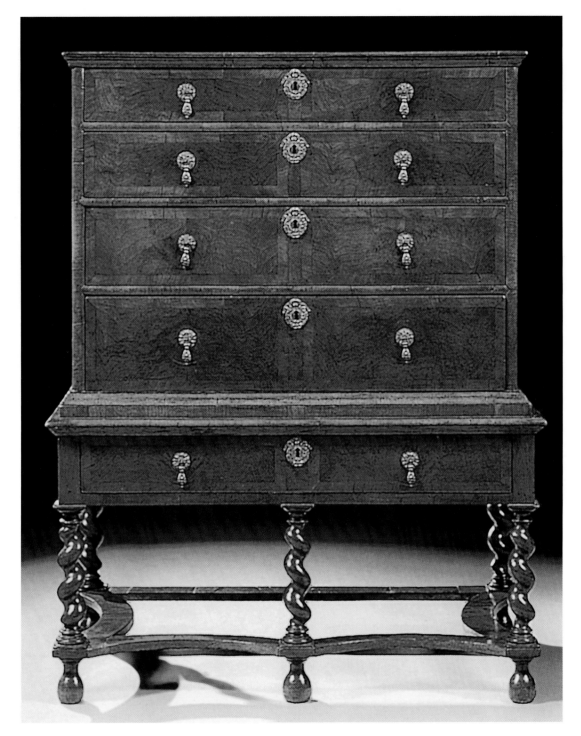

Plate 2:34. Chest on stand (c.1670-90). Figured walnut veneers on a deal carcase. The top moulding is inverted to form a 'cornice' Most chests of this form have long since lost their stands and consequently have had bun or bracket feet added.   SOTHEBY'S

common ovolo. This usually indicates that the chest was originally made to sit on a stand, so that the top moulding therefore 'reads' as a cornice rather than surbase moulding (2:34). Chests of drawers on stands or 'frames' feature regularly in contemporary documents, but most have long since been separated. It is always worth looking carefully at the feet of these chests to determine their originality.

Plate 2:35. Cabinet-on-stand, (c.1675-90). Cocus wood veneers on a deal carcase. It is relatively rare to find cocus wood used in this fashion after about 1680. By this time olivewood, walnut and marquetry were more common.
CHRISTIE'S

Oyster veneering

'Oyster' veneering describes the use of transverse or oblique cuts of small diameter timber to create a decorative surface. It was an economical way of using expensive woods of limited size, such as cocus or princeswood, and was also extended to more common woods, such as olive and walnut, whose small branch timber was otherwise of no value. Modern authorities commonly cite both laburnum and lignum vitae as being used for oyster veneers, but there is no contemporary evidence of their use. Whenever putative specimens have been subjected to microscopic analysis they have turned out to be something quite different, such as cocus or princeswood.

Plate 2:36. **Interior drawer** (c.1670).
The contrast between heartwood and sapwood makes a dramatic effect.
HAM HOUSE, THE NATIONAL TRUST

Cocus and princeswood were the favoured materials for oyster-veneered cabinets of the 1660s and early 1670s. The oysters were arranged in an essentially geometric style, mimicking the moulded panels of late Mannerist joinery and cabinet-work (2:10). When cut obliquely, both woods have a strong directional figure which lends itself to this decorative style. The same essentially rectilinear geometric arrangement was used on contemporary pendulum clock cases up to about 1675 (2:17). In other cases it was the contrast between sapwood and heartwood which provided the decorative impact (2:36).

Olive and walnut tended to be used rather differently. The oysters were usually cut transversely rather than obliquely, because in these woods the figure does not necessarily follow the grain so that it is not possible to get the same directional emphasis that could be achieved with cocus and princeswood. Instead, the decorative effect is gained by the contrast of concentric but rather erratic dark figuring on a light ground. Oysters were frequently combined with marquetry panels, or in circular/oval arrangements defined by light coloured bands or stringing lines (2:29-30).

Floral marquetry

The fashion for floral marquetry was imported from France, where the immigrant Dutch *ébéniste* Pierre Gole began to supply marquetry furniture to Louis XIV from about 1661 onwards (2:37).[30] Gole's style of decoration, with naturalistic sprays of flowers and foliage represented by coloured woods and other materials, quickly caught on and developed into a sophisticated art form which culminated in Boulle's magnificent showpieces of 1690-1700.

R.W. Symonds argued that floral marquetry furniture was made in England as early as 1664.[31] In support of this hypothesis he quoted John Evelyn, whose famous work *Silva* makes references both to *cabinet-makers* and to the technique of *inlaying*. However, Symonds drew on two separate editions of *Silva;* the first, of 1664, and the second, of 1670. The two texts have some small but perhaps significant differences. In the earlier edition Evelyn describes how walnut was used by *'the Cabinet-Maker for Inlayings,* especially the firm and close *Timber* about the *Roots,* which is admirable for *fleck'd* and *chambletted* works, and the older it is, the more estimable;…'.[32] This is certainly evidence that cabinet-makers were working in England in 1664, but it does not sound much like floral marquetry. Rather, it describes the use of naturally figured wood to decorative effect. The 1670 edition, on the other hand, contains specific references to the staining and colouring of woods by inlayers:

> … when they would imitate the natural turning of *Leaves* in their curious *Compartiments* and bordures of *Flower-works,* they effect it by dipping the pieces (first cut into shape and ready to *In-lay)* so far into hot *Sand,* as they would have the shadow and the heat of the *Sand* darkens it so gradually, without detriment or burning the thin Chip, as one would conceive it to be natural.[33]

These 'flower-works' do indeed sound like floral marquetry and the shading technique described has become well known to marqueteurs ever since. The differences between the two editions might suggest that floral marquetry, little known in 1664, was being made in England by 1670.[34] It was certainly well known by 1675 when Edward Traherne's stock-in-trade included numerous items of 'inlaid' and 'flower'd' furniture.[35]

30. Riccardi-Cubitt (1992), p. 86; Baarsen (2000), pp. 53-55.
31. Symonds (1929), pp. 41-3.
32. Evelyn (1664), p. 27.
33. Evelyn (1670), p. 200.
34. It may be that I am reading too much into the differences between the 1664 and 1670 editions of *Silva.* Many of the alterations and additions are very minor and are probably routine revisions or improvements whose value as evidence is debatable.
35. See note 10, above.

Plate 2:37. Cabinet-on-stand (c.1662) attributed to Pierre Gole. Ivory and marquetry veneers on oak and deal carcase. This stunning piece was probably made for the Palais Royale, Paris. The jewel-like quality of the floral marquetry is one which English marqueteurs tried hard to emulate.
VICTORIA AND ALBERT MUSEUM

Plate 2:38. Cabinet-on-stand (c.1675-85). Veneers of walnut and floral marquetry on a deal carcase. The panels of marquetry are self-contained, which suggests that they might have been bought in from a specialist supplier.

©Christie's Images Ltd. 2001

Plate 2:39. Cabinet-on-stand (c.1675-85). Olivewood and marquetry veneers on an oak and deal carcase. A very similar example to the previous one, this time with olivewood rather than walnut veneers. In both cases the marquetry is laid into an ebony ground.   SOTHEBY'S

A great deal of detailed research remains to be done on English marquetry, and without it we can only make very general observations about its development and putative dating. Clock historians date the earliest floral marquetry clock cases to the mid-1670s. These employ small reserves of marquetry in oval or quadrant panels applied to an otherwise conventional walnut or olivewood case. As the fashion and the skills developed, they argue, so the quality of the marquetry grew better and the area covered by it increased, so that by 1690 almost the entire case was decorated.[36]

It is tempting to follow the same line of argument with regard to case furniture. The same small, distinct marquetry panels are found on tables, cabinets and chests of drawers, whose general style suggests dates between c.1675 and c.1685 (2:38 and 2:39). However, the cabinet in 2:40 might suggest that the argument is fallacious. This cabinet was installed at Ham House between 1679

Plate 2:40. Cabinet (c.1680). Ebony and marquetry veneers on an oak and deal carcase. Unlike the previous examples this superb piece is almost entirely covered with marquetry. It is very difficult to envisage this being made from bought-in work, since the marquetry seems tailor-made for the piece.

HAM HOUSE, THE NATIONAL TRUST

and 1683, which makes it a relatively early example, and yet the work is highly sophisticated and covers most of the visible surface of the cabinet. The quality of the design and cutting is exemplary (2:41) and indeed it would be difficult to find a more accomplished example. The apparent differences in style and technique between this marquetry and that on 2:38 and 2:39 are very trivial, and the only substantive difference is in quantity, not quality. It is probable that marquetry laid in small panels and all-over floral marquetry were contemporary and the difference between them was essentially one of cost. Marquetry was an expensive and specialised product, and very few furniture makers can have had marqueteurs permanently employed. Instead, it is likely that the small panels were produced commercially and bought ready-made by case makers and cabinet-makers. For the best furniture, however, it was worth paying for marquetry to be purpose-made.

The quality of marquetry on all these examples is very high, which raises the question of where and how the marqueteurs were trained. The best has a jewel-like quality not unlike contemporary Italian *pietra dura,* and the naturalistic style is close to that of Gole's originals. It is possible that Dutch or French specialists were responsible, but, on the other hand, Evelyn's description of *'Flower-works',* part of which is quoted above, begins with the statement that it was done by 'Our Inlayers', which implies Englishmen.[37] Until firm evidence comes to light the question is unlikely to be resolved, but what is very striking is that the quality of work does not necessarily improve over time. This apparent paradox can be explained by a dilution of the general quality caused by increasing demand. Thus the small group of highly skilled artisans who were the original practitioners of the art were joined by numbers of less skilled opportunists who were able to supply floral marquetry of reduced quality at a reduced price. This, at least, is one explanation for the large quantity of marquetry furniture which varies in quality from the indifferent to the incompetent. 2:42 shows a chest on

Plate 2:41. Detail of 2:40. showing the front of one of the interior drawers. The ebony ground for the marquetry covers the entire drawer front, and is therefore tailor-made to the drawer. Note the wavy cut at the top and bottom, just above and to the right of the drawer handle. This is the 'way in', showing the line taken by the marqueteur's saw to start and finish the cutting of the ebony ground. From this it is apparent that the black and white stringing line was put in after the marquetry was laid.

stand of about 1685-1700. The entire front is veneered with marquetry whose exuberance compensates only partially for the poor quality of execution. The design too has suffered; subtlety of shading and perspective has been lost in the attempt to cram flowerheads and foliage into every available space. The effect is certainly impressive, but it does not compare to the delicacy and balance of top quality work. The cheapening of the market is also evident from the carcase work, which is often decidedly poor in both materials and workmanship. Even on good quality pieces floral marquetry of the later 1680s tends to suffer in design if not execution, as shown by the slightly cluttered style of decoration on many examples.

The technique of floral marquetry[38]

The first stage in producing floral marquetry was to draw the design on paper, and this acted as the master from which all subsequent copies were made. The most precise method of copying was 'pouncing'. The outline of the design was first pricked out with a fine needle, after which the master was laid on a clean sheet of paper. Using a 'pounce pad' coated with fine bitumen powder, the master was rubbed over until the powder had penetrated the perforations and passed through to the clean paper below. Fine graphite or coloured chalk might be used to the same effect, but the advantage of bitumen was that if it were gently heated, the powder would melt and fix irremovably to the paper.[39]

Once sufficient copies were made, either of the whole design or of sections of it, the individual elements – leaves, petals, stems, etc. – were cut out and glued on to their respective veneers. The veneers were then cut on a marqueteur's donkey, or jigsaw, and almost invariably were sawn in a packet of several veneers clamped together. The packet served two purposes: first, it allowed several identical pieces to be cut, so that if the design contained repeated motifs they could be cut simultaneously; second, it prevented the delicate veneers from tearing by clamping them between sections of scrap wood. As an additional security, the veneers were further strengthened by paper glued to one side. After cutting, the individual elements could be shaded (if desired) by dipping in hot sand. This was a simple technique, but capable of achieving very subtle effects.

If the marqueteurs were following what one might call the textbook method, used for the great masterpieces of the Louvre workshops, then the ground was also cut out from a copy of the master drawing. But it is apparent that the ground for most English floral marquetry was produced in a different way, as the table top in 2:43 demonstrates. This is divided into four quadrants around a central oval. The marquetry in each quadrant is similar, but not identical. Some components, such as the acanthus clasp from which the flower stems originate, are repeated, but others, such as the flowers, are not. So although the marqueteur duplicated some elements of the design by cutting them in a packet, he also introduced variety. By using different coloured woods in the same packet a design that appears in one quadrant as red-on-white appears in the next as white-on-red. And by transposing some elements, such as the flowerheads, from one part of the design to another, repetition was avoided. Thus a peony becomes a chrysanthemum, and a rose is changed to a tulip. These transpositions meant that the ground could not be cut in a packet of four identical quadrants, since each was slightly different. Instead the pieces in each quadrant were assembled (perhaps spot-glued) on to the ground which was then marked and sawn out separately. This combination of repetition and variety was employed even on

Furniture with any pretensions to quality employed either gilt iron or brass locks in the most visible places (2:52-53). These were usually screwed and often had three or four shoots. The decorative baluster which secures the 'splick' or pivot is a feature common to most good quality locks of the period, and indeed one that persists well into the eighteenth century.

Handles are perhaps the most vulnerable of all cabinet fittings and consequently the least likely to survive. However, it is often the case that where exterior handles have long since been replaced, those on the interior of cabinets and scriptors have remained largely unused. The earliest and grandest cabinets very often have handles that are unique, usually cast, and either gilt or silvered (2:54-56). This is primarily a reflection of the value attached to the cabinet, but it might also suggest that the trade of cabinet-founder was in its infancy and 'off the shelf' models were not widely available. Similarly, lock escutcheons also tend to be non-standard on high quality pieces (2:57), whereas others employ one or other of a limited number of patterns (2:58-61).

Plate 2:64. **Drawer handle** (1672-74). Gilt brass. This is the most common pattern of drawer handle found on cabinet-made furniture between c.1670 and c.1690. From the Duke of Lauderdale's library cabinet/scriptor.

Plate 2:65. **Drawer fixing** (1672-74). Iron. This is the fixing for the handle shown in 2:64.

Drawer handles of iron have a relatively good survival rate because they are strongly made (2:62 and 63), but these are more often found on joined furniture than cabinet-made. By far the most common type of handle found on early cabinets is the bifurcated scroll, and this remained popular until at least 1690 (2:64). It was fixed by an iron wire or strip, which was folded around the pivot of the drop, pushed back through the drawer front, flattened and punched into the wood (2:65). These handles were sand-cast, usually in brass, and then either lacquered or gilt. The fact that they are so common, and so similar in style, strongly suggests that they were mass-produced, and this in turn suggests a high demand. It is probable that by the early 1670s there had emerged in London a group of metal workers catering specifically for the furniture trade, and for cabinet-makers in particular. Among Edward Traherne's creditors in 1675 was an ironmonger, a locksmith and one Mr Wandall, who was owed £8 for 'boyling of silver and brasse worke'. Door bolts were standard fitments on most cabinets, and the most common form is shown in 2:66. They vary somewhat in detail, but the segmental knob is an almost universal type.

Gilding on metal

The technique of gilding on metal differed according to the base metal. For brass and copper fittings mercury or fire gilding was employed, using an emulsion of gold leaf suspended in mercury. Stalker and Parker described how the emulsion was made:

> Put the gold, and as much quick-silver as will cover it, into a gallipot. Let them stand for half and hour,... stirring them with a stick. This time being expired, strain 'em through a piece of leather, squeezing with your hand, till you have brought out as much quick-silver as will; be forc't through by your industry. Now that which remains in the leather looks more like silver than gold, yet tis that, and that alone, which must be employed in the succeeding operation.

The fittings to be gilded were either cast or cut from sheet metal. The drop-handles fitted to most cabinets and scrutores were cast, whereas hinges and lock plates were usually cut from sheet brass. The detail on castings could be sharpened up by chasing, and sheet metal was decorated by engraving, punching, or a combination of the two.

The piece to be gilded was first scrubbed with a wire brush to remove dirt and key the surface. In some cases the surface was also 'fettled', that is, scraped with a hard steel scraper. This had the effect of producing a slight ripple which, when gilt, enlivened the otherwise dead flat surface (see 7:75). The metal was then rubbed over with mercury mixed with nitric acid, and the mercury/gold emulsion applied with a brush. A little heat helped the liquid to spread as it was brushed and dabbed into every part of the fitting. This being done, it was then heated further to drive off the mercury, leaving the gold closely adhering to the base metal. Any remaining mercury was brushed off and the finishing touch was to suspend the piece in a boiling solution of salt, argal and brimstone in order to clean it and improve its colour.[45] This is perhaps the process for which Mr Wandall was owed money by Edward Traherne (see above). For a really thick, lustrous surface the whole process of fire gilding might have to be repeated several times. Since mercury is a highly toxic metal, mercury gilding was a dangerous job and has been illegal in England since the nineteenth century.

Plate 2:66. Door bolt (c. 1670-1700). Lacquered brass. This is a very common pattern. Note the small fixing pin – another is fixed at right-angles to it, into the bottom edge of the door.

Iron or steel fittings were gilded in a more straightforward manner. The surface was first hatched or roughened and then heated in a charcoal fire before gold leaf was laid directly on to the hot metal (2:45, 48 and 52). The resulting finish was much thicker than that achieved by mercury gilding, and was consequently 'four times as dear'.[46]

Lacquering on metal

Despite the relatively small quantities of gold used, gilding on metal was very expensive. A cheaper option was to polish plain brass fittings to a high lustre and then varnish them to prevent tarnishing. This process was called 'lackering'.

Common lacquers were based on shellac or seed-lac varnish, coloured with Turmeric or Dragon's blood. More expensive lacquers contained ingredients such as Gamboge, a gum-resin (soluble in both water and alcohol) obtained from Asian trees of the genus *Garcinia*.[47] The aim was to achieve a 'true golden colour', altering the appearance of the base metal to more closely resemble gold.[48] The result could be very convincing and one often has to look very hard to determine whether 'gilt' fittings are not in fact lacquered (2:58). Of course, the lacquer was effective only until it wore through in use, but tarnished fittings could always be re-polished and re-lacquered.

45. *Argal* – '… also Argol. Dried cattle dung used as fuel in the steppes of central Asia' *(Oxford English Dictionary)*; *brimstone* – sulphur.
46. Stalker and Parker (1688), p. 67.
47. Bristow (1996), p. 82.
48. Stalker and Parker (1688), p. 63.

Chapter Three
SEAT FURNITURE
1660–1689[1]

hairs of State and 'French' chairs

The Francophile tone of the Carolean court is immediately apparent from the bills for seat furniture ordered for the royal palaces during the 1660s and early 1670s. The two suppliers chiefly responsible were the upholsterer John Casbert and the joiner Richard Price. Casbert (fl.1660-1677) was almost certainly a French émigré.[2] Immediately after the Restoration he began to supply upholstered furniture to the crown even though the post of 'King's upholsterer' was formally held by an Englishman, John Baker. Baker's death allowed Casbert to succeed officially to the post in 1663.

One of Casbert's first commissions was to make the canopies and chairs of State for Charles' coronation in April 1661.[3] One of these chairs, made for William Juxon, Bishop of London, survives (3:1). Casbert's bill describes this as 'a rich purple velvt Chaire of State for the Bishop with a foot stoole and seat cusshon suitable: fringed w[TH] gold fringes and double gilt nailes w[TH] cases of Bayes... £04:00:00'.[4] Eighty-seven ounces of gold fringing were supplied by Ralph Silverson, fringe-maker, at a cost of £29.1s.8d.[5]

The form of this chair is an ancient one. It derives from the late medieval folding chair of state, of which several examples are known. By the 1660s any pretensions to mobility had been put aside; the frame is heavy and rigid and entirely covered with upholstery, so that no part of the wooden frame is exposed. A number of other chairs of this type survive, of which two are at Knole, in Kent. These bear inventory marks for Hampton Court Palace, dated 1661, and can also plausibly be attributed to John Casbert.[6]

As well as formal chairs of state, Casbert supplied seat furniture for more casual use, including numerous chairs described as 'French'.[7] These too were a relatively old model, dating from before the Civil War.[8] Although the square, boxy shape was common to upholstered chairs throughout Europe, the distinctive feature of this chair is the low, landscape-oriented back, without the carved finials which characterise contemporary Dutch chairs of the same basic form. Contemporary engravings show such chairs ranged around the walls of fashionable French apartments, the low backs reaching just to dado level.[9] Similar chairs without arms are often called 'farthingale' chairs (3:2), because it used to be thought they were made to accommodate the wide, hooped farthingale skirts worn by fashionable women around 1600. The name is a fanciful nineteenth century invention; the contemporary name for an upholstered chair without arms was 'backstool' or 'back-chair'.[10]

As an upholsterer, Casbert was concerned primarily with supplying fabrics and trimmings and making these up into all types of upholstered furniture, from footstools to state beds. The range of materials used was very wide, from inexpensive Turkey-work, linen and serge to costly velvets, silks and brocades. Seat furniture with any pretensions to fashion was invariably trimmed with fringes and these, as was the case with Bishop Juxon's chair, were sometimes of real gold and silver. The cost of these materials could be staggering. In 1672 the upholsterer Charles Bland supplied Catherine of Braganza's wardrobe with '2 Large elbowe Chaires of Needle worke richly wrought, one of Blew and gold the other of Silver and pincke', costing £60 the pair.[11] Compared with this, joiner's work came relatively cheap. The cost of materials – oak, beech, or walnut – was negligible when compared with upholstery fabrics, and the labour – joinery, turning and carving – was also inexpensive. A plain twist-turned backstool frame averaged about ten shillings, while a carved elbow chair frame 'wrought with scrowles' and other decoration, might cost £3.[12]

Chairs 'turned all over'

Many of the frames for Casbert's chairs were supplied by the joiner Richard Price, whose name appears in the Lord Chamberlain's accounts from 1670 to 1684.[13] Because they frequently describe the shape and decoration of the frame, instead of the covering, it is his bills, rather than those of John Casbert, which offer the most detailed information regarding the changing form of English chairs during the reign of Charles II.

As we have seen, the 'French' chairs of the 1660s were long established types, essentially unchanged over several decades. From about 1670 onwards the pace of stylistic change quickened and in 1671 Price supplied the first frames of chairs and stools 'turned all over'. Hitherto, backstools and elbow chairs had turned fore-legs and arm supports, and sometimes turned back legs, but the rest of the frame was square or rectangular in section (3:2). On chairs 'turned all over', all exposed elements of the frame were turned, including stretchers, fore-rail and rear posts. It is often assumed that these chairs were entirely of wood,[14] but the majority of Price's bills refer to chair *frames*, implying that upholstery of some sort was intended. The implication is reinforced by

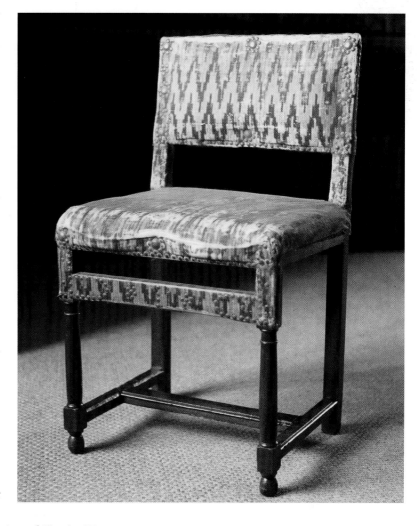

Plate 3:2. **'French' backstool** (1630-70), original silk upholstery, with walnut frame. Popularly called a 'farthingale' chair in the antiques trade, this was the commonest form of upholstered chair in use in the middle decades of the 17th century. The moulded stretchers, the lack of a rear stretcher and the high fore-rail suggest this example is probably French, but similar chairs were made for Charles II in England.   Treasurer's House, York The National Trust,

1. This chapter, together with the subsequent chapter on seat furniture, draws heavily on the evidence of the bills submitted by tradesmen responsible for furnishing the royal palaces to the Lord Chamberlain's office. These are housed in the Public Record Office at Kew. They survive in almost complete sequence from the 1660s onwards and provide a remarkable record of the development of English seat furniture over many decades.
2. For further details of Casbert's career see Beard and Gilbert (1986), p. 149; Beard (1997), pp. 82-85.
3. Beard (1997), p. 82.
4. Yorke (1999); PRO LC 2/8.

5. PRO LC 2/8.
6 Jackson-Stops (1977), II, p. 621; Yorke (1999).
7. PRO, LC 9/271-2.
8. In 1637 the royal upholsterer Ralph Grynder supplied Queen Henrietta Maria with 'French' chairs for her house at Greenwich in 1637 – 'For making 2 french Chayres being Covered all ovr. with figured Velvett & garnisht Round with silvr fringes... £02.00.00' [PRO LR 5/66].
9. Thornton (February 1974) discusses this type of chair in detail. The low-backed form is illustrated in Thornton (1984), fig. 34.
10. The meaning of these terms is discussed in detail in Thornton (February 1974), pp. 103-4; and (1978), pp. 185-87. Thornton states that the

backstool was by definition an upholstered chair and in most cases this seems to hold true, at least in a fashionable context. Randle Holme wrote that a backstool was '... a Chaire made up by an Imbrautherer... Some will call it a Turky worke Chaire. Some a stoole-chaire or backstoole... If the chair be made of all Joyner's work, as back and seate, then it is termed a Joynt chaire or Buffit chaire' [Randle Holme (1688). However, Thornton allows that 'from 1670 onwards... it seems that any chair without arms could be called a 'back stool' [Thornton (1978), p. 187]. Chinnery considers the term equally applicable to wooden and upholstered chairs [Chinnery (1978), pp. 276-79]. The japanned chairs at Ham are described in

the 1683 inventory as 'backstools', and Thomas Roberts occasionally submitted bills for caned backstools, both of which examples tend to support Chinnery's wider interpretation. The most probable hypothesis is that the term was originally specific to upholstered chairs but came in time to be more loosely applied.
11. PRO, LC 5/41, f. 13.
12. These and similar prices can be found in PRO LC 9/273 and 275.
13. For details of Price's career see Beard and Gilbert (1986), p. 716. Price also supplied bedsteads, tables, forms or benches and other joinery.
14. Symonds (Feb. 1934), pp. 86-87; Edwards (1954), II, p. 237.

Plate 3:3. Chair of State (1660-70), original sky blue silk upholstery, with painted ball-turned frame. This is a very rare survival, predating the much more common twist-turned chairs by a decade or so.

KNOLE, THE NATIONAL TRUST

the frequent use of the term 'backstool' and 'back-chaire' which, in a fashionable context, usually described an upholstered chair without arms.

Confusingly, many of Price's frames 'turned all over' were also described as 'French'. The term was applied both to a generic type of stool or chair – 'For 16 French foulding stooles frames turned all over at 5s. a peece' (1672) – and to the style of turning itself – 'For 12 back chaire frames french turned all over' (1672).[15] Some authorities consider that in this context the term 'French' implied spiral or twist-turning,[16] but Price was careful to distinguish in his bills between 'French' and 'twisted' frames, which suggests that the two were not the same. One possible candidate for 'French' turning is what is now called 'bobbin' or 'ball' turning. This common decorative device can be seen in French engravings of the period, and it also occurs on the stands of French and English cabinets made in the 1660s and early 1670s (cf. 2:7 and 2:10). The fact that few ball-turned chairs are found with later features such as carved crest and fore-rails tends to support an early date for this type of turning and is consistent with the date of Price's bills for 'French' turned chairs.

Ball-turned chairs occur in both wooden and upholstered forms. 3:3 is a rare survival of the latter, covered with its original sky blue silk. This chair probably originated in one of the Royal Palaces, and was later acquired by the Lord Sackville, sixth Earl of Dorset. The splayed back is uncommon, and usually denotes a Royal chair of state. Wooden ball-turned chairs are much more numerous. The example in 3:4 is from a large set of elbow chairs. The boxy shape, horizontal arms and 'landscape' oriented back all suggest an early date (perhaps 1660-70), as do the block terminals of the arms. The graduated spindles in the back are a nice refinement and indeed the whole chair is constructed from unusually slight members – most examples are more strongly built. The seat board is panelled into a groove cut into the rails, which is the usual method of construction, and it would almost certainly have been furnished with a loose cushion for comfort. It is possible that a cushion was also hung from the button finials on top of the back posts. 3:5 shows a more typical example, very strongly built, and with two parallel side stretchers. This is probably what Richard Price called 'double rayled'.[17]

Another 'double railed' backstool, this time with a Turkey-work cover, is shown in 3:6. Three dozen of these were bought in London in 1668 and delivered to Holyrood Palace, Edinburgh, the same year. The frame is of a standard design, with squared stretchers and back legs, and not 'turned all over'. It is interesting to compare this chair with an earlier model at Holyrood, probably made before the Restoration (3:7). The proportions are very similar, but the earlier chair has baluster-turned fore-legs without a fore-rail and no turning of the back posts between seat and back.[18]

15. PRO LC 9/273, f.46.

16. Forman (1988), p. 220.

17. For example: 'For one back chair double rayled and turned all over' (1673) [PRO LC 9/273, f.82].

18. Swain (1977). My interpretation differs from that given by Mrs Swain, who suggests that both the bobbin-turned and the baluster-turned chairs date from 1668. The Holyrood bills account for only eighty-four of the one

hundred and twenty chairs recorded at the Palace in 1685. Mrs Swain assumes that the missing three dozen chairs were also bought in 1668, although no bill survives. A more probable inference is that these three dozen

were already in the Palace in 1668. This would explain both the discrepancy between the bills and the 1685 inventory, and the stylistic differences between the two sets.

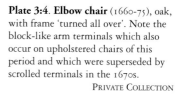

Plate 3:4. Elbow chair (1660-75), oak, with frame 'turned all over'. Note the block-like arm terminals which also occur on upholstered chairs of this period and which were superseded by scrolled terminals in the 1670s.
PRIVATE COLLECTION

Plate 3:5. Chair (1660-75), oak, with frame 'turned all over'. A very strongly made example, 'double-rayled' at the sides. It has lost its feet and therefore at least 2in. (50 mm) in height.
NOSTELL PRIORY, THE NATIONAL TRUST

Plate 3:6. Backstool (1668), one of three dozen sent from London to Holyrood Palace in 1668. This chair, with its plain side stretchers and rear legs, bears out the assertion made by the Joiners' Company in 1689 that Turkey-work chair frames had 'but little Work in the making, less Work in the Turning, and generally no Carving at all' (cf. page 84, below). The frame has been much repaired and the upholstery removed and replaced several times. HOLYROOD PALACE, THE ROYAL COLLECTION,© 2002 HER MAJESTY QUEEN ELIZABETH II PHOTOGRAPH: ANTONIA REEVE

Plate 3:7. Backstool (before 1688). These chairs were probably already at Holyrood when those in 3:6 were delivered in 1668. The baluster turned fore-legs and stretchers almost at ground level are typical of an earlier style, and these perhaps date from the 1640s or 1650s. HOLYROOD PALACE, THE ROYAL COLLECTION,© 2002 HER MAJESTY QUEEN ELIZABETH II PHOTOGRAPH: ANTONIA REEVE

Variations on ball-turning are common. Reel turning is one, but far more popular was the ring-and-ball turning shown on the couch in 3:8. Couches of this type were made over a very long period, and their simplicity and lack of embellishment afford few stylistic clues to dating. The low back and straight arms of this example suggest a relatively early date, probably before 1680, but it could be much later.

The 'twisted turn'

The sudden appearance of twist-turning on English chairs is traditionally ascribed to Dutch influence and it is certainly the case that twist-turning was employed in Holland before its use in England, but twist-turning was popular throughout Europe, and it is difficult to confirm its attribution to any one source. The twist-turned or 'Solomonic' column, so-called after the spiral pillars which once supported Solomon's temple in Jerusalem, was an ancient device revived and made popular by Italian baroque architects, notably Bernini, who employed it for the supports of the high altar canopy in St Peter's church at Rome (1633). Thereafter it became a standard feature of European baroque architecture from Sicily to Scandinavia. The use of twist-turning on furniture follows the long established convention of treating chair and table legs as columns in miniature.

Pictorial and documentary references both attest to the presence of twist-turned chairs in France and Holland before 1670,[19] but the first mention of such chairs in Richard Price's bills does not occur until 1672: 'For 12 Back Chaire frames turned all over wth the twisted turne wth great Heeles'. The cost was nine shillings each.[20] Interestingly, the date coincides closely with the first recorded use of twist turned columns on clock hoods (cf. 2:20), and on the stands of cabinets (cf. 2:25). The phrase 'great Heeles' is open to various interpretations. Most turned chairs of this date have ball, pear, or cup-shaped feet, so it is possible that the 'great Heele' was a back leg whose foot

19. See, for instance, Thornton (1974), fig 4; Jaffer (2001), pp 135-6.
20. PRO LC 9/273, f.58.
21. Symonds (1929), pp. 63.

Plate 3:8. Couch (1670-90), modern upholstery with walnut ring-and-ball turned frame.   MONTACUTE HOUSE, THE NATIONAL TRUST

Plate 3:9. **Chair** (1670-85), oak twist-turned frame. This is a very typical example of a frame turned all over with the 'twisted turne'. One of a pair.

terminated in a rectangular block. It is also possible that a 'great Heele' and a 'compass' or raked heel were the same thing. The only thing we can say with certainty is that the 'great Heele' implies that the front and back feet were different.

3:9 shows a twist-turned chair, 'turned all over' and with a panelled seat. It has the same boxy form and landscape back as contemporary bobbin-turned chairs, which suggests an early date, perhaps 1670-80. Its double-stretchered construction imparts great strength, which no doubt accounts for its survival in good original condition.

The turnings on this chair are of the 'double-bine' type, that is, having two spirals cut on the same shaft at one hundred-and-eighty degrees to each other. Conventional wisdom holds that the Continental twist-turning had a single spiral and the English version a double one,[21] but, like all rules of thumb, this must be treated with caution, since there are plenty of English examples of single-bine turning. It is nevertheless true that this style of turning is less common in England than on the Continent. The reason for this is obscure, but it may have to do with the widespread use of spiral turning lathes in England, which made the production of multi-bine turnings relatively easy.

Plate 3:10. Chair (1670-90), oak twist-turned frame. A strong but crudely made example, combining twist-turning in the upper frame with ring and ball turning in the lower.
<small>NOSTELL PRIORY, THE NATIONAL TRUST</small>

Plate 3:11. Detail of 3:10 showing the scars left by the rasp used to cut the spirals in the back rails.

22. Moxon (1678), p. 181.
23. Ibid., p. 177.
24. Ibid., p. 180.
25. Ibid., p. 179.

It is often assumed that twist-turning was carved by hand, and indeed one can sometimes discover evidence of hand work on twist-turned chairs (3:10-11). But hand-cutting spirals was a laborious and inefficient process, particularly when sets of eight, twelve or twenty-four chairs were needed. Far better, then, to cut the spirals on a lathe. This could be done on a modified screw-cutting lathe, a device which had been employed in Europe since medieval times (3:12). It operated by moving the workpiece against a stationary cutter, the pitch of the spiral being controlled by a lead screw, into which the workpiece was fixed.

Although many turners plied their trade independently of other furniture makers, inventory evidence reveals that few large joiners' shops were without their own lathes. From the 1670s onwards most fashionable chair frames were turned to some degree, and it was simply uneconomic not to house all the tools and machinery under the same roof. The simplest form of lathe was the pole lathe (3:13), usually a springy sapling or pole attached to the roof of the workshop and powered by a treadle. A string 'made of the Guts of Beasts' ran from the treadle around the workpiece and up to the pole. The thickness of the string depended on the size of work undertaken, and the pole was made 'longer or shorter, or bigger or smaller, according to the weight of the Work'.[22]

Although cheap and easy to set up, the pole lathe had one big drawback, which was that it cut only on the downstroke, thus limiting its efficiency. Its power was also limited by the strength of the operator's legs, ' For the thicker the Pole is, the harder must the Tread be to bring it down...'.[23] The treadle lathe made more efficient use of leg power by converting the reciprocating action of the treadle into a continuous drive. This lathe could also be geared to multiply the effort of the treadle but, 'not having the strength to carry heavy Work about', it was mainly used only for small work, such as 'Cane-heads, Small Boxes &c.'.[24]

Large workshops were usually equipped with at least one 'Great Wheel', which was both more efficient and more powerful than either the pole lathe or the treadle (3:14). The wheel, perhaps 5ft. or 6ft. in diameter (1.5m to 2m), was turned by a hand crank, and because of its great circumference it drove the workpiece at high speed. Despite needing at least two men to operate it (one to drive the wheel and one to do the cutting), the great wheel was a highly efficient machine; 'Besides commanding heavy Work about, the Wheel rids Work faster off than the Pole can do; because the springing up of the Pole makes an intermission in the running about of the Work, but with the *Wheel* the Work runs always the same way; so that the Tool need never be off it, unless it be to examine the work as it is doing'.[25]

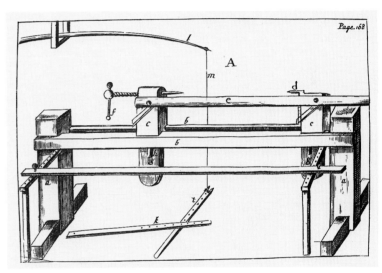

Plate 3:13. **The pole lathe,** from *Mechanick Exercises* (1678).

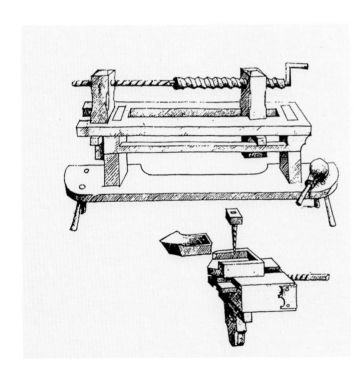

Plate 3:12. **Lathe for spiral turning.** This lathe works by moving the workpiece against a stationary cutter. At the right-hand side is the crank, whose shaft is threaded through the headstock. As the crank is turned it moves forward. The workpiece is fixed into the end of the crank, which therefore also moves forward, sliding freely through the tailstock (left). The cutting tool (shown in foreground) is either held by hand or in a tool holder, and cuts the spiral as the workpiece moves across it. By rotating the workpiece 180 degrees relative to the crank, another spiral can be cut on the same workpiece, producing the typical English double-bine spiral.

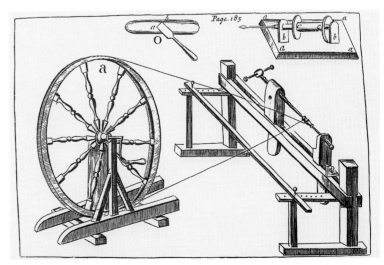

Plate 3:14. **The Great Wheel**, from *Mechanick Exercises* (1678). Note that the gut is crossed around the workpiece to give it purchase.

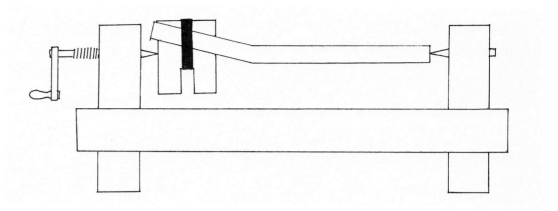

Plate 3:15. Lathe for two-centre turning. This drawing shows a conventional lathe-bed, powered either by a pole or a great wheel. The buckle and counter-weight form a false centre to which the raked section of leg is strapped while the horizontal section is turned. The assembly can then be reversed to turn the raked section.

The fashion for frames 'turned all over' presented the turner with at least one new technical problem. Because of the rake of the back posts above the seat, turners had to develop a lathe which could turn each end of the post (above and below the seat) separately. This 'two-centre' turning could be achieved in various ways, but perhaps the most straightforward solution is shown in 3:15. The wedge-shaped block strapped to one end of the workpiece acts as a false centre, allowing the other end of the post to be worked. When this is done, the workpiece is reversed and the other section turned in the same way.

Plate 3:16. Turkey-work, showing the individual knotting used to create the design. The black areas have been re-knotted. This is because the iron oxide used as a mordant for the black dye corrodes the wool leaving large areas of the design bare.

Turkey-work.

Turned chairs made entirely of wood have a relatively high survival rate, but were probably less common than those with some form of upholstery. The Upholsterers' petitions of 1689 and 1699 claimed an annual production of 192,000 and 300,000 upholstered chairs respectively.[26] Even allowing for some exaggeration, this staggering figure offers a thought-provoking measure of the scale of chair making in late seventeenth century London.

The most expensive chairs were furnished with silk, velvet and other luxurious fabrics, but most were covered with traditional woollen cloth – 'Serge, Perpetuanoes, Camlets, Bays, Kersies, *Norwich* cheniis, and *Kidderminster* Prints'.[27] The vast majority of these have perished, but a fair number of the most durable of these materials, known as Turkey-work, have survived. As its name implies, Turkey-work imitates the appearance and structure of Turkish carpets. It differs from embroidery in that it was not created with a needle and thread but was tied knot by knot on to a woollen warp in the same way as an Oriental carpet (3:16). The result was both colourful and hard-wearing, and the quantity of surviving examples is testament to its popularity and durability.

Turkey-work was also quite cheap. In 1673 John Casbert supplied '12 Back Chaires of Turkey-work' at 11s.6d. each, together with a matching 'great Chaire' (elbow chair) at £1.18s. This compared favourably with the cost of 6s.10s. for

PROSPECTUS INTRA CAMERAM STELLATAM.

uncovered back-chair frames supplied by Richard Price at this time.[28] The cost of supplying and fitting the Turkey-work appears therefore to have been not more than about 5s.6d. per chair. The combination of colour, durability and affordability ensured that Turkey-work was the single most common upholstery material in middle-class homes up to 1700, and this is borne out by the evidence of inventories from all parts of the country.

Unlike needlework or embroidery covers, which were often made at home, Turkey-work was manufactured commercially and to standard patterns. This explains the very similar design and structure of many surviving Turkey-work covers. Very little is known about Turkey-work manufacture, but a petition of about 1680 states that it was made in Yorkshire.[29] Two later petitions calculated that 72,000 Turkey-work chairs were produced in 1689 and 60,000 in 1699 out of a total production of upholstered chairs of 192,000 and 300,000 respectively. The drop in both absolute and relative terms (from 37.4% to 20% of total production) indicates a gradual decline in popularity, but Turkey-work chairs nevertheless continued to be made into the second quarter of the eighteenth century. A good proportion of English Turkey-work covers were exported and have been identified on chairs in Italy, Sweden and North America. There is also documentary evidence that Turkey-work covers were exported to France in the 1660s.[30]

Most Turkey-work backstools are rather conservative in design, with conventional square-section frames turned only on the fore-rails, fore-legs and sometimes the rear posts. A set of this type is shown in 3:17, which depicts the interior of the Star Chamber at the Royal Greenwich

Plate 3:17. Engraving, the Star Chamber at the Royal Greenwich Observatory (1670s). Turkey-work chairs with twist-turned frames are ranged around the walls.

MAGDALENE COLLEGE, CAMBRIDGE

26. BL, *For the Encouragement of the Consumption of the Woollen Manufacture of the Kingdom* (1689).
27. Ibid.
28. PRO LC 9/273, f. 129.
29. BL, *For the Encouragement of the Consumption of the Woollen Manufacture of the Kingdom* (1689).
30. Forman (1988), p. 195; Swain (1987), p. 51.

Plate 3:18. Great chair (1670-80), Turkey-work upholstery and twist-turned oak frame. A rather stiff, old-fashioned looking chair, but probably typical of many modestly-priced examples.

DURHAM CATHEDRAL

Plate 3:19. Backstool (1685), one of four dozen bought in London for Holyrood House in 1685. Compare with 3:6 and 3:7. Note the altered proportions, twist-turned frame and raked rear heels.

HOLYROOD PALACE, THE ROYAL COLLECTION,
© 2002 HER MAJESTY QUEEN ELIZABETH II. PHOTOGRAPHER: ANTONIA REEVE

31. Swain (1977).
32. This chair is discussed in detail in Gilbert (1998), p. 578.

Observatory. The chairs have twist-turned fore-rails, fore-legs and rear posts above the seat, and the backs are 'landscape' oriented. The 'great chair' or elbow chair in 3:18 is of the same basic pattern, and the straight, horizontal arms are typical, at a time when more fashionable upholstered and caned chairs were increasingly made with downcurved 'compass' arms. It is noticeable, too, that Turkey-work chairs were slow to follow the fashion for higher backs which was such an obvious feature of contemporary caned chairs, and indeed they never achieved the same extravagant heights. One possible explanation for this might be the inability of the Yorkshire producers to respond rapidly to stylistic change. Cloth production in the Pennines was still essentially a cottage industry, with hundreds or even thousands of small producers supplying wholesale merchants in towns like Halifax, Bradford and Leeds. Having established a standard size and style, it would not be easy to alter them to suit the rapidly changing London market. Nevertheless, later Turkey-work chairs do pay some lip-service to contemporary fashion. In 1685 four dozen backstools were ordered

Plate 3:20. Backstool (c.1680-90), original turkey-work upholstery and walnut frame. This is an exceptional survival, untouched and virtually entire. Note the fringed seat and back panel. These fragile trimmings are almost always lost in use.

TEMPLE NEWSAM HOUSE, LEEDS CITY ART GALLERIES

for Holyrood Palace to add to the three dozen bought in 1668.[31] A comparison between these chairs (3:19) and the earlier ones (3:6) shows that, although the structure of the chair is essentially unchanged, its proportions have altered significantly. The overall height and width are the same, but the later chair has an almost square, upright back. The later example also has a twist turned fore-rail, fore-leg and medial stretcher, and 'compass' heel. The backstool in 3:20 is perhaps later still. It is significantly higher overall (even without its feet), and the back is now 'portrait' oriented.[32]

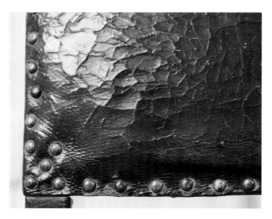

Plate 3:21. Russia leather. Note the typical hatched surface, and the pale colour of the leather showing through the patination. The domed tacks are original, and were originally gilt or lacquered.

Plate 3:22. Backstool (c.1670-85), original Russia leather upholstery and walnut frame. Note the leather applied to the forward faces of the rear posts, a common feature presumably done to create a visual link between seat and back. THE GEFFRYE MUSEUM, LONDON

Russia Leather

Even more durable than Turkey-work was leather, and leather covers are perhaps the most common type of original chair cover to survive. Documentary sources make frequent mention of both 'Russia' and 'Turkey' leather, although apart from their different nationalities the distinction between the two is unclear. Little or no research has been done on the trade in Turkey leather, but the importation of Russian hides from ports in the Baltic and from Archangel is well documented. Russia leather was highly regarded throughout Europe and was used on a large scale by English chairmakers. Its high quality was the result of long tanning, up to eighteen months and sometimes longer, during which time the leather was steeped in a bark liquor variously described as being made from oak, birch, willow or poplar.[33] This was augmented by a final impregnation with birch tar or oil, which not only enhanced suppleness and durability, but endowed the leather with an intense and unique aroma.

The surface of Russia leather was finished with a characteristic hatched or diapered pattern (3:21). *The Art of Tanning and Currying Leather* (1780) describes how the pattern was impressed with steel rollers weighted with stones. The roller was moulded with raised diagonal lines, so that two passes, one at ninety degrees to the other, produced '… a multitude of small lozenges… which

33. Garbett and Skelton (1987), pp. 26-27.
34. Ibid., p. 42.
35. Trent (1987), p. 46, fig. 26.
36. Agius, (1971), pl. 24B.

Plate 3:23. Backstool (1692), original leather upholstery and oak frame. Supplied to Christ Church, Oxford, by John Williams in 1692. Chairs like this illustrate the difficulty of dating semi-fashionable furniture. The frames are unchanged from those of the 1670s, and only the height of the back is indicative of a later date.
CHRIST CHURCH, OXFORD, BY KIND PERMISSION OF THE DEAN AND CHAPTER

Plate 3:24. Backstool (1690-1710), original leather upholstery and oak frame. The proportions of this chair are very similar to 3:23. The carved fore-rail is most unusual on plain leather backstools and is of a type fashionable on caned chairs from about 1685-90. VICTORIA AND ALBERT MUSEUM, V&A PICTURE LIBRARY

please the public eye'.[34] One suspects that the diapering also served to disguise blemishes in the hide. The high reputation of Russia leather spawned a host of imitators, even to the extent of imitating the diapered finish.[35] It is a fair bet that much of the 'Russia' leather recorded in seventeenth century documents was not the genuine article.

Backstools covered in Russia leather exhibit an identical pattern of stylistic and structural development to contemporary Turkey-work backstools (3:22-25). In many cases it is only the height of the back which gives any clue to their date – compare, for instance, 3:22, a backstool of about 1670-85, with 3:23, made for Christ Church, Oxford, in 1692.[36]

None of the leather or Turkey-work chairs so far discussed is decorated with carving in the same way as contemporary caned chairs. This bears out an observation in the Cane-Chairmakers' petition of 1690 (discussed below) that 'there is seldom or never any Carved work bestowed upon them'. Occasionally one finds examples with carved fore-rails, and this is a considerable help in dating them. The chair in 3:24 has a fore-rail of paired scrolls centred on a winged cherub's head and the same fore-rail can be found on caned and upholstered chairs of about 1685-1700. 3:25 is

Plate 3:25. **Backstool** (1700-20), modern leather upholstery and oak frame. One of a large set reputed to date from the founding of Chetham's Hospital in 1655, but the carved fore-rail, with its addorsed C scrolls, is not found on fashionable furniture much before 1700.　CHETHAM'S HOSPITAL, MANCHESTER

Plate 3:26. **Backstool**. This is a typical 19th century reconstruction. The thick, coarse leather is not original and the frame, which dates from about 1680, has been substantially rebuilt. Note the wear on the lower edge of the fore-rail, indicating that the rail has been turned to disguise it.　EAST RIDDLESDEN HALL, THE NATIONAL TRUST

later still, for the addorsed C-scroll fore-rail is unlikely to date from much before 1700 (cf. 8:60-8:61, below).

Having languished in cellars, attics and outhouses for most of the eighteenth century, leather backstools were rescued from oblivion by Victorian historicism. Thus the 'Cromwellian' chair was born – dour, unyielding, and an ideal set dressing for the halls and passageways of England's ancient mansions. The backstool in 3:26 has been completely reconstructed; the fore-rail has been turned to disguise the wear, and the leather is a stiff, thick hide, quite different from the supple Russia leather which it seeks to imitate. The colour is also very much darker than most genuine examples. Original Russia leather was frequently light tan in colour, sometimes a rich brown, but rarely black. The rich black-brown tones of old examples are the product of three centuries of oxidization, dirt and polish, but one can occasionally see a hint of the original colour on some hidden surface (3:21).

Plate 3:27. Backstool (1670-1700), original Russia leather upholstery and walnut frame. This is probably Dutch (see text). MONTACUTE HOUSE, THE NATIONAL TRUST

The same antiquarian hankerings encouraged the import of Continental backstools to make up the shortfall of genuine English ones. 3:27 shows a French or Dutch example of about 1675, which has at least four obvious differences from those in the preceding illustrations. The first is the very high fore-rail – on English chairs they are usually lower. The second is the single-bine turning centred on a ring and ball. This style of turning can certainly be found on contemporary Dutch examples. The third is the round-to-square joints between stretcher and leg. This last feature is by no means exclusively Continental and also occurs on English chairs, but in combination with the other two it is a good indication of Continental manufacture. The fourth difference is the high rear stretcher – none of the English backstools illustrated (both Turkey-work and leather) has a high rear stretcher. (This is in contrast to more fashionable caned and upholstered English chairs, which almost invariably have a rear stretcher mid-way between floor and seat.)

Caned chairs

Shortly after the Restoration the middle-market dominance of traditional Turkey-work and leather backstools was challenged by an exotic newcomer – the caned chair. Both the technique and the material of caning came from the Orient. The 'cane' was made from the trailing suckers of the Rotang or Rattan cane (*Calamus rotang*), a plant native to much of Asia. The suckers were split to produced long, narrow strips of great strength which were easily pliable when green or damp. Rattan was certainly known in Europe by the beginning of the seventeenth century and was apparently employed in making binding or twine long before it was used in furniture making,[37] but, according to the London Cane-Chairmakers' petition of 1690, caning for seat furniture did not come into fashion until 'about the year 1664'.[38]

If it is not clear why caned chairs had not been adopted in England before the Restoration,[39] their popularity thereafter is easily explained. Among their many virtues were '... Durableness, Lightness, and Cleanness from Dust, Worms, and Moths, which inseperably [*sic*] attend Turkey-work, Serge and other stuff chairs and couches, to the spoiling of them and all Furniture near them'.[40] Moreover, caned chairs were cheaper than their upholstered equivalents. Richard Price's bills show that in the 1680s caned chairs could be bought for as little as 10s. each. This fact alone goes a long way to explaining the extraordinary growth in caned chair manufacture in the late seventeenth and early eighteenth centuries. By the early 1680s the canes were being imported into London in large quantities – 4,500 in the month of January 1682, for instance. By 1698, the first year for which complete records survive, the figure had reached 894,205 canes per annum.[41] Most were imported in a raw state, but some were split and ready for use.[42]

Our best contemporary information about the caned chair manufactory comes from the Parliamentary petitions generated by disputes between the Cane-Chairmakers and the Upholsterers who, together with the Woollen Cloth Manufacturers, had hitherto had a virtual monopoly of the supply of cheap chairs and upholstery materials. The petitions were linked to various phases of legislation concerning the woollen trade, which went through Parliament in the 1680s and 1690s. The earliest of the petitions – 'For the Encouragement of the Woollen Manufacture of England' – probably dates from before 1689.[43] It does not mention caned chairs specifically, but argues for a general prohibition on covers other than woollen cloth for couches under the value of £4 and chairs and stools under 20 shillings. Interestingly, covers of leather were exempted from this prohibition, since they were 'the product of our Cloth from Turkey and Russia'. In other words, the woollen manufacturers wanted to avoid damaging counter-measures from these lucrative export markets. The protection extended to Russia leather is a consistent feature of all the subsequent upholsterers' petitions.

A second petition – 'For the Encouragement of the Consumption of the Woollen Manufacture of this Kingdom' – was presented to the House of Commons in December 1689.[44] This petition arose from a resolution of the Upholders' Company's Court of Assistants in October 1689, when £15 was voted to the Warden 'towards obteyning an Act of Parliament for prohibiting the making of Cane Chairs etc....'.[45] This was at a time when Parliament was itself debating a bill concerning the manufacture and export of wool. When the Cane-Chairmakers got wind of the petition, they asked the Joiners' Company to present a counter-petition 'on behalf of themselves and some thousands concerned in making the said Chaires...'.[46] This petition went before the House of Commons in 1690. The Joiners' Company calculated that the framing of 192,000 upholstered chairs per annum employed not more than one hundred and eighty joiners and thirty turners, 'there being but little Work in the making, less Work in the Turning, and generally no Carving at all in those Frames'.[47] The demand for caned chairs, on the other hand 'occasioned the Chair-Frame Makers and Turners to take many Apprentices; and Cane-Chairs, &c. coming in time to be Carved, many Carvers took Apprentices, and brought them to Carving of Cane-Chairs, Stools, Couches and Squobs only: And there were many Apprentices bound only to learn to Split the Canes, and Cane those Chaires, &c.'. As a result, the caned chair manufactory employed 'many Thousands of People', all of whom had invested substantially in training, premises and stock.

To reinforce their case, the Cane-Chairmakers pointed out that, compared with the enormous

37. Forman (1988), p. 229.
38. 'The CASE of the Cane-Chair makers...'(1690), quoted in Symonds (March 1951).
39. One possible explanation is that the fashion for caned chairs was directly linked to the general burgeoning of all East India trade. As with the West India trade, there were often more ships than freight in the Indies, and so Rattan, an inexpensive but widely available commodity, might have been carried even when more lucrative freights were lacking.
40. 'The CASE of the Cane-Chair makers...' (1690), quoted in Symonds (March 1951).
41. PRO Cust. 3.
42. Ibid.
43. B.L., L.R. 305.a.7.
44. B.L., 1605/622 (8).
45. G.L., 7191/1 22 October 1689.
46. G.L., 8046/2, 30 December 1689.
47. This means that each joiner produced 1,066.6 chair frames per annum which, assuming a working week of six days, amounted to 3.5 frames per day. The turners turned 20.5 frames per day.

output of upholstered chairs, caned chair production was relatively small. In 1690 the Cane-Chairmakers reckoned to make 72,000 chairs, stools and couches per annum, of which a third were exported. These went not only to Europe but to 'almost all the Hot Parts of the World, where Heat renders Turkey-work, Serge, Kidderminster and other stuffed Chairs and Couches useless'.[48] Caned chairs were recognised throughout Europe as a characteristically English product and in France were even known as 'chaises à l'Anglaise'.[49] Of those chairs that remained, many required 'Cushions or Quilts, which consume much Wooll and Silk'. Consequently, the damage to the wool trade was much less than woollen manufacturers claimed. If their trade was suffering at all, the real cause was the undoubted increase in imported fabrics, for 'whereas about Thirty Years ago there was One Dozen of Chairs covered with Velvet, Damask, Mohair and other Silks, now there are Four Dozens covered as aforesaid; which also occasions less Wool to be worked into Chairs'.[50]

The Cane-Chairmakers won their case, but the Woollen Manufacturers' petition was resurrected in 1699, when another bill concerning the trade in woollen cloth was before Parliament.[51] They argued for a clause to be added to the bill 'to prohibit the making and vending of *Cane Chairs, Stools* and *Couches*'.[52] The petitioners argued that the fashion for caned chairs had seriously damaged the market for woollen chair covers of all types, putting 'above 50,000 of His Majesties Subjects' out of work. Furthermore, the consumption of ancillary goods such as '*Silk Fringe… Nailes, Girt-Web, Sack-Cloth, Worsted Fringe, Flax, Hemp, Hair*, all of our own growth and Manufacture' had also been seriously affected. As in 1690, the petition failed.

The truth of these assertions and counter-assertions is impossible to verify, but the petitions of both sides agree in depicting a chair-making industry with a prodigious output and with a large export market. They also show clear subdivisions of labour between joiners, turners, carvers, caners and upholsterers. One of the principal differences between the making of caned and upholstered chairs was that whereas cheap upholstered chairs might be made in most large provincial towns, caned chairs were made almost exclusively in London.[53] This was naturally so, since the canes imported by the East India Company were landed at London, and London was also the primary entrepôt for the export market. The failure of the woollen manufacturers' petitions might simply have been due to the greater political weight of the Joiners' Company combined with the East India lobby, but it was also a sign of more fundamental change. The time when England was almost wholly dependent on wool for its export earnings was now past. Colonial trade and re-exports were now the main sources of economic growth.

Inventories give some idea of the spread of caned chairs around the country from about 1670. At Ham House, caned chairs were recorded in all inventories from 1677 onwards,[54] but they do not commonly appear in middle-class London households until the 1680s.[55] However, because most inventories are probate inventories, there is an inevitable time lag between the actual purchase of goods like caned chairs and their appearance in the inventories. At Oxford University, for instance, caned chairs do not occur in probate inventories until 1694, but one could reasonably assume that caned chairs had reached Oxford before this.[56] A letter written to an Oxford undergraduate in June 1685 proves the point:

> Child, I Heare my Cosen Denton Nicholas is come to Towne… You say Hee Hath
> bespoke a new Table and Cane chayres, wch will amount to £3 a peece between you,
> But I Do not understand why you should Bee at that unnecessary Charge, as long as
> you Have that wch will serve yr turne, neither Do I like the Vanity. You do not tell me
> whether you are matriculated yet or noe, and I am impatient till I know Thats done.
> You say you want money, wch I will supply you with very shortly, but not to Lay out in
> Vaine moveables, and so God Blesse you.[57]

Geography, or proximity to the sources of production, was obviously one of the factors influencing the adoption of caned chairs in English houses, but this was less important than wealth, status and pretensions to fashion. In 1688 Michael Warton, reputedly the richest man in Hull, had several sets of caned chairs in his new house near Beverley, in the East Riding of Yorkshire, whereas

48. 'The CASE of the Cane-Chair makers…' (1690), quoted in Symonds (March 1951).
49. Thornton (1975), pl. 195.
50. 'An act for better preventing the export of wooll, and encouraging the woollen manufacturers of this kingdom' [1 William & Mary, cap. 32].
51. 'An act to prevent the exportation of wool… and for the encouragement of the woollen manufacturers in the kingdom of England' [10 & 11 William III cap. 10].
52. B.L., 'For the Encouragement of the Consumption of the Woollen Manufacture of this Kingdom… (1699).
53. This was still the case in the eighteenth century when, despite the scale of their own manufactory, the Lancaster firm of Gillow was forced to source its caned chairs in London.
54. Thornton and Tomlin (1980).
55. Earle (1989), p. 294.
56. Agius [1971], p. 79.
57. Quoted in Symonds (March 1951), p. 10.

Plate 3:28. Elbow chair (1670-80), caned with walnut frame. This is the most common type of early caned chair. It is characterised by the square proportions, the wide mesh caning, flat arms and hexagonal blocks to the rear posts. The turned feet are missing.
BOUGHTON HOUSE,
THE DUKE OF BUCCLEUCH

Plate 3:29. Elbow chair (before 1677), cedarwood. This chair is one of two made for the Duke's library at Ham House, probably when the library was fitted out in the early 1670s. The overall shape and proportions are very similar to those of 3:28. The octagonal section of the fore-legs and rear posts immediately strikes one as unusual, but it does echo the section of the upper rear posts on contemporary caned chairs (cf. 3:28, 31, 33-35). The carved masks and paw feet are reminiscent of those found on Dutch backstools.
HAM HOUSE,
VICTORIA AND ALBERT MUSEUM

58. Hall (1986).
59. 'Inventory of all the goods etc. of Richard Legh…'. [Chetham's Library, Manchester, Raines Mss. Vol. 38, p. 461].
60. The first bill for a caned chair supplied to the Royal Household is as follows: 'For a Caned Chaire with Eares and Elbowes to move with Joynts and a Footestoole with Iron worke to fold… £6.10.0' [PRO LC 5/41, f. 179 (1680)]. This expensive article sounds very much like a sleeping chair, of the sort illustrated in Thornton (1978), figs 175-77.
61. Thornton and Tomlin (1980), p. 153.

Marmaduke Woodhouse, a master mariner of Hull worth only £131, had none.[58] In the same year the worthy Sir Richard Legh, whom we first encountered buying longcase clocks in London (above, page 44), also had numerous sets of caned chairs in his house at Lyme Park.[59] Both Warton and Legh were rich men with business and social connections in London, giving them exposure to the latest fashions in furniture and the means to afford them.

That money was not the only criterion governing the uptake of caned chairs is also shown by the fact that caned chairs are not recorded in the Lord Chamberlain's accounts before 1680, and not until the mid-1680s do they occur with any frequency.[60] One possible explanation for this is that the seat furniture made for the Royal Palaces was generally upholstered, and the fashion for lighter and cheaper caned chairs might have taken some time to be accepted at Court. It may also be significant that caned chairs were supplied by the joiner, Richard Price, and his successors, and not by

Plate 3:30. Elbow chair (c.1670-1700), caned with walnut frame. Although ostensibly similar to 3:28, the square posts and flared arm terminals might suggest a later date, perhaps 1690 (?).   BOUGHTON HOUSE, THE DUKE OF BUCCLEUCH

Plate 3:31. Chair (1670-80) caned with japanned oak frame. One of a set, including a daybed.   HARDWICK HALL, THE NATIONAL TRUST

the upholsterers. There might well have been strong resistance from John Casbert and his colleagues to the infringement of their monopoly of Royal seat furniture by the newfangled caned chairs.

The earliest surviving caned chairs are probably those which share the boxy proportions of contemporary wooden chairs and backstools. The example in 3:28 is a relatively common type, perhaps dating from c.1670-75. The back is square and dished or 'compassed' to accommodate the sitter. The flat, outcurved arms are typical and are also found on a documented pair of cedarwood chairs at Ham House, which share very similar proportions (3:29). These chairs are still in the Duke's library at Ham, where they have been recorded in inventories from 1677 onwards. They probably date from the time of the library's construction in the early 1670s.[61]

Another chair of this general type is shown in 3:30. Although superficially similar to 3:28, it has moulded arms with flared and scrolled terminals. These are not commonly found on upholstered chairs until the 1690s, which suggests that this may be up to twenty years later than the previous examples. On the other hand, both 3:28 and 3:30 have the same wide-mesh cane work in the back, which seems to be indicative of an early date (compare, for instance, with 3:44 and 3:45, below).

3:31 and 3:32 show one of a fine set of chairs with japanned frames. The design and proportions are similar to the previous examples, and it also has the same octagonal section rear posts with ball finials. Both these features appear to indicate an early date, probably before 1680, as do the delicate

Plate 3:32. Detail of 3:31 showing the delicate silver and gold decoration on the black japanned ground.

pear-shaped feet. These attributes are shared by the day-bed in 3:33, which is a relatively common type with an adjustable back. Both the day-bed and the chairs would have been furnished with loose cushions, and these are frequently noted in contemporary inventories. At Ham, for instance, the 1677 inventory records 'six Arme Kane Chaires of wallnuttree' in the Duke's dressing room, together with six cushions 'suitable to' (i.e. matching) the wall hangings.[62] Similarly, caned couches or day-beds are often described as having a 'bed' or mattress with bolsters.

Chairs 'cutt with scrowles'

The Cane-Chairmakers' petition states that caned chairs came 'in time' to be carved, and from 1675 onwards Richard Price's bills describe the style of carving quite clearly. In that year he supplied 'Four Elbowe chaires of the twisted-turn of walnutt wood with Lyon's foot with compass backs carved elbows... 18s. Each'.[63] Various other chairs with 'carved work' were delivered that year and in 1676 he supplied the first of numerous chairs 'cutt' or 'wrought' with 'scrowles'. These words describe the carved foliate decoration which characterises Carolean chairs made from about 1675 onwards.[64] In the early 1680s Price even renovated older chairs by replacing turned fore-rails with new 'scrowled' ones.

It seems logical that the first of these carved chairs possessed at least some of the attributes of earlier forms. The chairs in 3:34-35 have the same pear-shaped feet, octagonal rear posts and ball finials found on uncarved caned chairs, but the back is higher and the crest rail, lower cross-rail and fore-rail are carved with scrolling acanthus and rosettes. The arms of 3:34 are moulded and carved at the shoulder and terminal, and the terminal itself is scrolled over in a leafy whorl. The

Plate 3:33. Daybed (1670-80), caned with walnut frame. The adjustable back is common to most daybeds of this type. One of the most familiar Restoration archetypes, epitomising the 'politer way of living' extolled by John Evelyn.

CANONS ASHBY, THE NATIONAL TRUST

Plate 3:34. **Elbow chair** (1675-80), caned with walnut frame. One of a large set. The crisp, tightly controlled carving is typical of the earliest carved caned chairs (compare with 3:45-46, and the octagonal posts also suggest an early date. The scrolled and carved arm terminals are a new introduction of the 1670s.

DRAYTON HOUSE, PRIVATE COLLECTION

Plate 3:35. **Chair** (1675-80) caned with walnut frame, *en suite* with 3:34. These chairs bear the carvers' stamp IS (or SI), which has also been recorded on similar chairs in other collections.

DRAYTON HOUSE, PRIVATE COLLECTION

arms are down-curved or 'compassed' and the back is dished. The earliest record of both these features occurs in one of Richard Price's bills for 1673; 'for two Elbow Chaires with Compass backs and Compass elbows... £1.0s.6d'.[65]

A slightly later date, perhaps 1680, is suggested for the chair in 3:36, from a set of ten at Hardwick Hall, Derbyshire. The back is higher, the rear posts are squared and carved on the forward faces of the blocks, and the finials are also carved. The seat rails are carved with leaves in shallow relief. The wide, carved borders of the back panel have the effect of narrowing the caned centre, enhancing the impression of height. The carved shell which centres the crest and fore-rails is a common device and predates the 'boyes and crownes' motif of the later 1680s.

It is quite common to find journeymen's initials stamped on the frames of caned chairs and the Hardwick chairs are particularly well marked (P3:37-38). All the carved elements – crest rail, lower cross-rail, side splats and fore-rail – are stamped with initials of a carver (either BO or RW).

62. Ibid., p. 50.
63. Seat furniture of this description can be found in PRO LC 9/275.
64. For a more detailed discussion of the meaning of the phrase 'wrought with scrowles', see Bowett (1999), pp. 263-4.
65. P.R.O., LC 9/274, f. 107.

Plate 3:37. **Detail of** 3:36 showing joiner's stamp AB on the rear post at seat level. Journeymen's stamps on caned chairs are very common, and probably indicate a system of piece-work manufacturing (see text).

Plate 3:38. **Detail of** 3:36 showing carver's stamp RW on the back of the splat. Every carved element is similarly stamped (see text).

Plate 3:36. **Chair** (1675-85), caned with walnut frame. One of a set of ten. HARDWICK HALL, THE NATIONAL TRUST

In addition to these, the frames are stamped on the rear face of the back post with the initials of either the joiner or perhaps the chair caner (AB, RG, PH, MP).[66] There are also scribed initials on some chairs (B, E, G) whose significance is unclear. The purpose of these stamps was to identify the work of the individual workmen, in this case four joiners or caners and two carvers producing ten chairs altogether. This strongly suggests that the individuals involved were paid piece-rate rather than a daily or weekly wage, and that the production of the chairs was divided into separate processes of manufacture and assembly. It is also possible that the chairs were produced by more than one workshop, perhaps by independent journeymen supplying a prominent 'maker'. It is significant, too, that although journeymen's stamps are common on caned chairs, they do not occur on upholstered chairs, indicating that these were probably not produced by the same system. We might infer, therefore, that the Cane-Chairmakers were a breed apart. The petition of 1690 certainly appears to suggest that the Cane-Chairmakers were a distinct group either within the Joiners' Company or affiliated to it.

The quality of the Hardwick chairs is not impressive – the carving is shallow and perfunctory, with very little attempt to modify the rectangular outlines of the boards from which it is cut.

---

66. The fact that these initials are rarely, if ever, found on upholstered chairs, suggests that they might be caners' rather than joiners' marks.

Plate 3:39. Chair (1680-90), caned with walnut frame. This is a fine quality chair, with carving much superior to that on the previous example. Note the much looser style of carving compared to 3:34-35, and the carved feet.

SUDBURY HALL, THE NATIONAL TRUST

Plate 3:40. Elbow chair (1680-90), caned with walnut frame. Another fine example, with wonderfully fluid carving. The fore-rail is not original and the carved three-toed feet have been mutilated by hasty repairs. HADDON HALL

Clearly, these chairs were made to a price and, indeed, it is surprising that carvers were employed at all, for such crude carving could easily have been produced by joiners and in many cases probably was. By way of comparison, look at the chair in 3:39. The design is similar, but the quality of carving is very much higher. The rectangular outline of each board has been cut away as far as possible and the foliage is fully cut through in an attempt to realise its natural forms. 3:40 shows a fine elbow chair of even better quality. Every element evinces technical skill and attention to detail. The carving is pierced through and deeply undercut, the flowerheads are realistically modelled and the scrolling acanthus and swirling petals of the flowers impart a wonderful sense of movement to the design. This continues even on the faces of the rear post blocks and the turned-over, undercut finials. The central strut in the back gives strength to an inherently weak part of the frame and at the same time enhances the appearance of height. The feet have been replaced, but were originally of a three-toed form like those shown in 3:41 and 3:42.

Plate 3:41. Elbow chair (1688), caned with walnut frame. A good quality chair with the three-toed fore-feet typical of the 1680s. The significance of the dated inscription for 20 February 1687/8 is unclear. The cresting bears the Royal Stuart arms and the fore-rail is carved with a crown supported by 'boyes'.

Plate 3:42. Elbow chair (1685-90), caned with walnut frame. Another typical 'boyes and crownes' chair of the late 1680s. It is stamped RP several times on the carved elements. The crowned rear posts seem to be a signature of this maker (cf. 3:53). This and the previous examples demonstrate the extraordinary variety achieved by English chairmakers while working with the same basic forms and decorative vocabulary.

TEMPLE NEWSAM HOUSE, LEEDS CITY ART GALLERIES

'Boyes and crownes' chairs

3:41 shows a well-known elbow chair, bearing the Royal Stuart arms and inscribed on the seat rail *'Febuery ye 20 George Lewis 1687/8'*. The significance of the inscription is unclear,[67] but the royal symbolism is very obvious, and the date is certainly plausible. As well as the Stuart arms, there are cherubs holding aloft the crown in the fore-rail and either side of the back panel. The 'boyes and crownes', as this ensemble was known, epitomises the flamboyant yet regal image of the Carolean caned chair. Ironically, however, the documentary evidence suggests that the 'boyes and crownes' device was not introduced on seat furniture until after Charles' death.

The origins of the 'boyes and crownes' device can be traced back to the late 1670s. Paired cherubs flanking a bunch of grapes occur on a pair of documented chairs of about 1678 at Ham House (below, 3:47 and 3:48). There are also examples of caned chairs 'wrought with scrowles' and probably dating from the late 1670s to mid-1680s, which have fore-rails and crest rails carved with cherubs flanking a basket of flowers.[68] The substitution of a crown instead of the basket was almost certainly a later development and does not occur on any documented or otherwise datable chair before 1685. This surprising fact is borne out by the Lord Chamberlain's accounts, which reveal that

67. It has been suggested that the inscription refers to George Lewis, Elector of Hanover and the future George I of England. [Sotheby's sale catalogue, New York, 8 and 9 December 1989, lot 472.]
68. For example Edwards (1954), I, pp. 242-43, figs. 50 and 52. The latter chair bears the Royal Arms of Charles II, which ought to place the chair before 1685.
69. PRO LC 9/278, f. 20.

Plate 3: 44. Detail of 3:43. 'Boyes and crownes' in the crest rail, deftly executed with bold, vigorous cuts of the chisel. This is typical of the sort of carving performed by London chairmakers at this date, by which maximum effect is achieved with the minimum of work.

Plate 3:43. Elbow chair (1685-90), caned with walnut frame. The Carolean caned chair in its final and most familiar form, with a boyes and crownes.   THE BOWES MUSEUM

the first 'boyes and crownes' chairs were not supplied to the Royal Household until 1686. The bill was made out by Elizabeth Price, Richard's widow, and ran as follows: 'For 8 caine Chaires of Wallnuttree carved with Boyes and Crownes... 12s. Each... For 4 Elbow Chaires the same... 16s.'.[69]

The timing of this bill is intriguing. Could it be that the death of Charles II in February 1685 prompted the adoption of the 'boyes and crownes' device as a mark of loyal remembrance? On the other hand, it might have nothing to do with royalist sentiment, but was simply an attractive and engaging motif that caught the fashionable imagination. The most we can truthfully say is that from 1686 onwards the 'boyes and crownes' was probably the most popular design of crest and fore-rail for caned chairs, and remained so until about 1700. The early examples seem to be those with 'boyes and crownes' resting on acanthus foliage (3:42-44). This design gradually fell from favour and was replaced by the even more ubiquitous 'boyes and crownes' on stylised 'horsebone' or S scrolls (these are discussed in more detail in Chapter Eight).

Plate 3:45. Elbow chair (c.1675), red silk upholstery and walnut frame, one of a pair. The seat bears the inventory stamp from Whitehall Palace and the frames were probably supplied by Richard Price. It is not clear whether the present upholstery and fringing are original, since traces of sky-blue silk are discernible underneath.　　　　　KNOLE, THE NATIONAL TRUST

Plate 3:46. Stool (c.1675), red silk upholstery and walnut frame. One of six, *en suite* with 3:45. Note the tightly controlled, precise carving of the fore-rail, very different from the carving on caned chairs of the 1680s (cf. 3:40-44). The curious blank area at the top of the legs is explained by the loss of the original fringe (cf. 3:45).　　　　　KNOLE, THE NATIONAL TRUST

The double-scrolled leg

Upholstered chairs with twist-turned frames are very much less common than caned ones, probably because there were fewer of them made, and their survival rate has been lower. Once the covers and stuffing had decayed it was hardly worth recovering the outmoded frames and these, being usually of beech or walnut, were anyway prone to worm and/or rot. This fact makes the chair in 3:45 something of a rarity. This is one of a pair, *en suite* with six stools, bearing an inventory stamp from Whitehall Palace. The suite was probably made for the extensive refurbishment of the Palace which took place in the mid- to late 1670s. It is difficult to link the illustrated chair with any specific bill, but twist-turned frames, carved elbows, 'Lyons feet' and carved fore-rails all occur in numerous bills submitted by Richard Price in the years 1675-78.[70] The 'compass' arms and 'compass' back are also typical of this period. The stools (3:46) have carved rails back and front, a feature which might be described by the following bill of 1675: 'For six stools of [walnuttree] with double carved work... £13.10.00'.[71]

68. For example Edwards (1954), I, pp. 242-43, figs. 50 and 52. The latter chair bears the Royal Arms of Charles II, which ought to place the chair before 1685.
69. PRO LC 9/278, f. 20.
70. PRO LC 9/274, 275.
71. PRO LC 9/274, f. 376.
72. PRO LC 9/275, f. 284.
73 PRO LC 5/41, f. 130.
74. Thornton and Tomlin (1980), p. 150-51.

Plate 3:47. Sleeping chair (c.1678). Original upholstery (restored) and gilt walnut frame. This is one of a pair installed in the Queen's Closet at Ham House between 1677 and 1679. The upholstery is gold brocaded red satin, matching that used on the walls. The back is adjustable by mean of the quadrant just visible under the arm. These chairs, together with that shown in 3:49, are the first documented examples having the new-style moulded S-scroll stretchers and scrolled fore-rails.
HAM HOUSE,
VICTORIA AND ALBERT MUSEUM

Plate 3:48. Detail of 3:47 showing the 'broken'-scrolled fore-rail and paired cherubs. The gilding is not original.

In other bills of the late 1670s there are indications that the essentially rectilinear form of Carolean seat furniture was beginning to change. From 1678 onwards Price began to supply chairs that were not only 'cutt with scrowles' but also 'wrought with mouldings'. For example, in 1678 he supplied to Whitehall Palace 'six stooles of Wallnuttree wrought with mouldings and carved with scrowles at £1.10s a piece'.[72] The novelty of this development is made explicit in another bill of the same year, for furnishings at Windsor Castle: 'for Two Elbow Chaire frames and six Stoole frames wrought with mouldings after a new fashion...'.[73] It is apparent from both these bills that the chairs and stools were frames only, intended for upholstery, so the 'mouldings' must have been on the visible parts of the frame below the seat, that is, either the legs or the stretchers, or both.

What did these mouldings look like? A probable candidate is suggested by the chair in 3:47. This is one of a pair of sleeping chairs made for the Duke and Duchess of Lauderdale between 1677 and 1679.[74] The legs of the chair are of conventional twist-turned form, but the stretchers are entirely new. They take the form of moulded S scrolls, conjoined into what some authorities have

Plate 3:49. Elbow chair (c.1678).
Modern upholstery with black and gilt
beechwood frame. One of ten installed
in the Volury at Ham House between
1677 and 1679. This is the first
documented appearance of the double
scrolled leg and scrolled arm support
on an English chair. The slight
outward turn of the 'knee' is most
unusual, and not often repeated until
the advent of the 'corner horsebone' leg
in the 1690s. HAM HOUSE,
VICTORIA AND ALBERT MUSEUM

75. Thornton (1975), p. 104.
76. Ibid.
77. Thornton and Tomlin (1980), pp. 73-74.
78. PRO LC 9/278-9.
79. Roberts' career is summarised in Beard and
Gilbert (1986), pp. 752-54.

called a 'cupid's bow',[75] but which will be here referred to as 'double-S'. The double-S stretcher
was introduced from France, where similar stretchers were fitted to Parisian *fauteuils* from the late
1670s.[76] Another set of chairs at Ham, again dating from between 1677 and 1679, also has double-S
stretchers, together with moulded and scrolled arm supports and moulded reverse-curved legs
ending in scrolled feet (3:49).[77] The fore-rails of both these chairs are of a new type, carved as two
'broken' scrolls centred in the first case on a pair of cherubs (3:48), and in the second on a
cartouche.

At the time of writing, the chairs in 3:49 are the earliest documented English chairs with
curved and scrolled legs. At this date (c.1678) these were stylistically very advanced, but during
the early 1680s the scrolled leg became increasingly common. A set of japanned chairs with an
identical leg and arm design was supplied to the Duke of Hamilton by John Ridge in 1682 (see
5:14). It is probable that this form of leg is the one referred to in numerous bills in the Lord

Plate 3:50. **Elbow chair** (1684-88).
19th century red velvet upholstery
with gilt walnut frame. This is a mix of
old and new styles, combining double-
scrolled fore-legs and S-scroll fore-rail
with a twist-turned frame.

Chamberlain's accounts which describe chairs with 'double scrowles in the foot' (the term 'foot' applied to the entire member below the seat). The name seems apt, since the leg has a smooth, moulded reverse curve scrolled inwards at the top and bottom to form a knee and a toe, and hence 'double-scrolled' will be the term adopted here.[78]

References to 'double-scrowles in the foot' became particularly common, and perhaps dominant, after Thomas Roberts succeeded Richard Price as royal chairmaker in 1686.[79] An upholstered chair of about this date is shown in 3:50. This is one of a set of four at Belton House, Lincolnshire, which was built between 1684 and 1688. By the latter date the house was substantially complete and furnished, and an inventory of that year records numerous sets of chairs, of which this is probably one. The style is a mix of old and new, with a conventional twist-turned frame and a back carved with foliage and flowers, combined with new-style moulded arms on scrolled supports, a broken-scrolled fore-rail and double-scrolled legs.

Plate 3:51. Chair (1685-1700), caned with walnut frame. A typical 'boyes and crownes' chair with double-scrolled fore-legs and twist-turned frame.

DUNHAM MASSEY, THE NATIONAL TRUST

Plate 3:52. Chair (1680-1700), caned with walnut frame. This style of back is an early variant of the oval and banister-backed chairs of the 1690s, which employ scrolls as a dominant decorative motif. PRIVATE COLLECTION

80. A set of Parisian chairs with this type of stretcher is at Salsta, Sweden, and is illustrated in Thornton (1975), fig.1.

81. There is an interesting coincidence of timing between the widespread introduction of round-to-square joints in English chairs during the 1680s and the Revocation of the Edict of Nantes in 1686. Could this imply an influx of Huguenot immigrants, seeking work with English chairmakers?

Double-scrolled legs also appear on caned chairs of the 1680s. 3:53 is a typical example, identical in all respects save its scrolled fore-legs to the chairs in 3:42-44, above. In 3:52 and 3:53 the double-scrolled device is taken into the back, so that it becomes the dominant decorative motif. This style, the successor to the leafy scrolled Carolean version, continued to gain popularity into the 1690s. Interestingly, 3:53 is stamped by the same carver as 3:42, demonstrating the facility with which this artisan moved between contemporary decorative idioms.

Many scrolled-leg chairs have stretchers which are neither twist-turned nor moulded, but are turned concentrically (3:54). The turning profile matches that on some contemporary Parisian chairs and this is the most likely source for the new style.[80] The earliest documented English examples occur on the chairs made by John Ridge for the Duke of Hamilton (1682, 5:14), and they become increasingly common thereafter. The chair in 3:54 is a typical example and might have been made at any time between about 1685 and 1700.

Plate 3:54. Elbow chair (1680-1700), modern upholstery with japanned walnut frame. This is the most common form of double-scrolled elbow chair. Note the stretcher turnings, which are typical of the 1680s and 1690s.

DRUMLANRIG CASTLE, THE DUKE OF BUCCLEUCH

Plate 3:53. Chair (1685-1700), caned with walnut frame. This is essentially a more detailed version of 3:52. It bears the same carver's stamp as 3:44 (RP), and is probably contemporary with it. It is interesting to find a carver moving between two different styles, one old and one new.   PRIVATE COLLECTION

The subsequent phases of concentrically turned stretcher design will be discussed in detail in a later chapter, but it is worth considering here a point which often causes disagreement among furniture pundits. It has already been observed that round-to-square joints between stretcher and leg are often thought diagnostic of Continental rather than English manufacture. While this still holds true in a very general way, there are numerous exceptions, of which 3:50 and 3:54 are just two examples. These chairs are so typically English in all other respects that to propose a Continental origin flies in the face of common sense. Moreover, some documented chairs by English makers, such as those by John Ridge, also have round-to-square joints. It might be suggested that these chairs were made by Continental journeymen (perhaps Huguenots), working under an English master, but we lack evidence either to support or refute this.[81] The most we can say is that round-to-square stretcher to leg joints are not on their own sufficient to warrant an attribution to a Continental maker.

Plate 3:55. Engraving (1687), *The Enthronement of James II and Queen Mary*, by Francis Sandford. This is the first known depiction of the broken-scrolled or 'horsebone' leg. The 'break' is particularly pronounced on the rear legs.

Early 'horsebone' chairs[82]

Although the double-scrolled leg was clearly a popular form, it ultimately lost ground to the bulkier, broken-scrolled type which Thomas Roberts called 'horsebone'. The etymology of this curious term is uncertain. It could have zoomorphic connotations, or it could be a corruption of the French term 'os de mouton', which was used to describe the scrolled legs and stretchers of contemporary French chairs.

The 'broken' scroll appears first as a design for fore-rails in the late 1670s, such as those on the sleeping chairs at Ham (3:47). By the mid-1680s it had been adopted for both front and back legs, and also for arm supports. The first known depiction of an English chair with these features occurs in Francis Sandford's *History of the Coronation of James II and Queen Mary*, published in 1687 (3:55). The coronation chairs in this engraving are clearly of the scrolled-leg type, and the rear legs in particular have a marked 'break' and reverse scroll. In addition, the feet are scrolled up and outwards, unlike those on the double-scrolled leg, which were usually turned under.

The appearance of the broken-scrolled leg on the coronation chairs coincides with the first recorded use of the term 'horsebone' in the bills of Thomas Roberts: 'For a large Elbow Chair of Wallnuttree with horsebone elbows and varnished' (1686).[83] Subsequent bills refer specifically to

Plate 3:56. **Elbow chair** (1684-88), modern upholstery, japanned and gilt walnut frame. It is debatable whether this chair is a true 'horsebone' chair, since, although the legs have a pronounced 'break', the scrolled-under toes are more typical of the double-scrolled leg. Most horsebone chairs have outscrolled toes. Note that the original upholstery would have left a gap between the back and seat which has now been filled.   BURGHLEY HOUSE

Plate 3:57. **Detail of 3:56** showing the fore-rail with delightfully carved cherubic trumpeters resting on scrolls. The same fore-rail occurs on an identical set of chairs formerly at Glemham Hall, Suffolk, and illustrated in Edwards (1954), I, p. 251, and again on the chairs and stools made for James II by Thomas Roberts in 1688.

'horsebone' as a design for legs, stretchers and fore-rails: 'For 4 Stooles of Walnuttree with Horsebone foott and Rayles (1687)… For 2 Chairs of State made all of Wallnuttree with Horsebone foot and fore railes with a flower in the raile and a scrowle on topp of the back' (1689).[84]

The earliest extant horsebone chairs probably date from the early to mid-1680s. The example in 3:56 is from a set of chairs made for Burghley House, near Stamford, probably between 1684 and 1688.[85] The frame is carved, painted and parcel gilt. It has double-S stretchers and the legs are sharply 'broken' with an acute reverse curve. Unusually, the feet are scrolled under in the same manner as double-scrolled legs. The nicely detailed fore-rails are carved with cherubic trumpeters reclining on confronting scrolls (3:57).

One of the richest collections of early horsebone chairs survives at Knole in Kent. Most of these

82. The meaning of the term 'horsebone' is discussed in Bowett (1999). The account given here differs in some details, but in general the interpretation of style and chronology remains essentially unchanged.
83. PRO LC 9/278, f. 27.
84. PRO LC 9/278, f. 105; 9/279, f. 31.
85. Bowett (1999).

Plate 3:58. Elbow chair (1685-94), upholstered in original blue silk damask on a walnut frame. Possibly by Thomas Roberts. The shaped top to the back is most unusual on chairs made before c.1700. Probably removed to Knole in 1694.

KNOLE, THE NATIONAL TRUST

were acquired by Charles Sackville, sixth Earl of Dorset, while he was Lord Chamberlain of the Household to William III. One of the traditional perquisites of his post was to have his choice of royal furniture after the death of a monarch, and the death of Queen Mary in 1694 offered particularly rich pickings. Sackville virtually cleared the queen's apartments at Whitehall and appropriated the furniture for his own use.[86] Much of this ended up at Knole and, because of their royal provenance, the horsebone chairs there can be attributed with reasonable confidence to Thomas Roberts.

There is space here to discuss only a few of these outstanding chairs. The example in 3:58 is

Plate 3:59. Elbow chair (1685-88) upholstered in original midnight-blue figured velvet on a walnut frame. One of a pair probably supplied by Thomas Roberts to James II, *en suite* with a state bed. KNOLE, THE NATIONAL TRUST

highly unusual in having a shaped back at a time when upholstered chairs were almost invariably square topped. Otherwise the chair is very typical of the late 1680s, having 'horsebone' legs and arm supports, a 'boyes and crownes' fore-rail and horsebone stretchers. Another example, one of a pair, is shown in 3:59. This beautiful chair is covered with its original dark blue figured velvet, which matches that used for a State Bed at Kensington Palace, bearing the cipher of James II and Mary of Modena. It is probable that these chairs formed part of the seat furniture *en suite* to the bed, and if so, they can be dated between 1685 and 1688.[87]

86. Jackson Stops (1977), parts I and II.
87. Thornton (1977), p. 138.

Plate 3:60. 'The Venetian Ambassador's Bed' (1688), *en suite* with its chairs and stools, made for James II, whose monogram is carved in the cornice of the tester. Original blue-green figured velvet with carved and gilded frames. The frames were supplied by Thomas Roberts, the upholstery perhaps by Jean Poitevin.

KNOLE, NATIONAL TRUST PHOTOGRAPHIC LIBRARY/ANDREAS VON EINSIEDEL

Plate 3:61. **Elbow chair** (1688), original blue-green velvet and carved gilded frame. Supplied by Thomas Roberts *en suite* with the State bed in 3:61. The slightly splayed arm terminals herald the arrival of the splayed 'corner elbows' of the 1690s.

KNOLE, THE NATIONAL TRUST

Plate 3:62. **Stool** (1688), original blue-green velvet upholstery and carved and gilded frame, *en suite* with 3:61 and 62.

One of Roberts' last commissions for James II was to make a suite of two chairs and six stools to complement a new state bed (3:60-62). The bed was ordered in August 1688, but the chairs, 'richly carved with figures and gilt all over with gold', were not paid for until November 1689, by which time James had abandoned his throne to William of Orange.[88] Both the chairs and stools have figure-carved legs in place of the horsebone, but retain Roberts' characteristic leaf carved S-scrolled stretchers. In design terms the most significant feature of the chairs is the flared terminals of the arms. This stylish variation of the more usual 'in-line' form anticipates the development of the 'corner horsebone' in the 1690s.

88. The bed and its seat furniture are discussed in Jackson Stops (1977) and Beard (1997), pp. 92-93.

Chapter Four

TABLE, STANDS AND MIRRORS 1660–1689

ining tables

It is one of the many idiosyncrasies of the antiques trade that Restoration dining tables are invariably regarded as 'country' furniture and sold alongside dressers, coffers and wainscot chairs. This is primarily because their joined construction and solid timber (usually oak) are thought to be more consistent with vernacular than fashionable living. But this is a modern view, derived from an idealised division between 'fashionable' and 'country' furniture. The bills of both Richard Price and his successor Thomas Roberts show that Charles II's courtiers saw no inconsistency in dining off an oak table while sitting on silk upholstered chairs and surrounded by veneered, marquetry, and giltwood furniture.

At the time of the Restoration the notion of a separate dining room or dining parlour, rather than a general purpose parlour into which food was brought, was beginning generally to be accepted.[1] While grand or formal dinners were still held in great halls, or (in a newly-built house) in the saloon, informal or private dining took place in more intimate surroundings. At Ham there were two dining rooms – the Great Dining Room on the first floor and the smaller Marble Dining Room on the ground floor. The former room held eleven cedar dining tables and the latter only three, but this is probably where the majority of meals were eaten. The evidence of surviving inventories suggests that whereas the furnishings of parlours or other rooms where casual meals were taken were fairly informal, dining rooms tended towards a standard layout. As well as one or more dining tables, there were often side or serving tables and a set of dining chairs, which were frequently caned rather than upholstered. The Dining Room at Belton (1688) is typical of many noble houses at this date. It contained 'two ovall tables, two Armd caine chairs, fifteen single cane chairs, one child's chaire, two side board tables, one pendulum clock with an inlaid case'.[2] When not in use the room was probably rather bare, with the tables folded to one side and the chairs ranged around the walls. All this changed when prepared for dining, as the tables were opened out, covered with cloths and laid, the chairs drawn up and the sideboards laden with glass and plate.

The oval dining table, with folding or 'falling' leaves, became common in fashionable English houses around the middle of the seventeenth century.[3] Most were quite small, seating six or eight people. According to an observer at a dinner given for Charles II in 1669, the shape was 'convenient

Detail of 4:19 showing one of the four marquetry panels from the corners of the table.

1. Thornton (1984), pp. 18 and 51.
2. Lincoln Record Office, Belton Inventory, 8 November 1688.
3. Edwards (1954), II, pp. 234-5; Thornton and Tomlin (1980), pp. 11 and 15.
4. Edwards (1954), II, p. 220.

both for seeing and conversing'.[4] When not in use the tables were folded down and put away. At Michael Warton's new house near Beverley in 1688 the dining tables of cedarwood and fir were stored in the passage outside the dining room, which seems to have been quite common, since many inventories record dining rooms without tables.

The table in 4:1 is the only survivor of the fourteen dining tables recorded at Ham in 1677. Its construction conforms to a standard type, based on a frame of four boards. The base board is tenoned into sledge feet, as are the two vertical ends (4:2). Another board runs underneath the top, joined to the two ends with dovetails. The gates pivot on wooden pins socketed into the top and bottom boards. The top of the table is in three parts – a narrow centre, pegged into the frame below, and two hinged leaves, each of which is composed of three butt-jointed boards.

Tables of this type are relatively uncommon, perhaps because their design is not very robust. The Ham table has been strengthened, probably not long after it was made, by the addition of oak corner brackets. Moreover, it seats only four people, because the ends of the frame are placed too close to the table edge to accommodate a diner at this position. Similar drawbacks afflict all surviving examples, most of which have turned or profile-cut end supports rather than the

Plate 4:2. Detail of 4:1 showing the construction of the frame of the table. The small pins securing the tenons are just visible.

Plate 4:1. Dining table (c.1675), cedar and oak. This exceptionally rare table is the only survivor of fourteen cedar dining tables recorded in the Ham House inventories. The form is much less common than the ubiquitous open-frame gateleg (cf. 4:5–13) and they are generally smaller. This one seats a maximum of four people in comfort.

HAM HOUSE, VICTORIA AND ALBERT MUSEUM

Plate 4:3. Dining table (1670-1740), oak. Tables of this kind were made over a very long period and the baluster-shaped supports were perennially popular. This could be 17th century, but is probably later.
TREASURER'S HOUSE, YORK,
THE NATIONAL TRUST

Plate 4:4. Detail of 4:3. The construction is crude but effective. Note the gates socketed into the frame and the 'foxed' or wedged tenons used to secure the balusters to the trestle feet.

5. PRO LC 5/41, f. 144.
6. PRO LC 9/276, f. 34.
7. Moxon (1678), p. 22 and fig. 5; Randle Holme explains that this is called a dovetail hinge 'because it is broad at the ends like a Dove or Pigeon's Tail. It is used for small doors of Wainscot, Cubbards, Boxes and Trunks...' [Holme (1688), p. 302.].

false-panelled ends of the Ham table (4:3 and 4:4). Many are difficult to date with any certainty, the only clues being in the turning profiles of the end supports.

A more common type of Restoration dining table is the open-frame gateleg table, which is perhaps the most numerous of all late seventeenth century tables to survive (4:5). The Lord Chamberlain's accounts record many tables of this type being made for the Royal Palaces, and during the 1670s and 1680s most were made with twist-turned frames. In 1679 Richard Price supplied 'a very large Ovall Table of wainscot with twisted Pillars & lined with the same to fall on both sides...'.[5] Large tables were often made with a double gate for better stability (4:6), and these too occur in the Lord Chamberlain's accounts: 'For a very large strong ovall table with a double sett of twisted pillars... £3.10.0' (1680).[6]

The usual method of construction was based on an open rectangular frame joined with pegged mortise and tenon joints. The legs or 'pillars' were almost invariably turned, but the horizontal stretcher-rails were often left either plain or moulded on the upper surface. Where turned, the design of the stretchers did not necessarily conform to that of the legs. The gates pivoted in wooden pins socketed into the upper and lower rails. Drawers could be fitted into either or both ends, usually running on a central bearer.

The top was made of boards butt-jointed together. The centre was fixed to the frame by pegs driven into the tops of the legs and upper rails. The hinges fixing the leaves to the centre were of iron, generally splayed in what is now called a 'fishtail' shape, but which in the seventeenth century was known as a 'dovetail' hinge.[7] The hinges usually have five punched holes arranged in a quincunx, and were fixed with nails, not screws (4:7). On better quality examples the hinges were riveted through the central hole, and the head of the rivet concealed on the upper surface by a wooden plug.

The main problem associated with this type of table is the failure of the butt-joints in the leaves.

Plate 4:5. Gateleg dining table (1677-1700), walnut. This is the most common type of late 17th century dining table to survive, with a twist-turned frame. Most are of oak or, as in this case, of walnut. SOTHEBY'S

Plate 4:7. '**Dovetail' hinge,** late 17th or early 18th century. Note the five nails (not screws) arranged in a quincunx. The kerf marks of the pit-saw are clearly visible on the wood.

Plate 4:6. Gateleg dining table, with 'a double sett of pillars' (1675-1700), oak. The double-gate made for a much stronger and more stable table, but these are much less common than the single gate versions. COUNTRY LIFE LIBRARY

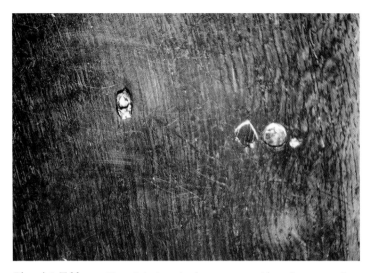

Plate 4:8. Table top. The original peg has been augmented by at least two nails which, even so, have failed to keep the top secured to the base.

PRIVATE COLLECTION

Plate 4:9. After the failure of several different nails and pegs, modern screws have been used to secure the top of this table. Note the 18th century hinge alongside the scars of the original five-hole dovetail hinge. The scars line up on both sides of the joint, proving that the top and leaf are contemporary. PRIVATE COLLECTION

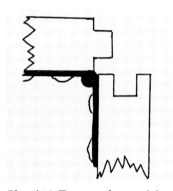

Plate 4:10. Tongue and groove joint between table centre and leaf. This type of joint offers support to the hinges when the table is opened.

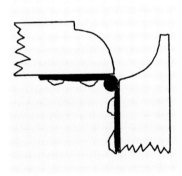

Plate 4:11. Rule joint between table centre and leaf. This is a typically 18th century feature and would be unusual on a 17th century table.

Because of this, many examples have had their leaves partly or wholly replaced, and most betray some evidence of repair. One common but rather ugly remedy was to screw wooden battens across the underside of the leaves to hold the boards together. Another weak point was the hinges themselves. The nails tended to work loose and in the course of time most have been replaced by screws. In the case of riveted hinges, however, there is a good chance that both the hinges and the leaves to which they are attached will be original. Finally, since the top was fixed to the frame only with pegs, it frequently worked loose, and many tables show evidence of re-pegging, often augmented with nails and screws. In some cases the top has been re-fixed from beneath in the eighteenth century fashion, either with glue blocks or with screws (4:8-9).

Most early gateleg tables have square or slightly rounded edges to the tops, rather than the quarter-round or ovolo edge, which became common in the eighteenth century. At the joint between the leaves and the centre the edges were either left square or tongued-and-grooved 4:10). The latter type made a much neater joint and provided some support to the hinges if the table were heavily laden. Rule joints (4:11) probably indicate an eighteenth rather than seventeenth century date.

Very few documented gateleg tables survive and because they are such a ubiquitous type the dating of undocumented examples is not an exact science. The only stylistic indicator is usually the style of turning on the pillars and rails, and for most of the period two styles dominate – either twist-turning or varieties of ball-turning. If the analysis of ball-turning given in Chapter Three is correct, then some ball-turned tables might date from the 1650s and 1660s, although most are likely to be later (4:12). Tables with twist-turned frames are unlikely to predate 1670 and the style certainly remained popular into the 1690s. Concentric 'banister' type turnings are also common and these are almost impossible to date with any accuracy since their popularity persisted well into the eighteenth century. A classic baluster profile, such as that in 4:13, could have been made at any time from the 1670s onwards. It is worth looking very closely at tables with anachronistic combinations of features, such as ovolo-moulded tops and twist-turned frames. The chances are that the top and frame did not start life together.

Plate 4:12. Gateleg table
(1670-1700), oak. The ring-and-ball turning is one of the most common surviving types.
PRIVATE COLLECTION

Plate 4:13. Gateleg table
(1670-1740), oak. The standard baluster turning profile, of the sort commonly used for staircases and balustrades, was popular over a very long period. BENINGBOROUGH HALL, THE NATIONAL TRUST

Plate 4:14. **Daniel Marot,** *Nouveaux Livre Da Partements* (1703), frontispiece. This engraving depicts William of Orange's dining room at Het Loo. At the end of the room is the serving area, with a sideboard table laden with cups and plate. A wine-cooler stands underneath.

Sideboard tables

As the Belton inventory shows, sideboard tables were a standard feature of Restoration dining rooms. They served two functions, one ceremonial and one practical. In their ceremonial role they were used as platforms for rich displays of silver and gold plate (4:14). Their practical purpose was to act as serving tables from which food and drink were served to the seated diners. Despite their apparent ubiquity, very few have survived from this early period. A notable exception is shown in 4:15. This is one of a pair installed at Ham House probably between c.1672 and 1677.[8] Each is fitted into a purpose-built niche in the Marble Dining Room. These rare and important survivals should not be considered exemplars of their type, however. The broken-scrolled leg is stylistically advanced for the date and the fleshy, auricular style of carving is most unusual and perhaps unique in England.

The 'triad'

The 'triad' is the modern name given to the suite of table, stands and looking glass which was such a common feature of Restoration houses. Most authorities suggest a French origin for this ensemble, which may be the case, but it quickly became a Europe-wide phenomenon. What is certainly true, however, is that in the hands of French designers such as Le Pautre, Bérain and Boulle the triad grew into a formidable apparatus of State furniture, its utilitarian function subsumed beneath rich sculptural forms, extraordinary workmanship and precious materials. Although some triads made for William III

8. Thornton and Tomlin (1980), p. 45.
9. Edwards (1954) (1954), III, p. 146; Beard & Gilbert (1986) P.571.
10. PRO LC 9/274 f. 108.

approach the French models in their scale and ambition (Chapter Six), most English examples are more domestic in scale, and generally conform to standardised and obviously widely popular designs.

Triads probably arrived in England in the early 1660s. Several pairs were supplied by Thomas Malin to the Royal Palaces in 1661-62, and one of the earliest domestic references comes from a letter written by Mary Verney in 1664, which mentions that she wants to acquire 'a table and stands'.[9] At Ham House there was nothing of this description in the inventory of 1654, save dressing tables in one or two bedchambers, but by 1677 there were at least nine triads in the principal rooms of the ground and first floors.

In many rooms triads were placed against the window piers and from this arrangement developed the eighteenth century pier table and glass. In State Apartments the triad was essentially a formal and static arrangement, but in a more domestic context it was more versatile, although its position remained roughly fixed by the placing of the mirror. The table functioned primarily as a dressing table and spent much of its life covered with a cloth. Light from the windows fell on to the sitters' face and was reflected in the looking glass, which was tilted well forward from the wall, while the flanking candlestands provided illumination at night. The disadvantage of this arrangement was that the proximity of the candle stands to the window curtains constituted a real fire hazard, and some contemporary engravings show the triad placed instead in the centre of one of the main walls.

The Royal Household accounts contain many bills for triads of varying quality. In the 1670s Richard Price charged £14.14s.0d. for 'an inlaid table and stands of Ebonie', whereas an olivewood version of the same cost only £5.10s.0d.[10] An olivewood looking glass *en suite* cost £4.10s.0d., which is some indication of the high cost of the glass. In the mid-1680s Gerrit Jensen and Richard Farneborough both supplied triads of all descriptions, ranging from walnut to olivewood, speckled wood, princeswood and ebony. Some were plain, others 'flower'd', 'inlay'd', or 'Markatree'.

Plate 4:15. Sideboard table (c.1675), cedar and marble. This is one of a pair installed in the Marble Dining Room at Ham House before 1677. The tops are not original, and indeed the lack of reference to the marble tops in the inventories might suggest that they were originally of cedar.

HAM HOUSE, THE NATIONAL TRUST

Plate 4:16. **Table and stands** (1660-75), princeswood. These are exceptionally rare and early examples of the type.

DRAYTON HOUSE, PRIVATE COLLECTION

Plate 4:17. **Detail of 4:16** showing the arrangement of veneers on the table top. Compare with 2:10.

DRAYTON HOUSE, PRIVATE COLLECTION

The table and stands in 4:16 might possibly date from before 1670. The ball-turning is certainly early and the geometric arrangement of veneers on the top matches that on the doors of early cocus wood and princeswood cabinets (4:17). Triads of this early form are rarities and tables with twist-turned legs are much more common. 4:18 shows a rare and beautiful example, veneered with ebony and garnished with repoussé silver mounts. The silver is not hallmarked, and so cannot be firmly dated, but the style of both the table and fittings suggests a date of perhaps 1670-85.

Plate 4:18. Table (1670-85), ebony veneers and ebonised wood with silver mounts. The combination of ebony and silver is both sombre and rich.
DRAYTON HOUSE, PRIVATE COLLECTION

Plate 4:19. Table (1684). Walnut and marquetry veneers. This neat table is probably from the set of 'Large wall[nut] flowerd Looking glass & Tables and stands flowered' supplied by Thomas Pistor (father or son) to James Grahme in 1684 at a cost of £9.0.0.

LEVENS HALL, PRIVATE COLLECTION

Plate 4:20. Detail of 4:19 showing the arrangement of marquetry reserves on the top. The corner panels use common components differently arranged to make four similar but different panels. Some of the same elements also occur in the central oval reserve. Note the damage on the left-hand side due to shrinkage of the main carcase relative to the side batten.

LEVENS HALL, PRIVATE COLLECTION

Plate 4:21. Table (1670-85), olivewood and marquetry with ash legs. This is the most common form of marquetry table, employing small reserves of marquetry framed by oyster-cut veneers. Although hard evidence is lacking, it is probable that marquetry of this type was bought in from specialist suppliers. MALLETT & SON (ANTIQUES) LTD.

Marquetry tables survive in considerable numbers and vary greatly in quality. The example in 4:19 and 4:20 was probably supplied by the London cabinet-maker Thomas Pistor to James Grahme, a friend and courtier to James, Duke of York (later James II), in 1684.[11] The form is absolutely conventional, and the marquetry is set into discrete reserves in the walnut veneer. Tables similarly inlaid with small reserves of floral marquetry are not uncommon, which suggests that they were relatively inexpensive, using bought-in panels mixed with routine oyster-work (4:21). Of greatly

11. Turpin (2000).

Plate 4:22. Table (c.1680), ebony, ebonised wood and marquetry. This superb table was installed at Ham between 1679 and 1683 and was probably made to match the cabinet in 2:40. HAM HOUSE, THE NATIONAL TRUST

12. Thornton and Tomlin (1980), pp. 105, 157.
13. Evelyn (1670), I, p. 40.

superior quality is the table in 4:22. This was installed at Ham House between 1679 and 1683, and was probably among the best of its kind available.[12] The marquetry occupies every available surface, even on the legs, where the lower parts are inlaid with marquetry in the round, a technically difficult and beautifully executed achievement. Tables of this quality are the yardstick by which others should be measured.

Much further down the scale of luxury and ambition are the numerous oyster-veneered tables

Plate 4:24. Detail of 4:23 showing the arrangement of veneers on the table top. The contrast between the olivewood oysters and the light coloured banding was originally much more intense. BENINGBOROUGH HALL, THE NATIONAL TRUST

Plate 4:23. Table (1675-95), olivewood and ash. A very typical example, of the sort recorded in numerous inventories throughout the country.
BENINGBOROUGH HALL, THE NATIONAL TRUST

and stands that survive in English collections. These are amazingly consistent in both style and form, rarely varying except in decorative detail. 4:23 and 4:24 show such a table in good original condition. It is of olivewood veneered on a deal carcase, and the legs are turned ash.

At first glance the use of ash strikes one as odd, but in fact almost all olivewood tables, candlestands and stands for cabinets have ash legs. The reason for this is that olivewood is rarely straight-grained enough or sound enough to be used for structural supports. Ash, on the other hand was straight, cheap and could be made to resemble olive. Some ash, known to cabinet-makers as 'olive-ash', is naturally figured to resemble olive (4:25). If not, it could be washed over with lampblack and oil, which emphasised the growth rings, making them appear as dark, wandering lines very similar to the figure in olivewood. The surface was then painted with a light brown stain and varnished to match the ground colour of olive. John Evelyn commented on both these phenomenon in 1670:

> Some Ash is curiously cambleted and veined; I say, so differently from othern timber,
> that our skilful cabinet-makers prize it equally with Ebony, and give it the name of
> Green Ebony, which their customers pay well for; and when our woodmen light upon
> it, they make what money they will of it: But to bring out that curious lustre, so as it
> is hardly to be distinguished from the most curiously diapered Olive, they varnish
> their work with the China varnish… which infinitely excels the linseed oil…[13]

The consistency of design and construction of these tables is such that anomalies are easily spotted. The table in 4:26 was formerly in a private collection and is now in a public museum. It has several anomalous features which should arouse suspicion. First, it has two drawers, which is most unusual. Second, it has a rail across the top of the drawers, whereas the usual practice was to fit the drawers directly under the top. Third, there is no *abacus* or cap at the top of the legs. Finally, the drawers have lapped dovetails and a raised bottom with rebated runners, a method of construction not generally found before about 1720 (4:27). The table is a fake – a well-made fake, certainly, but the combination of so many out-of-period features on one piece cannot be accidental.

Plate 4:25. Olive ash – a common figure in ash much prized by late 17th century cabinet-makers for its resemblance to olivewood.

Plate 4:26. Table (20th century), walnut and marquetry veneers. This is a deliberate fake, betrayed by errors in design and construction (see text).
RED LODGE,
BRISTOL MUSEUMS AND ART GALLERIES

Plate 4:27. Detail of 4:26 showing lapped dovetails. The drawer also has a raised rebated bottom and rebated runners, a method of construction not common until after 1720.   RED LODGE,
BRISTOL MUSEUMS AND ART GALLERIES

Plate 4:28. Table (1670-90), walnut. A nicely made example in solid walnut, combining stylish twist-turned legs with archaic ripple mouldings and pegged construction. Canons Ashby, The National Trust

Joiner-made interpretations of triad tables often combine features which, in a fashionable context, would have been anachronistic. The table in 4:28 has five twist-turned legs, an unusual configuration, but one employed even by the best makers. In 1677 Richard Price supplied the Crown with 'a frame for a table with 5 twisted pillars and a compass bottom of black china varnishe... £2.0.0'.[14] On the other hand, the ripple moulding placed below the drawer and around the base of the legs is an archaic vestige of a former style. Another clue to its less than up-to-the-minute character is the solid walnut construction, with cleated top and pegged mortise-and-tenon joints.

14. PRO LC 9/275, f. 116.

Plate 4:29. **Candlestand** (1670-90), olivewood, oak, deal and ash. This is one of the commonest types of candlestand, made as one of a pair, and with a table *en suite*. It was originally slightly higher, having lost its three bun feet dowelled into the underside of the legs.

HARDWICK HALL, THE NATIONAL TRUST

Plate 4:31. **Candlestand** (1670-90), olivewood, deal and ash. The scrolled feet are probably the commonest design for this type of stand.   HARDWICK HALL, THE NATIONAL TRUST

Candlestands

The number of triads which survive complete with candlestands is relatively small. Consequently one is likely to find candlestands either singly or, more rarely, in pairs. 4:29 shows a typical example with olive-wood veneered top and ash shaft. The legs were originally fitted with small turned feet under their extremities to lift them clear of the floor. The top of this example is veneered on an oak substrate with a segmental pine edge, although pine substrates are more common, and the manner of fixing the block with nails and glue is typical (4:30). A very similar stand is shown in 4:31, but in this case the ends of the feet are scrolled, which achieves the same effect as the buns on the previous example.

Plate 4:30. **Detail of 4:29** showing the underside of the top with its oak substrate and pine edging. The block is simply nailed and glued in position. HARDWICK HALL, THE NATIONAL TRUST

15. Plott (1686), p. 384.
16. Randle Holme (1688).

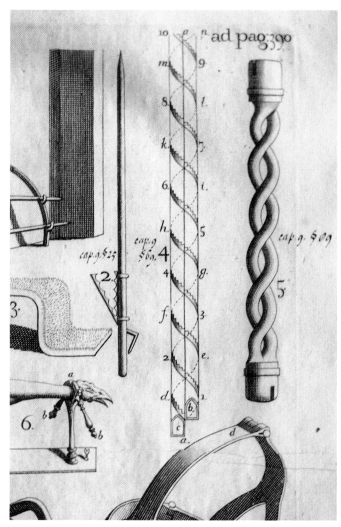

Plate 4:32. **Candlestand** (1670-90), walnut and deal with plumwood banding. The pierced turning is rare. Note the original bun feet and traces of ebonising on parts of the shaft.   PRIVATE COLLECTION

Plate 4:33. **Detail from an engraving,** from *The Natural History of Staffordshire*, by Dr.Robert Plott (1686), showing lathe-turned pierced double-bine turning.

The stand in 4:32 is a relatively rare example of pierced double-bine turning. These could be cut by hand, with some trouble, but were also lathe-turned. Robert Plott's *The Natural History of Staffordshire* shows an example of this work (4:33) turned on a machine devised by one John Ensor of Tamworth. Ensor claimed to be able to turn spirals 'not only of *two*, but of 3 or 4 *twists*, or more if he pleaseth; and that in so little time, that he can *turn* 20 of these, while one is cut or *rasp't...*'.[15] Like many candlestands of this date, it is made in sections which screw together (4:34). The threads are vulnerable to wear and damage, so that many examples which were once threaded have now been permanently glued.

Plate 4:34. **Detail of 4:32** showing the candlestand disassembled and the screw threads clearly visible.   PRIVATE COLLECTION

Plate 4:35. Candlestand (1670-90), walnut. This was made entirely on the lathe, with a solid walnut top and base. It lacks its original feet which were dowelled into the base. BENINGBOROUGH HALL, THE NATIONAL TRUST

Plate 4:36. Candlestand (1670-90), walnut and deal. Small stands of this kind were made for casual use about the house and were an ideal height for setting beside a chair. BENINGBOROUGH HALL, THE NATIONAL TRUST

Plate 4:37. Candlestand (1670-90), olivewood, cocus wood and deal with ash shaft and feet. BENINGBOROUGH HALL, THE NATIONAL TRUST

The chief difference between these three stands and the one in 4:35 is that this stand was made by a turner, not a cabinet-maker. Thus the top and base are turned from solid walnut, as is the shaft. The base was originally fitted with three small feet, dowelled into its underside at an angle so that they splayed out beyond the rim of the base.

Many candlestands were never part of a formal triad, but were made for casual use about the house. Randle Holme (1688) described them as 'a little round table, set upon one pillar or post, which in the foote branches itself out into three or four feet or toes... for its fast and steady standing'.[16] In many cases they seem to have been intended for use alongside a chair, so that they were considerably less tall than those made for a triad. 4:36-39 show three typical examples. It is impossible to date these objects with any precision – the twist turned examples were probably made over at least thirty years, from c.1670 to 1700. However, as 'banister' turned profiles became popular for chair backs at the end of the 1680s, similar profiles appeared on the shafts of candlestands

Plate 4:38. Detail of 4:37. Note the quartered cocus wood oysters in the centre of the top. These would originally have contrasted strongly with the much lighter olive and the white holly stringing. BENINGBOROUGH HALL, THE NATIONAL TRUST

Plate 4:39. Candlestand (1690-1710), olivewood and deal with ash shaft and feet. This turning profile suggests a later date than the previous examples. The inversely tapered section towards the base of the shaft mimics the same taper found on much grander stands such as those shown in 9:8-13.
BENINGBOROUGH HALL,
THE NATIONAL TRUST

Plate 4:40. 'Blackamoor' candlestand (before 1677), painted and gilt, one of a pair. These stands are described as 'Indians' in two of the Ham inventories. The feathered skirt and quiver of arrows are standard attributes of North American or Caribbean Indians, as depicted in numerous late 17th century engravings.
HAM HOUSE, THE NATIONAL TRUST,
V&A PICTURE LIBRARY

(4:39). Indeed, the turning profiles of short stands such as this are often matched by the upper sections of tall stands dating from the 1690s and later (some, perhaps many, have been cut down from taller stands).

Stands produced by carvers were in an entirely different league from turned ones and are extremely rare. One pair is shown in 1:4 and another, both turned and carved, in 4.42. Carvers were also responsible for the 'blackamoor' figures which were found in some grand houses. As early as 1638 Sir Henry Slingsby had 'a blackamore cast in led holding in either hand a candlestick to set a candle to give light to ye staircase'.[17] At Ham there were two such stands in the Great Dining Room, variously described in the inventories as 'Indian' or 'blackamore'.[18] Each of these holds aloft a plateau in the form of a tambourine, and was almost certainly intended to bear a candlestick (4:40). The function of those at Dyrham Park is less obvious (4:41). The servile pose and hollow, scallop-shell top suggest an offering of some sort, perhaps sweetmeats or cakes? They were intended to stand either side of a lacquered tea table in the Balcony Room (c.f. 5:4).[19] It is usual to state that blackamoor stands were 'Venetian', and although many were apparently made in Venice in the nineteenth century, there is no reason to suppose that the illustrated examples are anything other than English.

17. Edwards (1954), III, p. 146.
18. Thornton and Tomlin (1980), pp. 119-120.
19. Walton (1986), p. 44.

Plate 4:41. 'Blackamoor' candlestand (before 1700), painted and gilt, one of a pair. The chained ankle clearly indicates that this portrays an African slave. The stands arrived at Dyrham in 1700 but may be earlier, since they were sent by Thomas Povey, William Blathwayt's uncle. DYRHAM PARK, NATIONAL TRUST PHOTOGRAPHIC LIBRARY/ANDREAS VON EINSIEDEL

Plate 4:42. **Table and stands** (before 1677), ebonised beech and pine with cane tops. These were installed in the Duke's Dressing Room at Ham, where they still reside. The design is essentially French, although there is a hint in the Ham House bills that they might have been purchased in Holland in 1672.

HAM HOUSE, THE NATIONAL TRUST

20. Thornton and Tomlin (1980), p.p. 50-51.
21. Thornton (1984), figs. 56 and 57.
22. Thornton (1998), pp. 48-9.
23. National Trust Guide Book, Knole (1998), p.44.

Scrolled-leg tables

Ham House contains several documented triads or parts of triads, of which the earliest is probably that shown in 4:42. This table and stands stood in the Duke's Dressing Room at Ham and were recorded there in the inventory of 1677.[20] They are of ebonised wood with caned tops and were originally protected by leather covers. The style is emphatically French; both the scrolled legs with eagles' heads and the tripod stand with its scrolled base appear in a drawing of a Parisian triad by Nicodemus Tessin, while designs by Bérain also show stands with scrolled tripod bases and heavily decorated baluster shafts.[21] The silver stands made for the Countess of Dorset in 1676 (4:43) are of similar form. This magnificent triad introduces a new form of English table, for this is the earliest documented example with broken-scrolled legs. The 'broken' scroll was a decorative device commonly found in both Mannerist and Baroque art, but it was not until the last quarter of the seventeenth century that it was adopted as a significant motif by English furniture makers.[22] The dating of this triad is slightly puzzling, because the stands are hallmarked for 1676 and the table for 1680. There can be no doubt about the latter, since Gerrit Jensen's bill for the table, dated 1680, has recently come to light.[23]

Plate 4:43. Table, stands and looking glass (1676-80), sheet silver on a wooden core. The stands are hallmarked 1676 and the table 1680. All four pieces bear the monogram of Frances, Countess of Dorset. The table was supplied by Gerrit Jensen, and is the earliest firmly dated example having 'broken' scrolled legs.

KNOLE, NATIONAL TRUST PHOTOGRAPHIC LIBRARY/ANDREAS VON EINSIEDEL

Plate 4:44. Japanned table (c.1679), English 'Bantamwork' on a pine substrate. This might be the table recorded *en suite* with stands and a looking glass in the Withdrawing Room at Ham House in 1679.

HAM HOUSE, THE NATIONAL TRUST

24. Thornton and Tomlin (1980), pp. 68-9.
25. Wills (1965), p. 43; Edwards (1954), II, p. 311.
26. Edwards (1954), II, p. 311.
27. Steel mirrors are listed in the Books of Rates of 1642,1657 and 1660. These were the schedules of commonly imported commodities, together with their average values, from which import duty was calculated. Small steel mirrors were valued at 13s.4d. the dozen, large ones £1.6s.8d.
28. Wills (1965), p. 43.
29. Edwards (1954), II, p. 313,
30. Evelyn, *Diary*, 19 September 1676.
31. Wills (1965), p. 55. An example of such a room survives at the Château de Maisons.
32. Wills (1965, p. 55.
33. Ibid., pp. 57-58.
34. Edwards (1954), II, p. 313.
35. Quoted in Child (1990), p. 17.

The emergence of scrolled forms for table legs is coeval with parallel developments in seat furniture, on which curvilinear legs begin to emerge in the late 1670s and achieve maturity in the 1680s. Curiously, the term 'horsebone', which was used by Thomas Roberts to describe the broken-scrolled leg on chairs, was not applied to similar forms employed on tables. Another difference between its use on seat furniture and on tables is that tables were often made, as here, with the scrolls set at forty-five degrees to the frame, whereas on chairs this was not generally done until the 1690s.

A japanned table at Ham might conceivably predate the Knole example; 'a table & pr of stands & Looking glasse of Japan' were recorded in the Withdrawing Room in 1679, and this entry is assumed to refer to the table shown in 4:44.[24] Whether or not this is correct, it was not until the 1680s that the scrolled-leg table became common. A large number of surviving examples are japanned, which affords no clue to their date, but those decorated with marquetry can roughly be dated by its style. Significantly, floral marquetry is relatively uncommon, whereas 'seaweed' or 'arabesque' marquetry is very much more so, which confirms the impression that the scrolled-leg style became increasingly widespread in the late 1680s and 1690s. There are exact parallels with scrolled-leg stands for contemporary cabinets, of which several examples are shown in Chapter Seven.

Mirrors

Mirrors or 'looking glasses' were comparative rarities in England prior to the seventeenth century and there are no surviving glass examples known from before 1600. Documentary references to looking glasses occur with increasing frequency during the reign of Charles I and this is probably linked to the growth of domestic looking glass manufacture. In the sixteenth and early seventeenth centuries European looking glass manufacture was dominated by the great Venetian glass houses at Murano. This was a jealously guarded industry, but renegade Venetian glassmakers gradually spread Murano's secrets throughout Europe. In the 1620s the importation of foreign glass into England was briefly prohibited, as England's glassmakers struggled to compete against foreign importations, and in 1623 Sir Robert Mansell was awarded a monopoly for the production of all kinds of glass, including looking glasses. He claimed to employ five hundred people in the 'making, grinding and foyling of looking glasses'.[25] Charles I's several palaces had numerous looking glasses, predominantly in frames of ebony and needlework, and similar articles are cited in most inventories of noble houses.[26] But before the Restoration these were luxuries and many households made do with *specula* of polished steel, which were imported in quantity throughout the seventeenth century.[27]

In 1664 the Worshipful Company of Glass-sellers and Looking-glass Makers was incorporated and the same year the prohibition on imported glass was reintroduced.[28] The ban was lifted in 1668, however, probably because domestic production could not keep pace with the demand for window glass after the Great Fire, and it is known that in the 1670s looking glass plates were once more imported from Venice.[29]

In theory the Worshipful Company of Glass-sellers controlled and regulated the manufacture of all kinds of glass within a seven mile radius of the City of London, but their monopoly was compromised by a number of pre-existing patents for the production of looking glasses, such as that granted in 1663 to George Villiers, second Duke of Buckingham. Buckingham's manufactory was at Vauxhall, opposite Westminster on the south side of the River Thames, and 'Vauxhall' glass soon became a synonym for high quality mirror glass. John Evelyn visited the workshops there in 1676, and saw looking glasses 'far larger and better' than any he had seen in Venice thirty years previously.[30]

The rapid growth in domestic mirror manufacturing was undoubtedly stimulated by Restoration fashions. The looking glass was both literally and figuratively the focus of the fashionable 'triad', which was by 1670 a prerequisite for any fashionable apartment. For some a mere looking glass was not enough. In 1667 Sir Samuel Morland had an entire room panelled in Vauxhall glass, as did two of Charles II's mistresses, Nell Gwynne and the Duchess of Portsmouth.[31] As the plates became more widely available and (one assumes) cheaper, so mirrors percolated down the social scale. Inventories of the 1680s show that even in the houses of non-gentry – yeoman farmers, cloth merchants, blacksmiths and shopkeepers – one might expect to find one or more looking glasses, usually in a bedchamber. Fifty years previously this would have been exceptional.

The manufacture of looking glass plates

Seventeenth century English mirror plates were made by the 'broad' process. This began with the blowing of a large, sausage-shaped bubble of glass, a feat demanding strength, dexterity and tremendous lung power. The ends of the sausage were cut off to make a cylinder, and this was then slit down the middle and opened out flat. To make large plates by this method required considerable skill, and the wastage was high. Nevertheless, it was claimed that plates of 82in. x 48in. (208cm x 122cm) could be produced.[32] Few surviving plates are of this size and where very large mirrors were wanted they were usually composed of several plates. Large cast plates, made by pouring molten glass on to metal tables or moulds, were certainly made in France at this time, but despite an English patent for casting plates being taken out in 1691, there is no evidence that casting was widely practised in England before the second half of the eighteenth century.[33]

The glass-maker usually did no more than produce the glass plates. The laborious processes of grinding, polishing and 'foiling' were carried out by specialist looking glass makers, of which there were at least twenty in London in 1675.[34] The raw glass was neither flat nor transparent, so the plate had first to be ground flat and then polished to a clear transparency. The process is described in the following eighteenth century account:

> After looking glasses have been ground, they are to be polished, they still looking
> something like a slate. The polishing is perform'd in the following manner: the plate
> is laid down on a stone plac'd horizontally, and, in a bed of plaister of Paris calcin'd
> and pulveris'd very fine and sifted: which being made into a sort of paste by water, and
> then plaister'd up to the edges of the plate, dries and hardens, and so keeps it
> immoveable; then the workman fixing a strong bow of yew or some other tough wood,
> to a board fixed up to the ceiling of the room, fixes also the other end into a hole made
> in a wooden parallelopepid of about four inches long, cover'd with a sort of coarse
> woollen cloth well drenched with Tripoly, tempered with water, works it with this
> block and bow all over by strength of arm, till the plate has got a perfect politure.[35]

Plate 4:45. **Mirror plate**, late 17th century, showing the characteristic gritty appearance of mercury foiling.

Plate 4:46. **Mirror plate**, late 17th century, showing the 'bloom' caused by damp penetrating faults in the foiling.

Plate 4:47. This photograph reveals the red oxide backing of a modern mirror plate peeping through a crack in the back panel of a '17th century' mirror.

The final stage was to 'foil' the back of the plate with tin and mercury:

> A thin blotting paper is spread on a table, and sprinkled with fine chalk; and then a fine lamina or leaf of tin, called foil, is laid over the paper; upon this mercury is poured, which is equally to be distributed over the leaf with a hare's foot or cotton. Over the leaf is laid a clean paper, and over that the glass plate.
>
> The glass plate is press'd down with the right hand, and the paper is drawn gently out with the left; which being done, the plate is covered with a thicker paper, and loaden with greater weight, that the superfluous mercury may be driven out, and the tin adhere more closely to the glass.
>
> When it is dried, the weight is removed and the looking-glass is complete.[36]

Tin and mercury foiling gave the back of the mirror a matt grey colour and a rough, granular surface (4:45). Damp was its great enemy, which is one reason why so few seventeenth century mirrors retain their original plates. Moisture penetrates through minute faults in the foil, producing small circular grey blooms on the face of the mirror (4:46), and extreme damp caused the foil to fall off altogether. When the foil is in good condition, old glass has an attractive, soft and slightly grey reflection, very different from the hard, bright image produced by modern silvering. The latter process was introduced about 1840 and employs a thin film of silver instead of tin and mercury. It is protected by a coat of red lead, so that the back of the glass is a smooth and uniform rust-red or brown (4:47).

Hand blown glass is much thinner than modern plate glass. An approximate idea of a plate's thickness can be gained by placing the point of a pencil against the plate; the perceived distance between the point and its reflection is approximately the thickness of the glass. The greater thickness and weight of modern glass frequently causes problems when put into old frames. Toilet mirrors suffer badly in this respect because of the relatively weak joint between the mirror supports and the base.

The edges of old plates were sometimes 'diamond-cut' or bevelled. Since the bevel was produced by hand grinding it has an imprecise, rounded edge that is more easily seen than felt. By contrast, a modern machine-cut bevel is crisp and tangible. However, neither a soft bevel, nor a thin plate nor a granular back is a guarantee of authenticity, since they can all be reproduced and frequently are.

36. Quoted in Wills (1965), p. 63.
37. For further information on raised work, see Brooke (1992)
38. Brooke cites the *Thesaurus Sacrarum Historiam Veteris Testamenti*, published in 1685 by Gerard de Jode, as a particularly fruitful source [Brooke, p. 13].
39. Brooke (1992), p. 17.

Plate **4:48**. **Mirror** with raised-work frame (1650-85). The cartouche-shaped frame is a common design, ultimately deriving, like the needlework, from Mannerist engravings.　　CHRISTIE'S

Mirror frames of 'raised work'

'Raised work' is the contemporary term for what is often called 'stump-work'. It describes a type of needlework embroidery, much of whose surface is 'raised' by stuffing with cotton or wool waste, or even small pieces of wood. Mirror frames decorated by this technique are comparatively rare, and they were popular only for about three decades, from c.1650 to c.1680. A number of dated examples survive, bearing dates from 1662 to 1679.[37]

The designs for the embroidery were drawn in pencil on white satin. The motifs used, which recur repeatedly from mirror to mirror, were drawn from printed sources, and feature Old Testament scenes, exotic fauna and flora, and stylised landscapes. Some of the sources date back to the sixteenth century, which accounts for the archaic dress of some figures, but others were more contemporary.[38] One of the most common designs shows regal male and female figures standing either side of the mirror plate and these are traditionally identified as Charles II and his queen, Catherine of Braganza (4:48-50). However, modern scholarship suggests that this is somewhat fanciful and that these figures were essentially no more than stock characters from the standard repertoire.[39]

The sketched designs were commercially produced for sale to private customers. These were generally young gentlewomen, often no more than fourteen years old, who worked the designs with exquisite skill and patience to create what was probably their most technically accomplished work. The finished embroidery represented a significant moment in their lives, at the transition between childhood and womanhood, and perhaps coincided with the completion of their formal

Plate 4:49. Dressing table mirror (c.1670-85) with raised-work frame. This mirror was designed to stand on a table, with an easel support in the back. The oak case is original.   CHRISTIE'S

Plate 4:50. Mirror (c.1670-85). This is more conventional silk needlework, but the design is essentially similar. The tortoiseshell frame is laid in short sections, in a similar manner to the half-round carcase mouldings on contemporary cabinet-work.   SOTHEBY'S

Plate 4:51. Mirror (c.1670-85). This small mirror has an easel stand at the back, indicating its intended use as a dressing-table mirror. This very delicate japanning might be the work of an amateur hand.   SOTHEBY'S

education. Certainly these raised-work frames were precious objects, on a par with the beautiful raised-work caskets which were made by the same technique. The embroidery was sent to a framer to be professionally mounted and the mounts are themselves often highly decorative, bordered with tortoiseshell, lacquer or japan. Some were intended to hang on the wall, others were fitted with an easel frame to stand on a table, but in all cases the mirror was essentially a personal item and was not part of the formal ensemble of the triad.

Raised-work mirrors are generally of two forms. The first is in the shape of a stylised cartouche, with a heavily indented profile, lobed at the corners, straight on each side and with a shaped top and bottom (4:48). The second is rectangular, sometimes with a shallow arch in the top (4:49 and 4:50). The same break-arch frame can be found in other media, such as the exquisite tortoiseshell and japanned example in 4:51.

The scarcity of surviving raised-work mirror frames is probably due more to their fragility than to inherent rarity. On the other hand, the fine condition of some survivals is explained by the fact that they were invariably provided with protective wooden cases. The case might originally have served to keep the mirror safe during its journey from the framer, but some examples are decorated both internally and externally, which suggests that the case was more or less a permanent housing for the mirror. Hinged doors also suggest regular use, rather than a mere travelling container.

Plate 4:52. Mirror with ripple-moulded frame (1630-1680), ebonised pear wood (?). This type of frame was popular over many years, and is difficult to date with accuracy. PRIVATE COLLECTION

Plate 4:53. Ripple-moulded mirror frame (1630-80), ebony and ebonised wood. This was another perennially popular form, common to much of western Europe. DYRHAM PARK, THE NATIONAL TRUST

Ripple-moulded frames

From the 1630s to the 1670s the most common form of decoration for both picture and mirror frames was the so-called 'ripple moulding' (4:52 and 4:53). To modern eyes this looks distinctly odd and perhaps outlandish, but it was developed for a very specific purpose, which was to give life and movement to the otherwise sombre façades of ebony cabinets. The full effect is now largely lost to us, because we no longer rely on candlelight after dark, nor on the flickering flames of open fires.

A device for producing ripple mouldings was illustrated by both Moxon and Randle Holme (4:54). It was called a 'Waving Engine... wherewith Waved work is generally made upon small Frames for Pictures and Looking Glasses'.[40] The waving engine had a small blade, shaped to the desired profile, clamped vertically in a frame, and directly below this was a cam. The workpiece was glued to a wooden batten which was waved on its underside. As the workpiece was drawn manually through the frame its waved underside rode up and down over the cam, forcing the workpiece intermittently against the blade. By repeatedly drawing through the workpiece and at the same time gradually adjusting the height of the blade the ripple was formed. The device, though crude, was extremely effective on a hard, close-textured wood like ebony, but less so on a softer material such as walnut.

Evidence from Edward Traherne's inventory suggests he was still producing ripple moulded mirrors in large numbers in the early 1670s. Many of his mirror frames are described as 'black', often with the additional comment that they are two, three or four 'tymes about'. This intriguing phrase might refer to the several concentric lines of moulding which is such a characteristic feature of these frames. Also included in his stock were many dressing table mirrors, some with 'silver'

40. Moxon (1678), pp. 106-8, pl 5, fig 7; Holme (1688), p. 354.

Plate 4:55. Dressing table mirror (1670-80). Silver mounted on ebony. This mirror could either stand on its easel support or be hung from a ring.

HAM HOUSE, THE NATIONAL TRUST

frames perhaps similar to that in 4:55.

So long as ebony and other dark woods such as cocus remained popular, ripple mouldings continued to be employed, and it is probable that most of the ebony-framed looking glasses recorded in contemporary inventories had ripple-moulded frames. However, in fashionable houses the rippled frame was gradually superseded from the 1670s by cushion-framed mirrors decorated with figured veneers and/or marquetry.

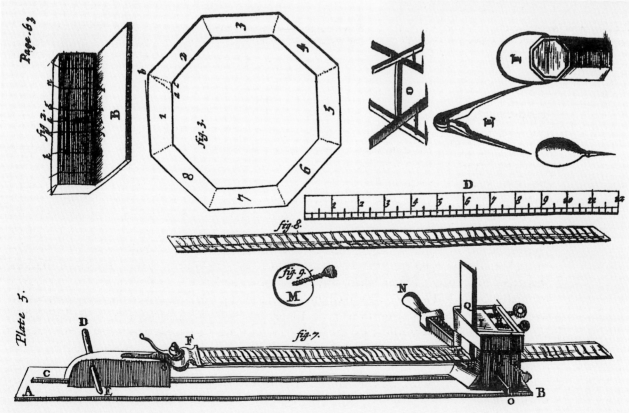

Plate 4:54. Engraving from *Mechanick Exercises* (1678), by John Moxon, showing (below) the 'Waving Engine' used to make ripple mouldings.

Plate 4:56. **Mirror** (c.1670-1710), olivewood and deal. The plate is not original. These cushion-framed mirrors were made over several decades and plain, uncrested examples are difficult to date with any precision.

NUNNINGTON HALL, THE NATIONAL TRUST

Plate 4:58. **Mirror** (c.1685-1700), walnut and marquetry on a deal frame. The style of the marquetry is typically 'late', crowded and not particularly well executed.

SOTHEBY'S

Plate 4:57. Detail of 4:56. The slots cut to house the cresting are clearly visible, but there is no evidence that one was ever fitted. NUNNINGTON HALL, THE NATIONAL TRUST

'Cushion' frames

Cushion-framed mirrors are the most numerous class of surviving seventeenth century looking glasses, and can be found made in every conceivable contemporary medium – walnut, olivewood, marquetry, lacquer and japan. The term 'cushion frame' is not contemporary, but it is apposite. It describes a rectangular frame of a broad ovolo section enclosing a rectangular glass plate (4:56). The frames are usually of deal, less often of oak, made in four sections half-lapped or butt-jointed at the corners. The joint is not evident from the front, because the convex outer face of the frame was a separate construction, mitred at the corners and glued on to the frame proper. The face was usually veneered oyster fashion and finished with a small ovolo on the outer edge. Sometimes the inner edge was also finished with an ogee section slip. An arched cresting was *de rigueur* in any formal setting, but many smaller mirrors were made without. Indeed, there is some evidence that the cresting was an optional extra, since one occasionally finds mirrors where provision for a cresting has been made but none appears ever to have been fitted (4:57).

Because they were made over such a long span of time, cushion-framed mirrors are difficult to date accurately, particularly if they have no other form of decoration other than veneers of walnut

Plate 4:59. **Mirror** (c.1680), ebony and
marquetry on a deal frame. This superb
mirror frame bears a ducal coronet and
was made *en suite* with the table in 4:22.
HAM HOUSE, THE NATIONAL TRUST,
V&A PICTURE LIBRARY

or olivewood. 4:58 shows a marquetry decorated mirror which has now lost its cresting. The style
of the marquetry is typically late, rather cramped and two-dimensional, which might suggest a
date in the late 1680s or even 1690s.

Crested frames are somewhat easier to date, since the style of both the cresting and the decoration
changed with the times. During the 1670s the crestings were wide and low, in the form of a
depressed arch, and usually shaped to some extent. A number of securely dated examples survive to
demonstrate that this style lasted into the 1680s (cf. 4:43) The fine quality mirror in 4:59 was
made for the Duke of Lauderdale in about 1680; it bears a Duke's coronet.[41]

41. Thornton and Tomlin (1980), p.157, figs. 139
and 140.

Plate 4:60. **Mirror** (1670-85),
scagliola. This is an exceptionally rare
example in superb condition.
DRAYTON HOUSE, PRIVATE COLLECTION

Of approximately similar date is the mirror in 4:60. This is exceptionally rare, because the frame
is veneered entirely in *scagliola*. This term describes a technique of simulating *pietra dura*, or
marquetry in stone, by the use of the powdered mineral selenite. The finely ground selenite was
mixed with water which could then be coloured as desired, before setting hard like plaster. There
are differing theories about how the decoration was actually applied, but most modern authorities
suggest that the ground was made first and allowed to harden. The design was then drawn on to
the ground and chopped out. The decoration – flowers, foliage, etc. – was inlaid as a semi-liquid
paste which was skilfully worked to create appropriate shading and colour. Once complete and
dried hard, the whole surface was scraped and polished smooth.

There are close similarities between the decoration of this mirror frame and that of the fireplace in
the Queen's Closet at Ham House. Surviving bills suggest that the fireplace was the work of an Italian

42. I am indebted to Maria Flemington for this
information.
43. Thornton and Tomlin (1980), pp. 68, 105,
125.

Plate 4:62. Mirror (1685-1700), Chinese lacquer on a deal frame. A high quality example with finely detailed lacquerwork, clearly recycled. Note the increased height of the cresting, and the fret pierced scrollwork, suggestive of arabesque marquetry. Both these features suggest a date after c.1685-90.   PHILLIPS

Plate 4:61. Mirror (1670-85), ebonised wood and gilt or lacquered brass. This is a relatively common type, showy without being prohibitively expensive. These were much copied in the 19th century.   KNOLE, THE NATIONAL TRUST

specialist, Baldassare Artima Romane, who was paid for a 'counterfitt marble chimney piece' in July 1673.[42] It is possible, therefore, that the Drayton mirror frame is by the same man – the date is certainly about right. The fact that Italian specialists like Romane pursued their careers here in the 1670s is yet another demonstration of the international draw created by the effulgent life of Restoration England.

Very much more common than scagliola are mirrors with frames embellished with repoussé brass mounts (4:61). The frames are usually of ebony or at least ebonised, chosen to contrast with the brilliance of lacquered or gilt brass. The inventories at Ham describe two such mirrors 'garnished wth brasse' and one of silver in the house in the late 1670s.[43]

Towards the end of the 1680s the height of the cresting tended to increase, and a new decorative style began to emerge with the introduction of arabesque scrollwork (4:62). This is a development which continued into the 1690s, and is further discussed in Chapter Nine.

Plate 4:63. Mirror (c.1664-85). Silvered and painted wood. The openwork carving is designed to allow the coloured background to be seen, contrasting with the silvered foliage. An almost identical mirror bearing the arms of Gough of Old Fallings Hall and Perry Hall, Staffordshire, granted in 1664, is in the Victoria & Albert collection. The design of the cartouche (which is missing its top) is similar to that of contemporary lock escutcheons. SOTHEBY'S

Plate 4:64. **Mirror** (c.1665-80). Carved and gilded wood. This is one of a rare pair of small mirrors exquisitely carved and gilt. Edward Traherne's inventory of 1675 reveals that mirror frames 'gilt with Gold and boyes' were one of the most common types. SOTHEBY'S

Plate 4:65. **Mirror** (c.1670-90). Carved and gilded wood. A slightly unusual example; the cherubs, shells and foliage are standard attributes, but the arms at the base are not and suggest a military connection. SOTHEBY'S

Carved frames

Carved mirror frames are less common than veneered ones. This might simply have been a question of cost, since carved frames involved considerable labour and a high degree of skill, although the materials used – deal, lime or peartree – were inexpensive.

Some frames were modelled on the same basic form as veneered ones, with broad, ovolo-section borders (4:63 and 4:64). The construction is layered, with the borders being carved before being fixed to the flat base frame. The carving was heavily pierced and undercut, so that much of the ground was visible through the carving, and so it was painted to provide a coloured background. The carved elements were either painted, silvered or gilt. The effect is similar to that created on the mirrors with pierced metal mounts.

One of the most popular decorative motifs used on carved mirrors was the *putto* or cherub, often in opposing pairs in the top or base of the mirror (4:63 and 4:65). These had a very long span of fashionable life. Mirror frames carved with 'boyes' occur in Edward Traherne's inventory of 1675, and they were still popular in the 1690s.

Plate 4:66. **Mirror** (c.1670-90).
Carved, silvered and gilded wood. The
laurel and berry border to the plate was
a popular one.   CHRISTIE'S

Another type of frame was more purely carvers' work and relates closely to contemporary picture
frames (4:65 and 4:66). Indeed, it is sometimes difficult to say whether some examples started life
as picture or mirror frames. These typically have a narrow carved border framing the plate, beyond
which is a wide margin of pierced and scrolling foliage, flowerheads and playful 'boyes'.

Finally, there are mirrors whose frames relate closely to the carved woodwork found on
contemporary overdoors and chimneypieces (4:67). These belong more to the tradition of the architectural carver and in many cases were integrated with fixed elements of the room panelling. The
style is naturalistic, often extremely lifelike, and clearly the work of a highly skilled carver. Many
of these frames are inevitably ascribed to Grinling Gibbons, but documented examples of Gibbons'
work are in fact relatively few and no mirror frames by him are known. One must be careful, too,
not to mistake a collection of reassembled fragments for the real thing.

Plate 4:67. Mirror (c.1670-1700). Carved and gilded wood. This has been heavily regilded, but is nevertheless a very finely carved frame whose style owes much to contemporary architectural carving of the sort made famous by Grinling Gibbons. The style is extremely naturalistic and the depth of detail could only be achieved by building up the design in layers. SOTHEBY'S

Chapter Five

LACQUER, JAPANNING AND OTHER FINISHES

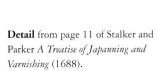

Detail from page 11 of Stalker and Parker *A Treatise of Japanning and Varnishing* (1688).

1. H. Jaeschke, 'Examination of Oriental Lacquer for Conservation', in Budden and Halahan (1994), pp. 6-10.
2. Ibid., p. 7.
3. 'The Committees for the Surat warehouse are desired to view the several sorts of lacquered wares now brought home on the *George* and *Rainbow* and to give direction for making such frames of chairs and other things as may be most proper to be sent in the next ship for Tonkin to be lacquered.' Minutes of the East Indian Company Board, 31 August 1687, quoted in Symonds (May 1934), p. 287.
4. Symonds (July-Dec 1934), pp. 41-42. Huth states that regular commercial relations between Holland and Japan commenced in 1639 [Huth, 1972, p. 14]. Stalker and Parker reckoned that Japanese lacquer was so superior to other types that 'no fiddling pretender could match or imitate it' [Stalker and Parker (1688), p. 6].
5. Thornton and Tomlin (1980).
6. Gloucestershire Record Office, E 254. I am grateful to Karin Walton for a sight of this inventory.

The trade in Oriental lacquerware

Lacquer cabinets like that in 5:1 were among the most highly prized of all Restoration furniture. Their exotic decoration and flawless finish held an exotic allure which both fascinated and charmed English observers, whilst their very high price ensured that they remained beyond the reach of all but the very rich.

The principal raw ingredient of Oriental lacquer is the sap of the lac tree, *Rhus verniciflua*. This is a natural polymer, which quickly gels and hardens in contact with air to create a tough, almost transparent coating. The carcases of Oriental lacquered furniture were almost invariably of soft-wood, carefully prepared and sometimes strengthened with cloth pasted over the entire surface to bind it. Layers of lacquer mixed with fine powdered clay, earth or sawdust were first applied to form a foundation. Once this was smoothed and sealed, the lacquer was applied in thin coats, each coat being allowed to harden before the next was applied. The process was lengthy – up to one hundred coats are commonly found – but the result was a wonderfully glossy surface of unmatched hardness and durability (5:2). If it remained undamaged, the lacquer was impervious to water, dilute alkalis, acids and most solvents.[1]

Raw lacquer is virtually transparent, but it could be coloured by the addition of pigments, as well as by the inclusion of powdered metals and other materials. Further decoration could either be applied directly with brush or pen, or in raised relief built up with fillers of clay powder, earth, or sawdust.[2]

The lacquered furniture surviving in English collections generally falls into one of several distinct categories. The first comprises genuine Oriental furniture, originally made for domestic consumption but increasingly, as demand in Europe grew, manufactured for export. The East India Company traded directly with several far-eastern ports, including Tonkin (now in Vietnam), Amoy and Canton (both in China). Much of the ware was sent first to India, where it was stored in the Company's warehouses before being shipped home.[3] Unlike the Dutch, the English did not trade directly with Japan, so Japanese lacquer, which most observers reckoned superior to all others, was bought at Dutch trading stations in Batavia (now part of Indonesia).[4] It is often said that much of the lacquerware imported into England came via Holland, but this is a fallacy, since the monopoly

Plate 5:1. Japanese lacquer cabinet (mid-17th century). This fine quality cabinet was one of the most sought-after status symbols of the age. In Japanese houses the cabinet stood on the floor, raised only by the low frame attached to its base.

TEMPLE NEWSAM HOUSE,
LEEDS CITY ART GALLERIES

of the English East India Company ensured that only they were permitted to import Oriental goods into England.

Most Oriental furniture was ill-suited for use in European houses, but one article which easily made the transition was the two-door cabinet enclosing small drawers and cupboards (5:1). In China and Japan these stood on or near the floor, but in Europe they were raised on a carved stand to create imposing centrepieces for important rooms. The severe, box-like form of these cabinets almost certainly influenced the design of contemporary English veneered cabinets and scriptors.

Another large piece of furniture which made the transition from east to west without modification was the lacquered screen, which acted variously as a room divider, draught ex-cluder, and decorative backdrop (5:3). No less than twelve 'Indian' and 'Japan' screens were recorded at Ham House in 1677.[5] Other commonly imported items included trays, hand screens, stands and small tables. The table shown in 5:4 is probably one of the several 'Japan' tables recorded in the inventory of 1703 at Dyrham Park.[6] The table is actually thought to be Javanese and several others of this form survive in English collections. One example at Ham House has been raised by the addition of twist-turned legs to conform more easily to English usage (see 1:12).

Because relatively few articles of Oriental furniture were suited to European domestic use, a second category of lacquered furniture consisted of pieces made in the Orient specifically for the European market. *A True Relation of the Rise and Progress of the East India Company* reveals that by

Plate 5:2. Detail of 5:1. The lacquer on this drawer front is unblemished after more than three centuries, a testament to the extraordinary durability of high quality lacquer. The loop handle with double fixings was employed in Japan decades before it became fashionable in England.

Plate 5:3. Chinese lacquer screen (late 17th century). This was one of the few large items of Oriental lacquerware which translated directly into English houses. Alternatively, the screens could be used as wall panelling, or broken up and used for making small furniture.

MALLETT & SON (ANTIQUES) LTD

the early 1670s it was Company policy to send out English artisans to ensure that many types of Oriental goods were made suitable for European markets:

> In Anno 72, or 73, several Artificers were sent over by the Company, with great quantities of English Patterns, to teach the Indians how to Manufacture Goods to make them vendible in England and the rest of the European Markets After which began the great Trade in Manufactured Goods from the Indies.[7]

This particular passage refers to the manufacture of cloth rather than furniture, but William Dampier recorded a similar practice relating specifically to lacquered furniture in 1688:

> Besides, our fashions of Utensils differ mightily from theirs, and for that reason Captain Pool, on his Second Voyage to the Country, brought an ingenious Joyner with him to make Fashionable Commodities to be lackered here, as also Deal-Boards, which are much better than the Pone-Wood of this country.[8]

The success of this policy eventually caused several prominent cabinet-makers to ask the Joiners' Company to petition Parliament against the trade in lacquered goods.[9] The petition, which was drawn up in April 1701, claimed that the 'Art of Cabinett Making' was in imminent danger of 'ruine and distruction' from greedy merchants who, 'minding only their private gain… [were] sending Modells or Paternes of the Inventions of your petitioners to India and severall other ports and places in or neare those parts from whouse great quantities of Cabinetts, Tables, Looking Glasse Frames and other Japaned Wares…are daily imported here…'. The petitioners therefore desired Parliament to bring in a bill to 'prohibite the importation of such Cabinetts from all forreigne parts'.[10] A second petition, probably drawn up in conjunction with the Japanners, is worth quoting at length:

7. *A True Relation…* (1697). Similar comments were made in *A Discourse of Trade, Coyn and Paper Credit;* 'After Anno 1670… *Throwsters, Weavers, Dyers* and such like Tradesmen, were sent out by the Company to teach the *Indians* to make all sorts of Manufactured Goods in such manner as might please the *Europeans*…'. Polloxfen (1697), p. 99.

8. Dampier (1729), II, p. 62.

9. G.L., Joiners' Company Minutes, 4 March 1701.

10. Ibid., 7 April 1701.

11. BL., 'THE CASE OF THE JOYNER'S COMPANY AGAINST the Importation of Manufactured CABINET-WORK from the EAST INDIES'.

12. Ibid. These figures probably represent the totals imported in the four years immediately prior to the petition, i.e., from 1697 to 1700 inclusive.

13. 12 & 13 *William III cap. 11.* (1701), 'An Act for granting his Majesty several duties upon low wines or spirits… and for improving the duties on japanned and lacquered goods'.

But several Merchants and others, Trading to the *East-Indies*, and to several Ports and Places thereabouts, have procured to be made in *London*, of late Years, and sent over to the *East Indies*, Patterns and Models of all Sorts of Cabinet Goods; and have Yearly return'd from thence such great Quantities of Cabinet-Wares, Manufactured there after the *English* Fashion, by our Models, that the said Trade in England is in great Danger of being utterly Ruined, being ingross'd by the said Merchants, and others, that Trade to and from those Parts, to so great a Degree, that they not only supply these Kingdoms with such Commodities, so Imported, but also spoil the EXPORTATION of the said *Joyners* and *Cabinet-Makers* Work to Foreign Parts, so that their Journey-men and Apprentices, in a manner, will be useless; which, if not timely prevented, will Reduce the said *Joyners, Cabinet-Makers*, and Thousands of other Poor Artificers depending on them, as the *Carvers, Turners, Coppersmiths, Glew-makers, Sawyers,* &c, to a deplorable Condition, who must perish for want of Work, or be maintain'd by their several Parishes.[11]

The Petition concluded with an account of lacquered furniture imported into England during the previous four years, which included 244 cabinets, 6,582 tea tables, 428 chests, 70 trunks, 52 screens, 589 looking glass frames, 655 tops for stands, 818 lacquered boards, 597 sconces and 4,120 dressing, comb and powder boxes.[12] Neither the argument nor the statistics persuaded Parliament, however. Not only was the East India trade of supreme importance to the nation as a whole, but many members of both Houses had interests in the East Indian trade. All that the aggrieved joiners got was a small concession stipulating that the import duties on Oriental goods should be charged according to their 'true and real value'.[13]

Another facet of the trade was the sending out of English-made goods to be lacquered in China. This might seem a tedious and expensive process, since the journey to China and back seldom took less than two years, but because there was usually excess cargo space on the outward voyage the freight was relatively cheap. In 1684 the Company sent a letter to one of its buyers at Tonkin:

Plate 5:4. Lacquer tea table (late 17th century). This is thought to be from Java. Several examples are known in English collections, and this one has been at Dyrham since c.1700.
DYRHAM PARK, THE NATIONAL TRUST

147

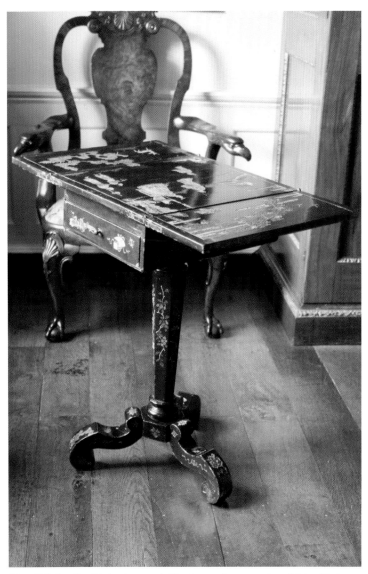

Plate 5:5. Small table (c.1690-1710). The form and construction of this table is typically English, but the decoration appears to be genuine incised lacquer. The dark aubergine colour is not one commonly used by English japanners, although common in China. Was this made in England and shipped out to be lacquered in China?   PRIVATE COLLECTION

Plate 5:6. The same table, with the top tilted and supported on a strut. The decoration of the top is rather better than that on the base.

> … we have Sent you (to help fill up y[e] Ship) Some quantity of Joyners ware to be Lackred there… we can give you no particular directions, they being things of Fancy, but we would have them well done and Substantiall that may hold for many yeares and with as much variety as may be, Some plain black, but most to be adorned with birds, fflowers or Imagery such as you Shall… think may be most acceptable in England…[14]

14. Quoted in Symonds (May 1934), p. 287.
15. Quoted in Symonds (July-Dec 1934), p. 39.
16. Huth (1972), p. 26.
17. Quoted in Symonds (July-Dec 1934), p. 40.
18. Gilbert and Beard (1986), p. 487.
19. PRO LC 9/282, *fol.* 79.
20. Sotheby's London, *Important English Furniture*, 10 July 1998, lot 116.

A few years later, in 1687, the Company directed that the 'frames of chairs and other things' were to be sent to Tonkin to be lacquered. But Tonkin lacquer was apparently not satisfactory and in 1690 the Company wrote to their Tonkin buyers instructing them to 'make it your business effectually to dispose of all our Goods which you have now lying by you… for your Laquer'd Ware is so slight and naught and of such low Esteem here, that it will not defray y[e] charges of y[e] ffreights.'[15] Thereafter most such shipments went to Canton and Amoy.[16]

Furniture of this kind, having an English-made carcase combined with true Oriental lacquer, is now very rare, or perhaps it just awaits identification. The small table in 5:5 and 5:6 is English in its design and construction, but the deep aubergine-coloured decoration appears to be genuine lacquer. Is this one of the East India Company's hybrid imports? To answer this question we would need to turn to science, both to identify whether the species of wood used for the carcase is European and to confirm whether the lacquer is indeed the genuine Chinese variety or an English imitation.

Yet another category of lacquered furniture comprises pieces of genuine lacquer re-fashioned into new forms by English joiners and cabinet-makers. One of the most common uses of lacquered screens was to make room panelling. In 1697 the supercargo of the Company ship *Nassau* was instructed to buy at Amoy 'Two hundred Lacker'd Boards finely lackered on both sides for screens or pannelling rooms'.[17] In order to make sure than the wood used was of the best quality, a hundred deals were sent out with the ship to be lacquered in China. A number of rooms panelled wholly or partially with Oriental lacquer survive in English houses, but most have succumbed to changing fashion. The Japan Closet at Chatsworth lasted a mere eight years; it was installed by Gerrit Jensen in 1692 and dismantled in 1700.[18]

One of the most celebrated instances of the recycling of Oriental lacquer is recorded in the Lord Chamberlain's accounts for 1704, when Gerrit Jensen was required to make substantial alterations to two 'Indian' cabinets at St James's Palace.[19] He began by dismantling them almost entirely, removing the tops, backs and the inside face of the doors, taking out the drawers and replacing them with shelves. The interiors of the cabinets were then quilted with crimson sarsenet and each placed on a carved and gilt stand. The drawers were used to fit out another pair of cabinets supplied for the gallery at Kensington Palace, while the tops were made into tables and fixed to carved frames (since the tops of the original cabinets were now above eye level, it made perfect sense to remove and re-use them). Most of these extraordinary hybrids have been lost, but the tables survive, having been acquired in the nineteenth century by the Earl of Warwick, in whose possession they remained until sold in London in 1998 (5:7 and 5:8).[20]

Plate 5:7. Table (1704). One of a pair supplied by Gerrit Jensen to St James's Palace in 1704. The tops are made from a dismantled lacquer cabinet. The pillar legs and stepped cross-stretchers are typical of Jensen's style. The apron bears the cipher of Queen Anne.   SOTHEBY'S

Plate 5:8. Detail of 5:7 showing the table top.   SOTHEBY'S

Plate 5:9. **Bantamwork cabinet** (late 17th century), the stand English, c.1675-90.   MALLETT & SON (ANTIQUES) LTD.

Plate 5:10. **Chest** (c.1670-1700). This is English, but constructed from imported Bantamwork panels.   TEMPLE NEWSAM HOUSE, LEEDS CITY ART GALLERIES

Plate 5:11. **Detail of 5:10** showing the side of the chest. The headless figures demonstrate that this has been made from recycled lacquer.

Bantamwork

Coromandel lacquer or Bantamwork is the name given to a different type of lacquerware on which the decoration, instead of being painted on to a smooth lacquered surface, was cut into a thick gesso-type ground (5:9). The incised design was then lacquered in colours and finished with a clear lacquer to protect it. The name Bantamwork derives from the Dutch colonial entrepôt in Batavia, while Coromandel refers to the coast of south-east India where much lacquer was transhipped on its way to England. According to one modern authority, the original source of this type of lacquerware was the Chinese province of Honan.[21] Although Stalker and Parker use the term 'Bantamwork', the contemporary layman usually called it 'cutt-work', 'cutt Japan' or 'hollow burnt Japan'.[22]

According to Stalker and Parker, by the late 1680s Bantamwork was 'almost obsolete, and out of fashion, out of use and neglected...'. They reckoned it was a very poor rival to polished lacquer, but admitted it was 'very pretty, and some are more fond of it, and prefer it to the other...'.[23] Despite these strictures, large quantities of Bantamwork have survived, which suggests that Stalker and Parker's disapproval was by no means shared by all.

As with ordinary lacquer, it was common to break up Bantamwork screens and recycle the panels into a more practical form, a practice famously lampooned by Stalker and Parker:

> I think no person is fond of it, or gives it house-room, except some who have made
> new Cabinets out of old Skreens. And from that large old piece, by the help of a
> Joyner, make little ones, such as Stands or Tables, but never consider the situation of
> their figures; so that in these things so torn and hacked to joint a new fancie, you may
> observe the finest hodgpodg and medley of Men and Trees turned topsie turvie, and
> instead of marching by Land you shall see them taking journeys through the Air, as if
> they had found Doctor Wilkinson's way of travelling to the Moon; others they have
> placed in such order by their ignorance, as if they were angling for Dolphins in a
> Wood, or pursuing the Stag, and chasing the Boar in the middle of the Ocean;... such
> irregular pieces as these can never certainly be acceptable, unless persons have an equal
> esteem for uglie, ill-contrived works, because rarities of their kind, as for the greatest
> performances of beautie and proportion.[24]

5:10 and 5:11 show a small chest made from a Bantamwork screen in this fashion, the sides exhibiting the chaotic results so strongly deplored by Stalker and Parker. The interior is standard

21. Huth (1972), p. 26.
22. Edwards (1954), II, pp. 267 and 271.
23. Stalker and Parker (1688), pp. 6-7.
24. Ibid, pp. 37-38.

Plate 5:12. Detail of 5:10 (interior).
The interior of the chest is conventional English work in oak with walnut veneers. The strong, slightly blurred figuring of the veneers is curious and could be due to fungal infection. It might, however, be produced by lampblack bleeding from the pores underneath the varnish.

first-phase English cabinet-work, which has survived in pristine condition (5:12). In more skilled hands the products of recycled Bantamwork were more impressive, as shown by the table and mirror in 5:13, attributed to Gerrit Jensen.

Japanning

Despite the growing scale of the trade in lacquered goods, it was not sufficient to satisfy a voracious demand. To make good the shortfall English furniture makers developed their own version of lacquer in imitation of the Oriental, and the word 'japanned' is now used to describe artefacts decorated with this false lacquer. The terms 'japann'd' or 'japan' also occur in contemporary records; in 1679 the upholsterer John Podevine supplied the Royal Household with 'two great arme Chaires of fine greene Japan'.[25] Another contemporary name for imitation lacquer was 'China varnish'. One of the earliest references occurs in the Lord Chamberlain's accounts for 1673, when Richard Price supplied a set of chairs 'of the China varnish'.[26] A few years later he made 'a frame for a table with 5 twisted pillars and a compass bottom of black china varnishe'.[27]

One of the earliest English descriptions of the technique of japanning occurs in the 1670 edition of *Silva*, 'the first time', boasted Evelyn, 'that so rare a secret has been imparted'.

> We conclude all, with that incomparable *Secret* of the *Japon or China-Vernishes*, which has hitherto been reserv'd so choicely among the *Virtuosi*; with which I shall suppose to have abundantly gratified the most curious employers of the finer woods.
>
> Take a *Pint* of the *Spirit* of *Wine* exquisitely *dephlegm'd*, four *Ounces* of *Gum-Lacq*, which thus clense: break it first from the sticks and rubbish, and roughly contusing it in a *Mortar*, put it to *steep* in Fountain water, ti'd up in a bag of course *Linnen*, together with a very small morsel of the best Castle-Sope, for 12 hours; then rub out all the *tincture* from it, to which add a little *Alum*, and reserve it apart: The *Gum-Lacq* remaining in the bag, with one *Ounce* of *Sandrac* (some add as much Mastic and White Amber) dissolve in a large *Matras* (well stopp'd) with the *Spirit* of *Wine* by a two dayes *digestion*, frequently agitating it, that it adhere not to the *Glasse*: Then *strain* and presse it forth into a lesser *Vessel*; Some, after the first *Infusion* upon the *Ashes* after twenty four hours, augment the *heat*, and transfer the Matras to the Sandbach, till the *Liquor* begins to *simper*; and when the upper part of the *Matras* grows a little *hot*, and that the *Gum-Lacq* is melted, which by that time (if the operation be heeded) commonly it is,

25. PRO LC 9/275.
26. PRO LC 9/273, f. 137.
27. PRO LC 5/41, f. 104 (1677).

Plate 5:14. **Japanned chair** (1682), one of a set supplied by John Ridge to the Duke of Hamilton. This is an early example of the scrolled-leg type. The design of the fore-rail corresponds to that on chairs at Ham, but is executed in profile to allow the surface to be japanned. The upholstery is modern.
HOLYROOD HOUSE,
THE ROYAL COLLECTION,© 2002 HER MAJESTY QUEEN ELIZABETH II,
PHOTOGRAPHER ANTONIA REEVE

Plate 5:15. **Japanned candlestand** (c.1670-1700). The scrolled shaft is an unusual form, but the flat surfaces allow the japanning to be seen to advantage.
HARDWICK HALL, THE NATIONAL TRUST

customers might require. The chair in 5:14 was supplied to the Duke of Hamilton by John Ridge in 1682. It was part of a suite comprising eight chairs, a footstool, table, mirror and two stands, all made for the Duchess's bedroom at Holyrood Palace.[34] 5:15 shows a candlestand with japanning of particularly nice quality. The top and base are of conventional form, but the S-shaped stem is unusual. These are but two examples – there was no article of furniture or indeed household utensil which could not be embellished by japanning. As well as wooden objects, japanning was widely applied to metalware, such as '*Mounteths, Punch-Bowls, Tea-Tables* and several sorts of *Iron-Ware…*'.[35]

A further advantage of japanned furniture was that it was a great deal cheaper than the lacquered equivalent. Whereas a fine Japanese cabinet might cost between £40 and £50, the japanned English equivalent, including its carved stand, cost less than £20. Nevertheless, £20 was still a great deal of money and japanned furniture took some while to become common in middle-class houses. It does not occur regularly in London inventories until the 1690s, and only after 1700 does it become commonplace.[36] While there may be an element of 'lag' in this data, since the inventories are mostly probate inventories, it might suggest that japanning was initially a rather

Plate 5:16. Japanned cabinet-on-stand (1675-1700). This is a wonderfully fresh and naïve example, the work of a not very competent japanner with a good imagination. The carved stand is likewise rather amateurish. CHASTLETON HOUSE, THE NATIONAL TRUST

Plate 5:17. Detail of 5:16. The dress and headgear of this figure are taken from contemporary prints depicting Indians from the Americas, not China. Note the gilt handle, with its double-petalled backplate.

specialised craft which was later taken up by more numerous and perhaps less skilled artisans.

English japanning encompasses many grades of quality. In some cases it consists of little more than paint varnished over with shellac, and this is scarcely surprising, since many japanners were at best semi-skilled. The Parliamentary petition of 1701 describes some as 'poor and Laborious Men, who (with their Families) wou'd otherwise have been very Burthensome and Chargeable on their respective Parishes'.[37] Much japanning is so inept as to be impossible to mistake for the real thing. The cabinet in 5:16 is a wonderfully fresh example, executed with naïve charm by someone who had obviously never seen China or a Chinaman. Three of the drawer fronts depict windmills, perhaps inspired by some Dutch blue and white ware which the japanner mistook for Chinese porcelain, while several of the figures represent North American Indians (5:17). At the other end of the scale are examples such the chair in 5:18 and 5:19, of which there are two sets at Ham House. These were made for the Duchess of Lauderdale, one set being installed in her Private Closet and probably used *en suite* with the lacquered tea table shown in 1:12.[38] The curious design probably derives from the Italian *sgabello* chair, of which a number of English–made examples are known.[39] The japanning is clearly not the work of an amateur, nor of a cheap workshop, and such skills were worth advertising. Philip Arbuthnot, whose business in the Strand flourished between 1702 and 1727, was proud to declare himself 'cabinet-maker and japanner'. His clients included Queen Anne and the Marquis of Annandale.[40]

The Japanners were not officially incorporated as a recognised trade and relied heavily on the Joiners' Company for commercial and political support. Both groups of artisans had enjoyed the fat years during the war against the French between 1689 and 1697, when trade with the East had been severely curtailed.[41] The resurgence of seaborne trade after the Peace of Ryswick in 1697 brought an unwelcome glut of lacquered goods on to the market, raising understandable fears

Plate 5:18. Japanned chair (c.1680), one of a set made for the Duchess of Lauderdale. The form is most unusual, but, like the candlestand in 5:15, it does allow the japanning to show well.
HAM HOUSE, THE NATIONAL TRUST

Plate 5:19. Detail of 5:18. Reverse of the chair, showing the wonderful colour which is not always apparent from the front.

37. 'THE CASE OF THE JAPANERS OF ENGLAND'. The B.L. catalogue gives a date of 1710 for this document, but this cannot be correct, since it refers to 'His Majesties Customs'. It was probably drawn up at the same time as the first Joiners' Company petition against imported lacquer cabinet-work (1701), and for essentially the same reasons.

38. The Ham inventories show that the set made for the Antechamber to the Queen's Bedchamber was installed between 1679 and 1683. The evidence for the set in the Private Closet is more ambiguous, but the most likely explanation is that it was installed at the same time.

39. Several are illustrated in Jackson-Stops, ed. (1985), pp. 134-135.

40. Beard and Gilbert (1986), pp. 16-17.

41. '…during [a] great part of the late War, the *East-India* trade was under some Discouragement, and while it was so, our *English* Manufactures flourished very much…'. *A True Relation…*(1697). See also 'THE CASE OF THE JAPANERS OF ENGLAND (1701)'.

among furniture makers and japanners alike. Following the Joiners' lead, in 1701 the Japanners submitted their own petition to Parliament demanding a prohibition on the importation of lacquered goods. This contains a wealth of detail about the trade of japanning, and is worth quoting at length:

THE CASE OF THE JAPANERS OF ENGLAND

The Curious and Ingenious Art and Mystery of Japaning, has been so much Imprv'd in *England* of late years, and has with all been so Beneficial to the Nation that those who have the most Knowledge thereof, humbly conceive it (with Submission) very fit and worthy to be supported and Encourag'd.

For it has afforded an honest Lively-hood, to several Hundreds of Families, of handy-crafts Men; as *Cabinet-makers, Turners, Goldbeaters* and *Copper-smiths;* besides its Benefit and Advantage to *Drugists, Distillers* and *Colour-men:* And has given Employment to many poor and Laborious men, who (with their Families) wou'd otherwise have been very Burthensome and Chargeable to their respective Parishes.

And many of the *Artificers,* in the said *Art* and *Mystery,* have brought it to so great Perfection, as to exceed all manner of *Indian Lacquer,* and to Equal the right Japan itself, by enduring the *Fire* in the Boyling of *Liquors.*

Also it will if Encourag'd vastly Improve both the *Wood* and *Iron* Trades for *Cisterns, Mounteths, Punch-Bowls, Tea-Tables,* and several sorts of *Iron-Ware;* which wou'd be Useless, if not Improved by our *English Lacquer.*

But the *Merchants* sending over our *English Patterns,* and *Models* to *India,* and bringing in such vast Quantities of *Indian Lacquer'd Wares;* (especially within the last two years,) a great number of Families are by that means reduced to Miserable Poverty.

And the large quantities of Japan'd Goods expected shortly to be brought from the *Indies,* will not only tend to the Ruine of the Japan-Trade here in England, but also Obstruct the Transportation of our *English Lacquer* to all *Europe,* which is a considerable advancement to his Majesties Customes…

Some corroboration of the Japanners' claims comes from contemporary critiques of the East India trade, of which there were many. *England's Almanack* (1700) showed that whereas only fifty-two English ships had sailed to the East Indies in the seven years between December 1690 and December 1697, the same number had already sailed since February 1698.[42] As we have seen, neither the Joiners' nor the Japanners' complaints were received sympathetically in Parliament and stood little chance against the powerful East India interest. The recommencement of war in 1702 and the subsequent reduction in seaborne trade perhaps brought relief to some.

Good japanning can be very difficult to distinguish from genuine lacquer, but in most cases English work is easily discovered by the materials and construction of carcases and drawers. Oriental carcases are pine, not oak, and the same is true of the drawers. The construction of Chinese and Japanese drawers is also very different from English (5:22-24). In those (admittedly rare) cases where an English carcase has been shipped out and lacquered in China, then one must look at the lacquer itself. Some museums now use infra-red analysis to identify the constituent part of the lacquered or japanned surface, and this provides definitive proof in either case. The same technique can also distinguish between lacquer made in different workshops or areas, due to the slight differences in composition of the lacquer.[43] This type of analysis is still in its infancy, but has great potential for many kinds of surface investigation. Even without embarking on such high-tech investigation, a practised eye can usually distinguish lacquer from japanning by looking at the surface itself, because lacquer and varnish degrade in different ways. English japanning crackles and flakes like any other shellac-based varnish, whereas lacquer tends to separate cleanly from the carcase with the lacquer 'skin' essentially intact (5:20 and 5:21). Both lacquer and shellac degrade

42. *England's Almanack, shewing how the East Indies Trade is Prejuditiall to this Kingdom* (30 March 1701).
43. Derrick *et al.,* 1985.
44. Readers are not encouraged to try this at home.

Plate 5:20. Lacquered drawer, showing the tendency of lacquer to separate from the substrate without crackling or crazing.

Plate 5:21. Degraded japanning, showing the crazed, flaky surface typical of shellac-based varnishes.

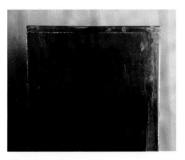

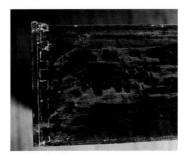

Plate 5:22. Drawer from a mid-17th century Japanese cabinet, showing the drawer constructed without dovetails. The positions of nails are just visible through the lacquer.

Plate 5:23. Base of an English drawer, showing the thin black wash imitating an Oriental lacquered drawer.

Plate 5:24. Chinese drawer, late 17th century. The numerous almost square dovetails are quite different from contemporary English work.

badly in sunlight, but, unlike shellac, lacquer can be buffed up or repolished. One simple way to tell the difference between lacquer and japanning is to apply modern paint stripper – true lacquer is impervious, but japanning is not.[44]

Bantamwork was also imitated in England, though perhaps less commonly than ordinary lacquer. Stalker and Parker provide the following instructions:

> The carved or in cut work, is done after this manner: Your Cabinet or Table, be it whatsoever you please to work on, should be made of Deal, or some other coarse wood; then take Whiting and Size, as before taught, lay it over your work, permitting it to drie between every wash; this must be so often done, till your primer or whiting lie almost a quarter of an inch thick; but always remember to mix your whiting and size thinner than formerly, and lay it therefore over the oftener; for if tis too thick, it will not only lie rough and unseemly, but twill be apt to flie off And crackle. Having primed it to its due thickness, being drie, water-plain it, that is, as we have hinted before, rub it with a fine, wet cloth: in some time after rush it very smooth; lay on your blacks, and varnish it up with a good body, and next of all in some space polish it sufficiently, though with a gentle and easie hand. Being thus far advanced, trace and strike out your design with vermillions and gum water, in that very manner which you intend to cut and carve it, and very exactly; your figures, Trees, Houses, and Rocks, in

their due proportions, with foldage of Garments, leafing of Trees, and in a word, draw it as if it were to stand so without any alteration. This finished, exercise your Graver, and other instruments, which are made of shapes, differing according to each workman's fancie;: with these cut your work deep or shallow, as you think best, but never carving deeper than the whiting lies, for tis a great error to pass through that and carve your wood, which by no means ought to feel the edg of your instrument…

When you have finished your carved work, and cut it clean and smooth, with your pencils lay the colours, well and purely mixt, into your carved work, in the manner which your ingenuity shal suggest, or the nature of it absolutely require. When the colours are finished, the gold may be laid in those places where you have designed it, with powder-gold, or brass—dust mixt with gum-water, but that looks not so bright

Plate 5:26. Detail of 5:25. Drawer of imitation Bantamwork. The design is carved directly into the wooden drawer front, rather than into gesso. The handle is not original.

Plate 5:25. English Bantamwork cabinet. Externally, this is a passable imitation of the real thing, but the interior drawers (5:26) clearly reveal its English manufacture.   NEWBY HALL

45. Stalker and Parker, p. 37-38.
46. Stalker and Parker (1688), pp. 37-38.
47. Quoted in the National Trust guide book for Lyme Park, Cheshire (1998), pp. 33-4.

Plate 5:27. Japanned table (c.1670-90). This is perhaps an example of amateur japanning. The floral decoration is nicely handled but does not have the finesse one would expect from professional work
LYME PARK, THE NATIONAL TRUST

Plate 5:28. Japanned candlestand (c.1670-90). One of a pair, *en suite* to the table. Note the small turned feet dowelled at an angle into the base.

and rich as Leaf-gold, which the Bantam Artists always employ;... Having thus finished your work, you must very carefully clear up your black with oil, but touch not your colours, lest you should quite rub them of, or soil them; for this is not secured, as other Bantam flat-work is; if wet come at this, the colours will be ruined, and peel off.[45]

Much English Bantamwork is rather crude. On the cabinet shown in 5:25 the outer carcase has a passable imitation of Oriental work, but the fronts of the interior drawers have not even been gessoed. Instead, the design has been cut directly into the wood (5:26).

As well as being a thriving branch of the furniture trade, japanning was promoted as a domestic pastime, suitable for amateurs and young women. Professional japanners like Stalker and Parker scorned the pretensions of 'those whiffling, impotent fellows, who pretend to teach young Ladies that Art, in which they themselves have need to be instructed...'.[46] Nevertheless, there were certainly some who made a living at it, and there were pupils eager to learn. It was on this head that in 1689 Edmund Verney wrote a charming letter to his daughter Molly:

> I find you have a desire to learn Jappan, as you call it, and I approve of it; and so I shall of anything that is Good and Virtuous, therefore learn in God's name all the Good Things, & I will willingly be at the Charge so farr as I am able – tho' They come from Japan & from never so farr & Looke of an Indian Hue & Odour, for I admire all accomplishments that will render you considerable & Lovely in the sight of God and man; & therefore I hope you will perform y[R] part according to y[R] word & employ y[R] time well, & so I pray God blesse you.

In 1681 Elizabeth Legh, wife of Richard Legh of Lyme Park, Cheshire, was sent some varnish by her sister in London 'for a Tryall'. She must have been satisfied with the results, because in 1684 she wrote to her husband: 'I would desire thee to rit out the receet [recipe] of Japanning for Sa. Banks' (her sister-in-law).[47] The table and stands in 5:27 and 5:28, which are at Lyme Park, could well be her handiwork.

Plate 5:29. Lacquer cabinet-on-stand (c.1660?). One of a pair in the Green Closet at Ham House. The cabinet is Japanese, c.1625-50, and it is possible that the low stand dates from before the Restoration. Its relative simplicity contrasts with the exuberant sophistication of later examples. HAM HOUSE, THE NATIONAL TRUST

Plate 5:30. Bantamwork cabinet-on-stand (c.1680). Several Oriental cabinets were installed at Ham between 1679 and 1683, of which this might be one. The stand is sophisticated in design and beautifully executed. HAM HOUSE, THE NATIONAL TRUST

The chronology of lacquered and japanned cabinets

Since the outward form of cabinets varied so little over the period under discussion, their dating presents particular problems. In the case of genuine lacquer, there is no necessary correlation between the date of the cabinet and the date of its introduction into England, and it is quite usual, for instance, to find a mid-seventeenth century Japanese cabinet on a mid-eighteenth century English stand. With japanned pieces we are little better off, since the construction of these cabinets did not change significantly until after 1700 – first phase carcases and drawers were standard throughout the early period. In the case of both Oriental and English cabinets, therefore, it is not the cabinet but the stand which affords the best clues to dating.

The dating of carved and gilded stands presents its own problems. In the first place, we must be sure that the stand is original to the piece. This is no easy task and, unless documentary or pictorial evidence survives, one must rely on a subjective assessment of style, form, proportion and size. Does the cabinet fit its stand? This is an obvious but rather fundamental consideration. Is the design of the stand appropriate for the proposed date? Very little research has been done on this question and our notion of the stylistic progression of stand design is still rather vague. Is the

48. Thornton and Tomlin (1980), pp. 33-34.

stand even old? Gesso and gold leaf can disguise any number of repairs, alterations and additions and, since regilding was common, the notion of originality is rather nebulous. Often the age of the stand can only be estimated by microscopic sectional analysis of the many layers of gesso, bole, gilt and varnish which make up the complex stratigraphy of its surface.

It is not surprising to find that the design of early stands derives directly from contemporary side or pier tables, for placing the cabinet on a table was the easiest way to raise it from the floor. It has been cogently argued that the stand shown in 5:29 (one of a pair in the Green Closet at Ham House) dates from between 1654 and 1672. It closely matches several tables also at Ham dating from the same period.[48] Common to all are the outward-leaning caryatid supports, flat compass stretchers and small, carved apron consisting of a pair of addorsed volutes with scrolling acanthus.

Between 1679 and 1683 several more lacquered cabinets were acquired for Ham, of which 5:30 is probably one. The stand is considerably more ornate than the previous examples, but it again has parallels with contemporary side tables. The zoomorphic head and reverse scroll of the leg resemble those on an ebonised and caned table dating from the early 1670s (cf. 4:42).

Increasingly, however, stands developed a flamboyant style of their own, in keeping with the luxurious nature of the cabinets they supported. The twist-turned stands typical of veneered walnut and marquetry cabinets are rarely found. Instead, they are heavily carved with the full repertoire of baroque ornament. One of the most common forms employs supports carved as the head and torso of a fat-bellied putto, whose lower part descends in a leafy reverse curve to a tightly-scrolled foot (5:31 and 5:32). The carving of the apron varies considerably in style and content, but certain conventions appear to reflect contemporary cane chair design (or perhaps vice versa). The central scallop shell was a popular motif from about 1675-80, and from the middle of the 1680s 'boyes and crowns' were fashionable.

Plate 5:31. Bantamwork cabinet-on-stand (c.1675-95).SOTHEBY'S   **Plate 5:32. Japanned cabinet-on stand** (c.1675-95).   CHRISTIE'S

Plate 5:33. Japanned cabinet-on-stand (c.1700-20). The pillar leg, cross-stretcher stand was introduced in the 1690s and remained popular until at least 1720. Several stands of almost identical form are known. Note the purpose-built plinths for porcelain in the centre of each stretcher. The cabinet itself is second-phase cabinet-work and probably dates from 1710 or later.   SALTRAM, THE NATIONAL TRUST

With the introduction of the pillar leg we are on rather firmer ground. Analogies with contemporary chair and pier table design suggest that stands with this form of leg are unlikely to date from before 1690 and most are probably early eighteenth century. 5:33 is a textbook example, having both pillar legs and scrolling cross stretchers; the curious bifurcated foot can be found on many pier tables of the early 1700s (cf. 9:26). 5:34 is a much simplified and undoubtedly cheaper version. The double-arched apron with its beaded lower edge suggests a date of about 1710 or later.

Plate 5:34. Japanned cabinet-on-stand (c.1710-30). This much simpler form of stand matches the rather simpler and less opulent japanning. The arcaded stand with its cockbeaded lower edge is typical of the first twenty years after 1700, although the pulvinated frieze to the stand is unusual.   PRIVATE COLLECTION

Varnishing and polishing on wood

Modern usage tends to blur the distinction between 'varnish' and 'polish', but in the seventeenth century these words had distinct and specific meanings. 'Varnish' was a hard, semi-transparent coating, usually shellac-based, intended to protect and beautify furniture. 'Polish' or 'polishing' was the physical activity of burnishing a surface by friction, often with the help of abrasive materials.

Until the seventeenth century traditional wood finishes were either oil or wax-based. The most commonly used oil was linseed, squeezed from the seed of the flax plant (*Linum usitatissiumum*), but others included walnut oil and olive oil. Walnut oil was particularly valued by painters, because it did not have the yellowing effect of linseed. Wax finishes were derived from beeswax, either raw or with oil, turpentine and other agents added. The purpose of most of these additives was either to aid application or to improve hardness and hasten drying.

Although both oil and wax finishes were satisfactory for general woodwork and common furniture, they had some inherent disadvantages. Both took time to harden and wax in particular was easily marked. Linseed tended to darken the natural colour of any wood, which was not always desirable, and both oil and wax rapidly oxidised, becoming first yellow and then progressively darker over time. With the introduction of veneered and marquetry furniture, there was a need for a clear, hard finish which both protected and enhanced the natural wood, did not discolour it and did not become dull or opaque over time. In the case of marquetry, it was also desirable to have a finish which, if possible, actually saturated the colours and heightened the effect of grain in the various woods employed. All these factors led to the widespread introduction of lac-based varnishes.

Lac was obtained from the sticky exudations of an Indian insect, *Laccifer lacca*, which was gathered from the twigs and branches of the tree on which it lived. It was bought variously as *stick-lac*, *seed-lac* and *shell-lac* (5:35 and 5:36). The first was the raw material, still adhering to its native twigs; the second was a refined version, looking like small semi-transparent pearls or seeds, and the third was similar, but in the form of small flakes or cakes.[49]

Stalker and Parker's *Treatise* contains a great deal of information about how these varnishes were made and applied. Most were based either on seed-lac or shell-lac dissolved in spirits of wine, usually with other gums or resins added to improve hardness, clarity and durability.[50] Much depended on the purity of the ingredients and, as a general rule, the clearer and thinner the varnish the better it was. Clarity was achieved through a lengthy process of heating and filtering. Thicker, less pure varnishes were quicker to prepare and easier to use, and since they had more body they built up a surface more rapidly. Stalker and Parker had much to say about the relative merits of shell-lac and seed-lac in this respect:

> Whosoever designs a neat, glossy piece of work, must banish [shell-lac] as unserviceable... tis commonly used by those that imploy themselves in varnishing ordinary woods, as Olive, Walnut and the like... Your common Varnish-dawbers frequently use it, for tis doubly advantageous to them: having a greater body than the Seed-Lacc, less labour and varnish goes into the perfecting of their work... if with a pint of this varnish you mix two ounces or more of Venice-turpentine, it will harden well, and be a varnish good enough for the insides of Drawers, frames of tables, Stanpillars, frames of Chairs, Stools, or the like.[51]

49. *Encyclopaedia Britannica* (1771), II, p. 858.
50. A gum was soluble in water, while a resin was soluble in alcohol.
51. Stalker and Parker, p. 10.
52. Ibid., p. 10.
53. Ibid., p. 18.
54. See note 28, above.

Plate 5:35. **Stick-lac**. This is the naturally occurring form, with flakes and globules of shellac adhering to the twigs on which the insect *Laccifer lacca*, lived.

Plate 5:36. **Shell-lac** (left) and **seed-lac** (right). Both are preparations of the raw stick-lac.

Plate 5:37. Sandarac. This was made from the sap of the thuya tree (*Tetraclinis articulata*), which is indigenous to the mountains of North Africa. It produces a much lighter and clearer varnish than shellac.

Finer, paler and clearer than either shell-lac or seed-lac was 'best white varnish', which was made with sandarac rather than shellac as the principal agent (5:37).[52] 5:38 shows jars of seed-lac and best white varnish prepared according to Stalker and Parker's instructions. Both are much darker than modern bleached shellac varnishes; the seed-lac is 'a reddish tawny colour',[53] while the 'best white' is paler but still relatively opaque. Because of this high opacity, the varnish had to be applied as thinly as possible, and this is one reason for the repeated smoothing or 'rushing off' described below:

> What remains then, but that from Precept we proceed to Practise, that from mean and ordinary endeavours we successively rise to the excellence and perfection of this Art.
> To begin with Olive-wood, which for Tables, Stands, cabinets, &c., has been highly in request amongst us; that which is cleanly workt off, void of flaws, cracks, and asperities, is a fit subject for our skill to be exercised in. Having rushed it all over diligently, set it by a weak fire, or some place where it may receive heat; and in this warm condition, wash it over ten or twelve times with Seed-Lacc-varnish,... let it thoroughly dry between every wash; and if any roughness come in sight, rush 'em off as fast as you meet with them. After all this welcom it with your Rush until tis smooth, and when very dry, anoint it six several times with the top or finest part of the aforesaid Seed-Lacc-varnish.

Having applied the varnish in many thin coats and cut it back repeatedly with rushes, it was time to polish the work. This was done with powdered Tripoly,[54] lubricated with water:

> After three days standing call for Tripolee scraped with a knife; and with a cloth, dipt first in water, then powdered Tripolee, polish and rub it till it acquires a smoothness and gloss: but be circumspect and shie of rubbing too much, which will fret and wear off the varnish, that cannot easily be repair'd: If when you have labour'd for some time, you use the rag often wetted, without Tripolee, you will obtain a better gloss.

Plate 5:38. Seed-lac varnish (left) and **Best White varnish** (right). Both are considerably more opaque than modern bleached varnishes, which meant that they had to be applied very thinly in order not to disguise the natural colour of the wood.

5:39 shows the effect of seed-lac and best white varnishes on walnut, varnished and polished in the manner described above. 5:42 shows a replica drawer front of olivewood, part-veneered and part-varnished with best white varnish. The brilliancy and luminosity of the finish is remarkable, as is the high contrast between light and dark wood. Furniture veneered and varnished in this way must have had an extraordinary visual impact when new, quite different from the mellow and subdued tones favourerd by modern collectors.

Stalker and Parker's instructions clearly refute the commonly held notion that lac-based varnish, now commonly called 'French polish', was not used until the nineteenth century. On the contrary, lac was the principal ingredient of varnishes for veneered furniture in the late seventeenth century. The difference between seventeenth and nineteenth century varnishes lies not in the ingredients but in the process. Stalker and Parker's method involves varnishing first and polishing second. 'French' polishing combines the two tasks in one, by using a 'rubber' both to apply the varnish and to polish it in a continuous action. A further difference is that for French polishing to be successful, the pores of the wood had first to be filled with whiting or plaster of Paris, in order to achieve a truly smooth and glossy surface. Stalker and Parker's method, on the other hand, did not require the grain to be filled, for this occurred gradually during the process of polishing. The residue of fine powdered varnish filled the pores in the wood, and this sometimes required that the surface be 'cleared up with lampblack and oil':

> Then wipe of your Tripolee with a spunge
> full of water, the water with a dry rag;
> grease it with Lampblack and Oil all
> over: wipe that off with a cloth and clear it up with another...

As 5:41 shows, this last application of lampblack and oil had the effect not only of knocking back the yellowing tendency of the seed-lac, but also of heightening the figure of the wood by washing lampblack into any remaining open pores. It also ensured that any white residue left in the pores was effectively disguised. When used on best white varnish it has the opposite effect, tending to muddy the surface and disguise both colour and grain. The different performance of seed-lac and best white varnish gives rise to the possibility that they were used for different applications. For ordinary woods, such as olive or walnut, Stalker and Parker recommended seed-lac 'cleared up' with lampblack. But; 'Should anyone desire to keep the true natural, and genuine colour of the wood, I council him to employ the white varnish...'.[55] Hence to varnish marquetry, in which pure colours and subtleties of grain were essential, white varnish was probably more suitable.

There is evidence to suggest that some woods, such as walnut, were treated before varnishing to enhance their colour and figure. John Evelyn described the preparation of walnut as follows: 'To render this wood the better coloured, joiners put the boards into an oven after the batch is forth, or lay them in a warm stable; and when they work it, polish it over with its own oil very hot, which makes it look black and sleek'.[56] It is not clear how heat would encourage the wood to look 'black and sleek', but the effect of the ammonia rising from the floor of a warm stable would certainly tend to heighten the colour and figure of the wood. Modern furniture makers, restorers and fakers achieve the same effect by 'fuming' wood, particularly oak, with ammonia to make it look old.

Gilding on wood
The extensive use of gilding on Stuart furniture may look showy to modern eyes, but in the days before electric light gilding was a way of enlivening the gloom of dim, candle-lit interiors. Moreover, as has already been observed in relation to gilding on metal, gold kept its colour and brightness long after other finishes had faded or become discoloured. The methods of gilding on wood explained by Stalker and Parker are essentially the same as those used today. There are two basic methods, oil gilding and water gilding.

Oil gilding was used invariably where work was exposed to the weather, such as on buildings, railings and other exterior applications. Because it was rather easier and cheaper to execute than water gilding, it was also commonly used on furniture.

55. Stalker and Parker (1688), p. 18.
56. Evelyn (1670), p. 55.
57. Stalker and Parker (1688), p. 54.
58. Ibid., p. 55.
59. Ibid., p. 56.
60. Ibid., p. 59.
61. Ibid., p. 64.

Before gilding could begin, the carcase or ground had first to be prepared with several coats of gesso, well smoothed. To make the gold adhere to the gesso a mordant was needed, in this case a 'fat oyl'; this was raw linseed left to dry for several months until it thickened – 'if it arrive to the consistence of butter, that it may almost be cut with a knife, reserve it carefully, and as the best for use that can possibly be made'.[57]

The mordant was mixed with an ochre of the appropriate colour – yellow or buff – to make a size which was then brushed on to the ground, 'jobbing and striking the point of the pencil into the hollow places of the carved work, that no place, creek or corner of your work may escape the salutation'.[58] The size was left to cure for a day or two until it became tacky. Finally, the gold was laid leaf by leaf and brushed into all the folds and crevices of the work: 'These Rules being strictly observed, your undertaking… will appear with a dazzling and unusual lustre, and its beauty will be so durable, so well fortified against the injuries of wind and weather, that the attempts of many Ages will not be able to deface it'.[59]

The one great disadvantage of oil gilding was that it could not be burnished, so if this was desired only water gilding would answer. In water gilding the gold was laid on a gesso ground as before, but required a different type of size, made from parchment size mixed with clay to produce a bole. The bole could be variously coloured yellow, red or orange to enhance the colour of the thin gold leaf. This also served to disguise omissions; 'for the yellow colour first laid on is nearer in colour to the gold, so that if in guilding you miss any, the fault will not so soon be discovered'.[60] To lay the gold, the ground was wetted with cold water and the leaf applied gradually, with repeated wettings, until the whole ground was covered. When dry the gold could then be burnished as desired with a dog's tooth agate or other suitable stone.

Water gilding permitted the different parts of the gilding to be finished in different ways. Some parts were burnished and others left matt, giving variety and life to the work. Yet others could be brushed with coloured shellac varnish to deepen the contrast between burnished and unburnished areas.

Silvering

Because of the expense of real gold leaf, a great number of gilt finishes were actually silvered and washed over with a gold-coloured varnish. Silvering was carried out in exactly the same way as water gilding, but with a suitably coloured bole (Stalker and Parker suggested pipe-clay and black lead). The surface might be left silver coloured, but because silver was apt to tarnish it had to be protected by a varnish.

If the intention was to make the silvered furniture appear gilt then the varnish was coloured, so that 'unless narrowly surveyed, [it] will put a fallacy upon and deceive curious, discerning eyes'.[61] So long as the varnish lasted the deception was unlikely to be discovered and many articles 'gilded' in this way survive to this day. If the varnish failed, or wore through, the silver rapidly discoloured and became unsightly. For this reason many pieces of furniture which were originally silvered are now gilt, having been smartened up at a later date.

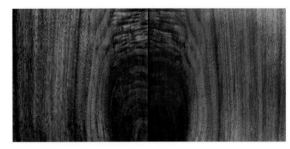

Plate 5:39. A walnut board varnished with Best White varnish (left) and seed-lac (right). The Best White varnish is considerably more successful in preserving the true colour of the wood.

Plate 5:40. Drawer (c.1700-20), burr walnut. The surface of this drawer is more or less untouched. The natural colouring suggests a sandarac-base varnish might have been used. Note the semi-matt finish, which is very characteristic. The lengthy varnishing process was controllable at every stage and allowed different degrees of finish to be achieved.

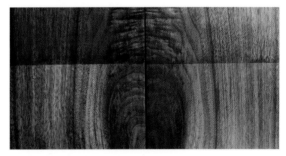

Plate 5:41. Best white varnish (left) and **seed-lac varnish** (right), 'cleared up' with **lampblack** (top). This enhances the figure when used on the seed-lac, but seems to muddy the Best White varnish.

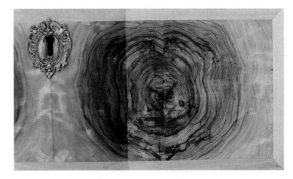

Plate 5:42. Drawer front from a replica chest of drawers, part veneered with olivewood and part varnished with best white varnish. The varnish has the effect of heightening the colour and dramatic contrast in the wood.

Chapter Six

FURNISHING THE WILLIAMITE COURT

Plate 6:1. Portrait of William III on horseback, by Sir Godfrey Kneller (1646-1723).
THE ROYAL COLLECTION ©2002, HER MAJESTY QUEEN ELIZABETH II

Dutch and Anglo-Dutch

The reign of William III (1689-1702) is often held to mark a peak of Dutch influence on English art and design, so much so that furniture of this period is often characterised as 'Anglo-Dutch' (6:1). But while William's reign united England and Holland[1] in a common political aim (that of halting French ambitions towards a European hegemony), it does not necessarily follow that the furniture of the two nations acquired some amorphous, trans-national quality which made the one indistinguishable from the other. Like many generalisations, the term 'Anglo-Dutch' becomes less meaningful the closer it is applied; more often than not it disguises a profound lack of real information and is frequently used as a catch-all for furniture which is essentially English in form but whose baroque or mannered style is somehow felt to be 'un-English'. In such cases the term is positively unhelpful, since it simply fudges the issue of correct identification, but even where it is used in a more considered and scholarly context, it still betrays a want of hard facts. In a general book such as this it is not possible to do much more than highlight the deficiency and perhaps identify some of the more obvious anomalies that the term 'Anglo-Dutch' encompasses.

William III was the hereditary ruler of the Dutch principality of Orange, and he was also Stadhouder or leader of the seven United Provinces that made up the free Protestant states of Holland. He married Mary, eldest daughter of the Duke of York (later James II) in 1677. The marriage was naturally a political one, intended to cement an Anglo-Dutch Treaty ratified the following year, and it was personal triumph for William, since it marked a major step towards his goal of binding England firmly to the Protestant, pro-Dutch and anti-French cause.

The question of religion was of fundamental importance in seventeenth century Europe, and the fact that both Holland and England were Protestant countries inevitably gave them common cause against the great Catholic powers of France and Spain. This was still true in the latter part of the century, despite the repeated attempts of both Charles II and James II to extract financial, political and military support from Louis XIV. Many in England were highly suspicious of the Anglo-French treaties of 1667 and 1670, seeing them as inimical to the national interest and tending inevitably towards the restoration of the Catholic religion and all that this entailed in terms of political absolutism. Indeed, it was this very fear which led to William being invited over from Holland to seize the throne from James II in 1688.

1. Although Holland was only one of the seven provinces which made up the United Provinces of the Free Netherlands, the English habitually referred to the whole country as Holland. This reflected the overwhelming commercial and political dominance of Holland, with Amsterdam as its commercial capital and The Hague as the seat of government for the whole United Provinces.
2. Wells-Cole (1997), pp. 43-124; Thornton (1999), *passim.*
3. Wells-Cole (1985).
4. Lane (1948); Wilson (1972); Thornton (1978), pp. 247-252.

Common religious values were underpinned by a longstanding commercial relationship, dictated both by the close proximity of Holland across the North Sea and by Dutch dominance of European seaborne trade. The fruits of this commercial intercourse were as much cultural as economic, and were evident in the widespread adoption in England of the Netherlandish Mannerist style in architecture and the applied arts from about 1560 onwards. Notwithstanding the Italianate brilliance of Inigo Jones, who created the court style of James I (1603-25) and Charles I (1625-49), most Englishmen acquired their knowledge of classical art and architecture at second hand, through the printing presses of Antwerp, Haarlem and Amsterdam.[2] Thus the first English translation of Book IV of Serlio's great architectural treatise, published in Venice in 1537, was derived from an Amsterdam edition of 1606.[3]

From about 1650, however, relations with Holland cooled rapidly, as England began systematically to assert control over her overseas and colonial trade, which inevitably entailed conflict with the Dutch. After three wars in quick succession between 1651 and 1674, it took all of William's dogged patience and diplomacy to reverse the trend by concluding the Treaty of 1678, and then to arrive at the point where, in 1689, he was invited to assume the crown of England in James's place. It would be wrong, however, to infer from this that William brought with him a renaissance of Dutch influence in the arts. As we have seen in the first part of this book, the chief stylistic impulse in English applied arts from 1660 onwards was overwhelmingly French, and William's arrival did nothing to change this. Indeed, in his desire to emulate and, if possible, to overreach Louis XIV, William initiated a renewed spate of building and furnishing at Hampton Court and elsewhere which was almost wholly French in its inspiration. It is often forgotten that Daniel Marot, William's self-appointed 'architect' and designer to whom much of the inspiration for the 'Anglo-Dutch' style is now credited, was a Frenchman, bred and trained in the French court style. Marot's contribution to English furniture will be discussed in due course, but it is worth pointing out that the phrase 'in the style of' or 'after' Daniel Marot is often used as a synonym for 'Anglo-Dutch'. This is surely nonsense.

The predominantly French influence in English arts does not preclude the presence of Dutch artefacts in many English houses. One of the most highly visible accessories to any fashionable apartment after the Restoration was Oriental blue and white porcelain, or its cheaper imitation, Dutch Delftware. The popularity of porcelain and Delft appears to have reached its height after 1689, inspired largely by the example of Queen Mary, whose personal penchant for it was well known.[4] It was Queen Mary who introduced the Dutch fashion for devoting entire rooms to blue and white ware, massed in extravagant display on walls, chimneypieces and cornices (6:2):

Plate 6:2. Daniel Marot, design for a chimney-piece, from *Nouvelles Cheminées,* published in the Hague, 1703. The fashion for covering every available surface with Oriental porcelain was reputedly brought to England by Queen Mary – japanned wall panels continue the exotic theme. Note the overmantel mirror and the cross-stretchered stool, both introductions of the 1690s.

> The Queen brought in the Custom or Humour, as I may call it, of furnishing Houses
> with Chinaware, which increased to a strange degree afterwards, piling their China
> upon tops of Cabinets, Scrutores, and every Chymney-Piece, to the tops of the
> Ceilings, and even setting up Shelves for their China-ware, where they wanted such
> places, till it became a grievance in the Expense of it, and even Injurious to their
> Families and Estates.
>
> Daniel Defoe, *A Tour thro' the Whole Island of Great Britain* (1724-7)

Another commonplace domestic article was the rush-seated 'Dutch' chair, probably with either a ladder or spindle back, which one finds in household inventories throughout the late seventeenth and early eighteenth centuries. These chairs, often described specifically as 'matted' or rush-seated, occur in bills of lading and customs data throughout the period; in the five years between 1698

5. PRO, Cust. 3.
6. For instance; 'For 42 Dutch Matted bottom'd Chairs for ye Bed Chamber Women… £25. 4. 0.' (1711) [PRgf. 16.]
7. The bill quoted in note 4 reveals that Thomas Roberts charged 12 shillings apiece for 'Dutch' chairs. There are occasional references in Price's bills of the early 1680s to chairs with frames of 'Dutch' turning, but it is not clear what this implied. For instance; 'For two fformes of Wallnutt wood wrought with mouldings and scrowles with great Bases on the foot and of the Dutch turne' (1681). [PRO LC 9/276, f. 20].
8. Loudon (1828), p. 1099-1100.
9. Houghton (1683).
10. Baarsen (1993), p. 30.
11. PRO, Cust. 3.
12. Baarsen (2000), p. 44.

and 1702 nearly 2,000 were imported, both into London and provincial ports.[5] It possible that they were also made in England, since bills for 'Dutch' chairs survive in the accounts of several English furniture makers.[6] Similarly, 'Dutch' tables also occur in inventories but were not necessarily Dutch made. They can be likened to the 'French' chairs and tables supplied in large numbers by Richard Price in the 1660s and 1670s, which were French in style but not manufacture. There was, however, one important difference between 'French' and 'Dutch' chairs, in that the former were used in the Royal apartments, whereas the latter, costing between five and twelve shillings apiece, were generally confined to the backstairs.[7]

A number of English collections contain carved benches of the type shown in 6:3. These are undoubtedly a Dutch type, intended to stand in the entrance halls or passages of Dutch houses. However, this example bears the arms of the Booth family, Earls of Warrington, and was probably made for George Booth (1675-1758). This suggests it was either made in England or made in Holland with blank reserves to be carved after purchase. One must bear in mind that designs for any type of artefact from anywhere in Europe could be bought at print sellers in London.

Other Dutch seating types found in England are discussed in detail in Chapter Eight, where it is argued that most of them arrived in the nineteenth century, when Dutch chairs were highly fashionable among creators of 'Elizabethan' interiors.[8] Indeed, one suspects that it was about this time that the notion of an 'Anglo-Dutch' style was first conceived.

Plate 6:3. Carved walnut hall bench, English or Dutch c.1700. This type of bench is known to have been popular in Holland, but several examples survive in England. In this case the bench is carved with the arms of the Booth family. It was probably made for George Booth (1675-1758), Earl of Warrington.

DUNHAM MASSEY, NATIONAL TRUST PHOTOGRAPHIC LIBRARY/ANDREAS VON EINSIEDEL

One of the assumptions underlying popular conceptions of 'Anglo-Dutch' is that the traffic was all one way, from Holland to England. But it is clear that this was not the case, and that certain English furniture types were not only exported to Holland but were instrumental in changing Dutch fashions. One of these was the longcase clock. It is ironic that although the pendulum clock was invented by a Dutchman, Christian Huygens, in 1656, it was England which took the lead in manufacturing and exporting longcase clocks. In just the first two months of 1683, 1,380 clock movements were exported from London, together with thirteen cases.[9] While their destinations are not recorded, it is known that Dutch makers initially relied on English movements and, indeed, the first recorded longcase clock-maker in Amsterdam (c.1680) was an Englishman, Joseph Norris. Not until about 1689 did the first Dutch maker, Steven Huygens, become established there.[10] The design of early Dutch cases is based closely on English examples and distinctively Dutch forms did not develop until the beginning of the eighteenth century (6:4). Even so, English cases continued to be exported to Holland in considerable numbers – between 1698 and 1702 cases worth £699 were sent to Holland, averaging £2 to £3 a case.[11]

Another English form adopted by Dutch furniture-makers was the fall-front scriptor. The great cabinet-making tradition of Antwerp did not extend into the Protestant northern provinces. Most Amsterdam 'cabinets' of this period are actually cupboards, with two doors enclosing a few open shelves (6:5).[12] However, English-style scriptors are certainly found and are clearly based on

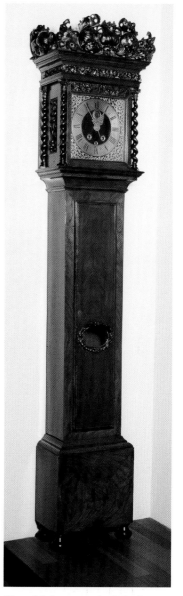

Plate 6:4. Longcase clock, by Steven Huygens, Amsterdam, c.1700. Huygens was the first recorded Dutch clockmaker to make longcase clocks. The walnut veneered case may be English, since substantial numbers of cases were exported to Holland, but the old-fashioned style, the oval glass in the door and the carved hood suggest a Dutch maker.
RIJKSMUSEUM, AMSTERDAM

Plate 6:5. Cabinet, olivewood veneers on an oak carcase, Dutch, c.1680-1710. This form of cabinet is typical of the Protestant northern provinces. Unlike contemporary English cabinets it does not have a closely-fitted interior, containing only broad shelves and drawers.
RIJKSMUSEUM, AMSTERDAM

English models. The customs returns show that scriptors and cabinets were regularly sent to Holland, most of them of the plain walnut variety costing between £8 and £10.[13] The resemblance between Dutch and English models is often very close indeed, and a Dutch origin can often only be established by looking at details of construction and metalwork (6:6).

The popular successor to the scriptor, the desk-and-bookcase, was also exported to Holland, where references to the 'Engels Cantoor Cabinet' occur with some frequency in the early eighteenth century.[14] Dutch furniture makers soon produced their own version and in The Hague every cabinet-maker's apprentice was required to make a cabinet 'in the English style' as his masterpiece.[15] Archaic-looking high baroque examples, usually with elaborately moulded double-arched cornices and more ornament than is thought proper, are often described as 'Dutch' or

13. PRO, Cust. 3.
14. Baarsen (1993), p. 86.
15. Riccardi-Cubitt (1992), p. 129.
16. PRO, Cust. 3.
17. Baarsen (1993), p. 82.
18. PRO, Cust. 3.

Plate 6:6. Scriptor, walnut veneers on an oak carcase, Dutch, c.1690-1710. This scriptor is taken directly from contemporary English models. In this case, identification was made easier by handwritten Dutch inscriptions on the cabinet's interior drawers. Other typically Dutch features are the heavy oak carcase, the cavetto waist and base mouldings, and the metalware. Note how the lock escutcheons are placed to accommodate the deeper Dutch locks. TENNANTS

Plate 6:7. Daniel Marot, frontispiece of the *Second Livre d'Appartements,* published in The Hague, 1703. The State bed is flanked by a suite of 'horsebone' chairs, typically English in their design, of the sort made in large numbers by Thomas Roberts and his contemporaries.

'Anglo-Dutch' in auction sale catalogues merely on the basis of their 'un-English' appearance. Some of these are indeed Dutch, but a great deal more research is needed before such attributions can be made with confidence.

English influence is equally evident in the design of some Dutch seat furniture. Chairs were the most numerous class of furniture sent to Holland, amounting in value to more than £1,150 between 1698 and 1702.[16] Dutch sale notices around the turn of the seventeenth and eighteenth centuries repeatedly mention 'English chairs', although it is not clear precisely which type is meant.[17] It may well be that the oval-backed cane chairs discussed in Chapter Eight were inspired by English models. If so, the Dutch versions were sufficiently different in style and construction to make it easy to distinguish between the two. While cane chairs are known to have been exported in numbers, upholstered chairs may also be implied in the phrase 'English chairs'. 'Upholstery ware' occurs in the customs returns for 1700-1702, amounting to £1,268 in value.[18] The 'horsebone' chairs depicted in Marot's interiors of Het Loo are typically English in style, and it is worth considering whether they were not supplied by English makers (6:7).

Taken in aggregate, the English customs returns for the five years of peace between 1698 and 1702 show the balance of trade in furniture to be heavily in England's favour. Dutch imports, primarily chairs, 'tea tables' (trays) and slate or marble slabs, amounted to something over £1,300 in value. English exports to Holland totalled £5,121.[19] The most significant commodities were chairs, cabinet-ware, looking glasses, clock cases and 'upholstery ware'.

William III at Hampton Court Palace

The political consequences of James II's flight into exile are still with us today; its artistic impact was less momentous, but undoubtedly significant. Had James remained in power, it is difficult to envisage him leaving any significant mark on English arts, for he was by all accounts a prosaic individual with few aesthetic interests. William, by contrast, regarded art and politics as indivisible. Architecture, horticulture, painting, sculpture, fine furniture and tapestries – all these were the outward and visible manifestations of political power. Thus in his native Holland William's rise to political dominance, first as Prince of Orange, then as Stadhouder of the United Provinces, was mirrored by the transformation of Het Loo, a former hunting lodge, into a palace of kingly splendour. The assumption of the English throne in 1689 allowed William to realise his ambitions on a much larger scale. With England's financial and military resources behind him, he could at last build an alliance to curb France's relentless territorial aggrandizement, while at Hampton Court he hoped to create a palace to rival Versailles (6:8 and 6:9).

19. PRO, Cust. 3. Figures rounded down to whole numbers.
20. Quoted in Jenkins (1994), p. 5.
21. Jenkins *et al.* (1994).

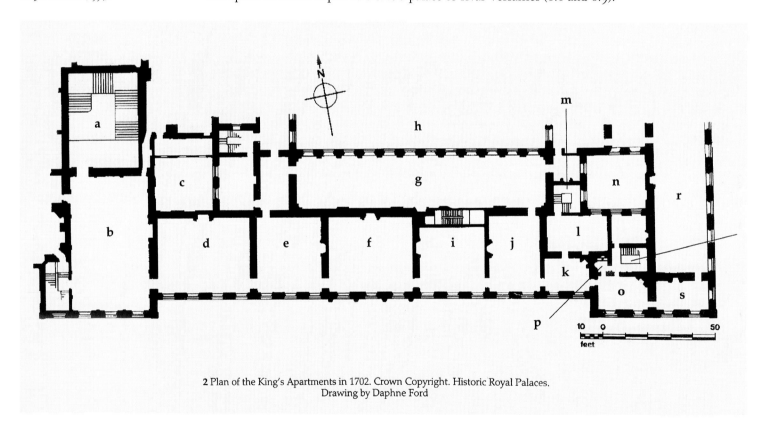

2 Plan of the King's Apartments in 1702. Crown Copyright. Historic Royal Palaces. Drawing by Daphne Ford

a – Great Stair; b – King's Guard Chamber; c – Court; d – King's Presence Chamber; e – King's Eating Room; f – King's Privy Chamber; g – Cartoon Gallery; h – Fountain Court; i – King's Withdrawing Room; j – King's Great Bedchamber; k – King's Little Bedchamber; l – Gentlemen of the Bedchamber; m – The Backstairs; n – Court; o – King's Closet; p – King's Garderobe; q – King's Backstairs; r – King's Private Gallery.

Plate 6:8. Hampton Court Palace, plan of the King's Apartments, 1702. This is a classic exposition of the French-style apartment in enfilade, with each room giving on to the next and progressing from the public areas of the Great Stair and Guard Chamber through progressively richer rooms to the Great Bedchamber, behind which were the more intimate surroundings of the king's private apartments. CROWN COPYRIGHT: HISTORIC ROYAL PALACES

Plate 6:9. Hampton Court Palace, the King's Apartments. Designed by Sir Christopher Wren and built between 1689 and 1694. The interiors were not completed until 1701.   CROWN COPYRIGHT: HISTORIC ROYAL PALACES

Horace Walpole wrote that William III 'contributed nothing to the advance of the arts'. Modern scholars take a different view and recent research into the building of the King's Apartments at Hampton Court Palace has shown William to have been closely concerned in all aspects of their design and decoration.[21] In the early years of his reign William was preoccupied with establishing his political position in England and in prosecuting the war against France, so that it was Queen Mary who was most closely concerned with Hampton Court. It was at this time that the Queen's own apartments, together with her riverside Water Gallery and Dairy, were completed. After Mary's death from smallpox in December 1694, work on the Palace virtually ceased and renewed impetus did not come until 1697, when William seized the opportunity afforded by the Peace of Ryswick to make urgent progress. Although work was by no means finished, the first formal residence of William's court in the new Apartments took place from April to July 1700.

Almost every element of William's artistic taste was deeply imbued with the example of his powerful rival and adversary, Louis XIV. He took pains to recruit French artists and artisans, particularly those with experience of Louis XIV's palaces and workshops. For the decorative painting of walls and ceilings, he chose Antonio Verrio and Louis Laguerre; for decorative metal-work, Jean Tijou; for carved pier tables, candlestands and other furniture, Jean Pelletier. Both Verrio and Laguerre had worked at Versailles and William had perhaps seen their work at first hand in Ralph Montagu's house at Bloomsbury. Tijou was almost certainly French trained and might have worked under Luchet or Delobel at Versailles. The Huguenot Jean Pelletier was also French trained and, having settled in England in 1682, had established a thriving business with his two sons, René and Thomas. Despite his long residence in England, Pelletier's style remained un-equivocally French.[22]

One must be careful, however, not to overstate the degree to which Hampton Court reflected purely French taste and talent, for William also employed a large body of English professionals. In this he had little choice, since all the Royal Palaces came within the remit of the Office of Works. William had therefore to tread carefully and work within the long-established system he had inherited, and indeed accepted, when he took the crown of England. The architects in charge were initially Sir Christopher Wren and, from 1699 onwards, William Talman. The elevations designed by Wren are typically balanced and quiet expressions of the English baroque, and the interiors, with the exception of Verrio's extraordinary King's Staircase, are also relatively restrained. The apartments are panelled in wainscot, with relatively plain mouldings, pilasters and cornices in most rooms reflecting the constraints of time and money within which Talman had to work. One suspects that in many areas the work fell short of William's original ambitions, but William had little time to rue the lack, for he died after falling from his horse in March 1702.

The craftsmen involved in the fitting out of Hampton Court – carpenters, joiners, glaziers, stonemasons, carvers and sculptors – were, with some notable exceptions already mentioned, Englishmen contracted to the Office of Works. A similar long-established bureaucracy controlled by the Lord Chamberlain supplied most of William's furniture. This is not to say that the king had no choice in his furniture, but that the furnishing of most apartments, particularly those with a public or state function, was determined by precedent and accepted form. Warrants were issued primarily to established contractors such as William Farneborough and Gerrit Jensen (cabinet-makers), Thomas Roberts (joiner and chairmaker), Richard Bealing (upholsterer), and Jean Pelletier (carver and gilder). Indeed, it is notable that top-flight foreign craftsmen like Francis Lapiere and Jean Poitevin were not involved in the King's Apartments at Hampton Court, although they did fulfil occasional contracts to other Royal Palaces and Lapiere supplied five 'French' beds for secondary rooms at Hampton Court in 1693-4.[23] The reason, perhaps, was merely a shortage of time and money, but it does mean that the furnishing of the King's Apartments of Hampton Court was predominantly an English affair.

The results, while perhaps not matching the extravagant opulence of Versailles, were not unimpressive. The State rooms were hung with tapestries from dado to cornice. These were already antique, having been purchased by successive English monarchs from Henry VIII onwards, and were chosen not only for their visual splendour but for their connection with England's past monarchs.[24] Against this rich background, new silks and velvets were employed for the standing furnishings of State – canopies, chairs of State, and the State bed, increasing in richness as one progressed through the enfilade towards the State bedchamber (6:10).[25] Red was the dominant colour, trimmed with fringes of gold. Under their canopies the chairs of State, together with their companion stools, were placed on a low dais covered with a 'Portugal mat'. This floor covering is very commonly found in contemporary inventories but, rather surprisingly, we do not know exactly what a Portugal mat looked like.[26] It was clearly an object of some worth and status, for another such mat was placed beneath the State bed. The rest of the floor was left bare, so there was a clear demarcation between this and the matted area made sacrosanct by the Royal person. The

Plate 6:10. Hampton Court Palace, the Privy Chamber. The crimson silk canopy is original, as is the tapestry. The seat furniture is not original, but illustrates the usual arrangement, the chair of state flanked by stools.

CROWN COPYRIGHT: HISTORIC ROYAL PALACES

22. The work of the Pelletier family is discussed in detail in Murdoch (1997 & 1998).
23. Further details of both these men's work in the 1690s can be found in Beard (1997), pp. 88-89, 95-97. For Lapiere see also Beard and Westman (1993).
24. For more on the Hampton Court tapestries see Campbell (1994).
25. Westman (1994), p. 40.
26. Thornton (1977), pp. 118, 146.

Plate 6:11. Hampton Court Palace, the King's Eating Room. This room was used by the king for occasional dining in public. The pier glasses were probably supplied by Gerrit Jensen and the candlestands by Jean Pelletier. The tables are not the originals. The white silk curtains are new, based on surviving fragments of the originals. Note the plain oak panelling and restrained cornice – the apartments were completed in haste and on a restricted budget. CROWN COPYRIGHT: HISTORIC ROYAL PALACES

27. Ibid., p. 42.

window curtains in most State rooms were white, with plain cornices (6:11). They probably functioned as sunblinds and were designed to pull up, rather than aside, as is made clear in Thomas Roberts' bills, which describe the cornices as having 'laths for Pull up Window Curtaines with box holes for ye Strings to play in'.[27]

The most richly appointed room was the State bedchamber (6:12). Here the tapestry-hung walls were complemented by a ceiling painted in perspective to give the impression of greater height. The furnishings were dominated by the State bed, covered in red velvet trimmed with gold. The bed was actually second-hand, bought from the Earl of Jersey in 1699, perhaps because time and money were short. Its simple, box-like profile, matching those of the canopies of state, is typically French, and very different from the sculpted baroque beds shown in the designs of Daniel Marot. The seat furniture was supplied by Thomas Roberts, but appears to have been modelled on a French original. The pier glass, table and stands in this room were the most splendid of all (6:13). The only major feature missing from the room is the fireplace and chimneypiece by John Nost, which is now in the Queen's Gallery (6:14).

Visiting the State rooms today one is struck by how large and empty they are, despite the ancient tapestries and expensive silks and velvets. The ceilings are high, the furniture sparse and formal, the floors a great expanse of bare boards. But one must remember that when in use these rooms were full of people, richly dressed in the full panoply of State. The State apartments were essentially a series of static sets, in which the rituals of monarchy were staged with deliberate

Plate 6:12. Hampton Court Palace, the Great Bedchamber. This richly decorated room is more or less as it was in 1700. The bed, of typically French form, was bought from the Earl of Jersey in 1699. The outer case curtains protect the precious velvet from light and air. The seat furniture is presumably by Thomas Roberts, probably based on a French model. The cornice is the richest of all the Apartments, with a carved frieze by Grinling Gibbons, and the ceiling was painted by Antonio Verrio.

CROWN COPYRIGHT: HISTORIC ROYAL PALACES

Plate 6:13. Hampton Court Palace, the Great Bedchamber. The huge pier glasses bordered with blue glass slips and rosettes were supplied by Gerrit Jensen in 1699. The table is not original, but the stands were supplied by Jean Pelletier between 1699 and 1702.

CROWN COPYRIGHT: HISTORIC ROYAL PALACES

Plate 6:14. Hampton Court Palace, chimneypiece by John Nost. This was originally in the Great Bedchamber. This beautifully designed and executed work is typical of the routinely high level of design and craftsmanship expected of the Office of Works' contractors.

CROWN COPYRIGHT: HISTORIC ROYAL PALACES

Plate 6:15. Hampton Court Palace, the King's Little Bedchamber. This was the king's private bedroom, as opposed to the more ceremonial function of the Great Bedchamber. The fabrics are entirely new, re-created from the surviving documentation. The ceiling is again by Verrio.
CROWN COPYRIGHT:
HISTORIC ROYAL PALACES

theatricality. The contrast between these rooms and the smaller, more intimate rooms which lay beyond is striking. On the far side of the State bedchamber was another, smaller bedchamber where the king usually slept. Although smaller in scale, it was equally well appointed, and appears richer, because concentrated in a smaller space. The bed, portière and window curtains were done out in rich yellow silk damask (6:15). The ceiling was painted, and the coved cornice enriched with carving. Each doorway had a painted overdoor and in the corner was a corner fireplace with mirror and tiered shelves for porcelain.

In the closet or private study beyond was William's desk, together with his barometer and longcase clock, all of which survive (6:16 and 17) There was access to a private staircase and, most private of all, the king's Stoolroom containing his velvet covered close-stool.

Plate 6:17. Barometer by Thomas Tompion. This bears William's cipher, and was made for him in 1700. The case is burr maple, probably treated with *aqua fortis* and lampblack.

The Hampton Court style, if we may call it that, was not exclusive to Royalty. A number of noble houses built or rebuilt around this time followed William's lead, in many cases employing the same architects and craftsmen. Significantly, many of these noblemen were closely connected with the court, and in some cases had been instrumental in bringing William to the throne. For his part in this drama William Cavendish was created Duke of Devonshire in 1694 and at Chatsworth the Duke had already engaged William Talman to design his new south and east fronts. Furniture for the new apartments was supplied by, among others, Gerrit Jensen and John Gumley. The owner of Boughton House, Ralph Montagu, was created Earl by William in 1689. He was also made master of the Great Wardrobe, which meant he not only controlled all the contracts for furnishings at Court, but was almost certainly able to influence the choice of workmen and their output. Montagu employed Jensen and the Pelletiers to work at both his principal houses. Another courtier who closely followed William's lead was Thomas Coningsby, Paymaster of William's forces in Ireland and owner of Hampton Court in Leominster. During the 1690s and early 1700s Coningsby rebuilt and refurnished his house in considerable style, and the red silk damask used for his State bed and its attendant seat furniture was exactly the same as that used in the King's Presence Chamber at Hampton Court Palace.[28]

There were relatively few men who could afford to build and furnish on this princely scale, but just as the minor apartments at Hampton Court were equipped with walnut and japanned furniture rather than lacquer and gilt, so more modest houses could be furnished less lavishly but no less fashionably. Tradesmen's bills and inventories even of the 'middling sort' are full of the stylistic cues which suggest a period of rapid change between 1690 and 1714, resulting in the disappearance of many established Carolean forms. Thus 'bannister backs' replaced the 'twisted-turne' for chairbacks, 'horsebone' legs gave way to pillar legs and cross-stretchers, 'bewroes' were introduced from France and scriptors were superseded by desks-and-bookcases.

There was one important aspect of furnishing in which French taste was not slavishly followed, for during the 1690s the design of English State beds diverged considerably from French models. A fascinating exchange of letters between William and the Earl of Portland, his ambassador to Louis XIV, reveals that by 1698 the simple, rectilinear shape of French beds was regarded as *démodé*. Portland wrote; 'I have found nothing… made here to Your Majesty's taste… The beds are completely square on the outside, right to the top, that is to say, there is no [cornice] above, where they are larger than the base, which has no basement [of carved woodwork], but an old-fashioned souspente [skirt or valance]'. Portland thought he could buy better beds and cheaper in England.[29]

This letter is intriguing, not least because William chose a conventional square French bed for the King's Bedchamber at Hampton Court Palace (6:12). More importantly, it raises questions about the stylistic origins of the extraordinary, high baroque State beds made between c.1690 and c.1715, of which at least a dozen English examples survive, wholly or in part. The inspiration for these beds is often attributed to Daniel Marot, whose published designs are certainly the most numerous and complete expressions of the style. However, there are indications that the rectilinear mould of the State bed was already breaking in the 1680s, as shown by that made for James II in 1688, which is fitted with an elaborately carved and projecting cornice (3:60). The flared profile of the cornice with its prominent corners is repeated in a more emphatic manner on later English examples, such as those made for the Duke of Devonshire and the Earl of Melville (6:18) in the 1690s. Both these are attributed to Francis Lapiere, and one wonders whether the 'fantasy' beds made for the Trianon de

28. White (1982).
29. Translated and paraphrased from the French, and quoted in Jackson-Stops (1971), pp. 122-4. Although having an English title, the Earl of Portland was a Dutchman, William Bentinck, and one of the King's oldest friends and supporters.

Plate 6:18. State bed, 1697-1700. The headboard bears the cipher of George, first Earl of Melville and his wife. It is upholstered with white Chinese silk and crimson silk velvet, trimmed with crimson silk braid. Attributed to Francis Lapiere.
VICTORIA AND ALBERT MUSEUM, V&A PICTURE LIBRARY

Plate 6:19. Daniel Marot, design for a State bed). This is plate 1 from *Nouveaux Livre de Licts de differents pensées*. This book of engravings was not included in either the 1703 or the 1712 editions of Marot's work and therefore probably postdates 1712. It illustrates the typically ponderous style favoured by Marot for his later bed designs.

Plate 6:20. State bed, 1703-10. This was supplied to William Blathwayt of Dyrham Park, and is currently attributed to Francis Lapiere. The red and yellow velvet upholstery is original. The rather more architectural style is characteristic of English beds after 1700 (compare with 6:18).

DYRHAM PARK, NATIONAL TRUST PHOTOGRAPHIC LIBRARY/ANDREAS VON EINSIEDEL

30. Thornton (1974), p. 17-18; Clinton (1979); White (1982); Beard (1997), pp 89, 95-6.31. Ward Jackson (1958), p. 6; Westman (1994), p. 40.
32. PRO, Treasury Calendars XVI, p. 402; XV, p. 373; XVII, p. 1050.
33. Jackson-Stops (1980); Lane (1949), pp. 23-4.
34. Lane (1948).
35. The evidence for Marot's involvement in these houses is summarised in Jackson-Stops (1996), pp. 58-61.
36. Ibid., p. 61.

Porcelaine at Versailles in the 1670s had any influence on his work.[30] Marot's contribution to the design of these beds is unclear. The fact that they occur in many of his engravings demonstrates only that he was aware of and approved the type, not that he actually created it. In the absence of documentary or other evidence, any connection between Marot's designs and similar beds in English collections is merely generic. However, Marot was almost certainly instrumental in promoting these State beds in Holland, where they remained in vogue for many years (6:19 and 6:20).

The role and influence of Daniel Marot

Discussions of Hampton Court, and of William and Mary furniture in general, inevitably ascribe a central role to the designer Daniel Marot (1661-1752). Marot was French Huguenot, the son of the prominent architect and designer Jean Marot. It is thought that Daniel trained under Jean Bérain,

Louis XIV's chief designer at the Menus-Plaisirs, the design workshop responsible for the French court's entertainments and miscellaneous decorative works. His career in France ended with the Revocation of the Edict of Nantes and in 1686 he fled to Holland. There he was soon employed by the future William III as an architect and designer, and was responsible for much of the interior decoration and furnishing of William's palace at Het Loo. After 1689 Marot spent time in both England and Holland. He was married in Amsterdam in 1694, but came to England the same year, and two of his children were baptised in London in 1695 and 1696. In 1697 he was back in Amsterdam, where a third child was baptised, but it is possible he returned briefly to England the following year. From 1698 he was settled in Holland, first in The Hague and then, after 1704, in Amsterdam.

The chief difficulty in estimating Marot's influence on English art and design, particularly in the field of furniture, is the wide gulf between the claims made on his behalf and the evidence presented to support those claims. His supporters pull no punches, describing Marot as the man who 'probably played a greater part than any other artist in introducing into England the classicizing baroque style which flourished in France during the last part of Louis XIV's reign', and 'the most important and prolific architect-designer of his age'.[31] These are impressive claims and might possibly hold good in Holland, where Marot's work is reasonably well documented, but in England they are not matched by any significant body of surviving work. Although frequently credited with a major role at Hampton Court, there is in fact no convincing evidence that Marot was in any way involved in the King's Apartments which, in any case, were fitted out and furnished after he had returned to Holland.

Despite using the title of 'architect' to William III, Marot held no official position in England. Payments recorded in the Treasury Calendar reveal that he was described as one of Queen Mary's 'servants', and employed as a member of her household.[32] None of the many thousands of bills and other documents relating to the building and furnishing of the King's Apartments makes any reference to Marot, and indeed it is difficult to see how Marot would have fitted into the departmental organisations of the Office of Works or the Royal Wardrobe. The only firm evidence of any work carried out by Marot for Hampton Court is a drawing for the parterre dated August 1689, and a payment for unspecified work connected with the gardens in 1698.[33] There are also reasonable grounds for attributing the design of some Delft tiles and flower vases, probably made for Hampton Court, to his hand.[34] That is the sum total of Marot's known contribution, none of it relating to the King's Apartments.

Aside from his putative links with Hampton Court, Marot's name is found in documents relating to two great houses belonging to the Francophile Duke of Montagu – Boughton in Northamptonshire and Montagu House in London, and a third belonging to Montagu's step-daughter, Petworth House in Sussex.[35] Among the collection at Boughton is a remarkable pair of mirrors, attributed to Jean Pelletier and corresponding reasonably closely to some of Marot's published designs (6:21 and 6:22). At Petworth there is a table, stands and mirror also bearing similarities to Marot's work; both these examples might be taken as evidence of Marot's influence, but sceptics might suggest that any resemblance is merely generic, being typical of the French-inspired style of the 1690s of which Marot was but one exponent. Hard evidence for Marot's direct involvement is slight and is clouded by the fact that Daniel's youngest brother Isaac was also working as a designer or draughtsman in England. Thus references to Marot may refer to Isaac and not Daniel, particularly at Boughton, where a payment to 'Marot' was made in 1706, at which time Daniel is known to have been resident in Amsterdam while Isaac remained in England.[36]

Specialists in this field may argue about the relative weight given to these various pieces of

Plate 6:21. Mirror sconce, c.1690-1705. One of a pair attributed to Jean Pelletier. The design bears some resemblance to Marot's engraving (6:22). BOUGHTON HOUSE, THE DUKE OF BUCCLEUCH

Plate 6:22. Daniel Marot, designs for mirrors and sconces (1703). This is plate three from *Nouveaux Livre d'Ornaments*. The style is typically French, and bears comparison with the sconce in 6:21.

evidence and about the relationship between certain objects, decorations or buildings and Marot's published designs. But the sum total is totally insufficient to justify the common assumption that Marot was the presiding genius of his age. In real terms his 'all pervasive' influence amounts to a few scattered documents, numerous tantalising stylistic analogies, and a great deal of art-historical speculation.

Like Hepplewhite and Sheraton in a later age, Marot's reputation in England arises not from any extant body of work, but from his published designs. These are certainly important, comprising over two hundred and thirty engravings of buildings, furniture, interiors, sculpture, metalware, gardens, wall hangings, clocks and fireplaces. In their number, range and variety they are un-equalled by any other designer of the period. Most were initially issued in *Livres* of six engravings each and were later gathered into collected editions issued in 1703 and 1712.[37] A further, much expanded two-volume edition was issued at a later, unknown date.[38]

The designs cover at least twenty years of Marot's professional life, from c.1689 to c.1710, although it is fairly certain he did not begin publishing them until c.1700-02. Ten *Livres* famously depict furniture and related objects and are used as primary source material by furniture historians, but a number of questions about them have yet to be resolved. We do not know to what extent they represent Marot's original talent and to what extent they merely record designs or objects observed. For instance, the 'horsebone' and cross-frame chairs depicted in the *Nouveau Livre* and *Second Livre d'Appartements* were well established types at the time of publication, familiar to most English and perhaps Dutch furniture makers. Similarly, we have seen that the high baroque State beds which are often regarded as Marot's defining *oeuvres* were a type already produced in England by upholsterers such as Francis Lapiere and Jean Poitevin. More importantly perhaps, we have no way of knowing what degree of popularity or influence the designs enjoyed in England, or even whether they were available. The evidence suggests that they were directed at a Continental clientele, whose names are indeed inscribed on some of the engravings. No English edition was produced and at the time of writing only one complete early edition is known to survive in an English collection.[39] The assumption that Marot's designs were of primary importance in defining the 'William and Mary' style is therefore highly questionable. Equally unwarranted are the constant attributions 'after' or 'in the style of' Daniel Marot found in modern auction house catalogues, usually based on a tenuous stylistic link between the object in question and some detail to be found in one of Marot's designs. The same details can be found in baroque designs published all over Europe between about 1680 and 1720.

One final point is worth making, which is that at the time they were published many of Marot's engravings were already out of date. One of the most striking aspects of his work as a whole is that it is firmly rooted in the style of the late 1680s and 1690s and barely acknowledges the new stylistic impulses emanating from France after 1700. Marot remained wedded to the ponderous baroque of Le Pautre and Bérain well into the eighteenth century and nothing in his published work matches the forward-looking originality of André-Charles Boulle. Boulle's own output began to change significantly around 1700 and his designs, published from 1707 onwards, inaugurated a new era of furniture design in France and, within a few years, in England.[40]

The work of Gerrit Jensen

A number of prominent cabinet-makers supplied furniture to William and Mary, but the man most closely associated with the 'William and Mary' style is Gerrit Jensen, who was re-appointed 'Cabbinet maker in Ordinary' to the Crown in 1689.[41] In fact Jensen's career spanned nearly half a century, from 1667 to 1714, so his work between 1689 and 1702 represented only a small part of his output. It is, however, particularly well documented and a number of pieces attributed to Jensen survive in the Royal Collection.

Jensen's name is closely linked to the decorative technique of arabesque marquetry, to the extent that virtually any competently executed example is attributed to him. One firmly attributed piece is the bureau in 6:23, which is probably that described in a bill of 1691, 'for a large Bouro of fine markatree wth drawers to stand upon the Top carved and gilt pillars... £80.00.00.'.[42] Although

37. *Oeuvres du Sr. D. Marot,* The Hague (1703), Amsterdam (1712). Original editions of Marot are very rare, but the designs were reprinted in a 19th century German edition, *Das Ornamentwerk des Daniel Marot,* Berlin (1892).
38. *De Werken van Daniel Marot, Architect van wylen zyn Koninglyke Majestyt van Groot Bretagne, Willem de Darde,* Holland (n.d.).
39. This volume of 1703 was originally in possession of the architect James Gibbs, and is now in the Bodleian Library, Oxford. Another incomplete volume of uncertain date survives in the library at Boughton House.
40. André-Charles Boulle, *Desseins de meubles et ouvrages de bronze et de marqueterie inventés et gravés par André-Charles Boulle,* Paris 1707-30.
41. A full summary of the known details of Jensen's career and output can be found in Beard and Gilbert (1986), pp. 485-87.
42. PRO LC 9/280, f. 43. My attribution is different from that given in the DEF and DEFM, which cite a bill of 1690 for 'a Folding writing table fine Markatree with a Crowne and Cypher', made for Queen Mary's use at Kensington Palace at a cost of £22.10s. Although the bureau does bear a crown and cipher, it is definitely a 'Bouro' in the French manner, and has a separate case of drawers 'to stand on top' as described in the 1691 bill. Moreover, the price of £80, also given in the 1691 bill, is consistent with the extraordinary quality of this piece.

Plates 6:24, 24a, 24b: Details of 6:23. This drawer construction is exceptional in every respect and closely resembles that found on furniture made for Louis XIV by André-Charles Boulle. The drawer front shows evidence of having originally been fitted with a small central handle. The locks are superb, and are fitted in the English manner with the escutcheon close to the top edge, but others are fitted centrally in the French way. Note that the drawer front is veneered on all four faces, disguising the oak core, which can be seen in the side view. The rest of the drawer is constructed from an unidentified tropical hardwood.

Plate 6:23. Writing table, decorated with marquetry of walnut and holly, 1690. This was almost certainly supplied by Gerrit Jensen for Queen Mary's use at Kensington Palace. The legs are replacements and were originally pillar legs with carved capitals. WINDSOR CASTLE, THE ROYAL COLLECTION, ©2002 HER MAJESTY QUEEN ELIZABETH II

firmly documented, the attribution of this piece to Jensen's workshop is not straightforward, for nothing about it is standard English work. The overall form is decidedly French, and this is explicitly acknowledged in the term 'Bouro', cited in the bill. It originally stood on gilt pillars; these were replaced with the present twist-turned ones in the nineteenth century. The construction of the carcase and drawers is of quite exceptional quality. The former is conventionally made of fine wainscot, but the drawers are unlike anything else made in England at this or any other time (6:24). The oak drawer fronts are veneered on all four faces, and the linings are of a fine textured orange/pink tropical wood. On the underside of each drawer is a narrow runner strip, which engages with a similar strip on the upper surface of the corresponding dustboard and ensures a smooth, accurate drawer action. Each drawer also has a fine brass and gilt lock, tailor-made to the size of each drawer, and the keyholes are located centrally, in the French manner.

43. PRO LC 9/280, f. 214.
44. Cornelius Gole worked for Queen Mary in Holland, and followed her to London after 1688. Several commissions are recorded in the Lord Chamberlain's accounts for 1691, although no documented pieces have so far come to light.
45. Beard and Gilbert (1986), p. 487.

Plate 6:25. Writing table, decorated with marquetry in metal, c.1695. This piece bears the royal cipher of William III and is attributed to Gerrit Jensen, but the attribution is not straightforward (see text). The tapered pillar legs were highly fashionable in the 1690s. WINDSOR CASTLE, THE ROYAL COLLECTION, ©2002 HER MAJESTY QUEEN ELIZABETH II

To find an analogous drawer construction we must look to France, and specifically to the work of André-Charles Boulle. A number of cabinets attributed to Boulle have a very similar drawer construction, with linings of tropical woods and fronts veneered on all faces. Could Jensen's bureau also be French? In view of his known connections with the Parisian furniture maker Pierre Gole, Boulle's illustrious predecessor, the idea is a distinct possibility. Moreover, this is not the only Jensen piece to have a French look to its construction. The metal marquetry table with drawers shown in 6:25 is probably the 'fine writing desk table inlaid wth mettall' supplied for Kensington Palace in 1695 at the enormous cost of £75.[43] This piece is often considered as the touchstone of Jensen's work, exhibiting the highest degree of technical refinement and encapsulating his mastery of contemporary French style. But the piece is manifestly a marriage. This is most evident in the frieze, where the foliate scrolls below the royal monogram have been truncated in order not to interfere with the working of the drawer below. It then becomes apparent that the marquetry of the top and frieze differs from that of the lower carcase. In particular, the geometric strapwork on the drawer fronts, rails and stiles is not repeated in the frieze, whose design is more foliate and flowing. The discrepancies are reflected in the construction, for the lower carcase is of pine, with pine drawer linings, whereas the upper carcase is of oak, with oak drawer linings. Recent conservation work has revealed that the top and frieze were originally made for a different base, and have been adapted to fit the present lower carcase, which is probably French (the locks are mounted in the French manner, with the keyholes centrally placed).

When did this marriage take place? Quite possibly in 1695, for both parts are stylistically contemporary, and this raises the strong possibility that Jensen imported and adapted a French carcase to take a new top. Or was the carcase supplied by a Frenchman working in England, perhaps Pierre Gole's son Cornelius, who was working in England in the 1690s?[44] The puzzle is compounded by the fact that the top of the writing desk matches closely a design by Daniel Marot, and indeed this is the only known piece of documented 'English' furniture for which a close Marot analogy survives.

The full story behind William's writing desk will probably never be known, but it does have an important bearing on other furniture hitherto confidently attributed to Jensen. At Boughton House there is a pair of small commodes of almost identical style and form, except that these retain their original tops (6:26). One of the mirrors *en suite* bears the crest of Ralph, Earl Montagu, which dates them to between 1689 and 1705, at which time Jensen is known to have been supplying furnishings.[45] Did Jensen supply these commodes and glasses? Possibly, but it is most unlikely that they were made in his workshop. As with the Kensington Palace example, the materials, construction and fittings are typically French. Given Ralph Montagu's known Francophile leanings, it would not be surprising to find him buying French furniture in the 1690s, but the attribution to Jensen cannot be regarded as sound.

In addition to these puzzling bureaux, there are

Plate 6:26. Writing table or bureau and looking-glass, French, c.1690-1700. Marquetry of metal and wood on a deal carcase. This is one of a pair supplied to the Duke of Montagu, and the similarities between this and the table in 6:25 have long been regarded as indicative of Gerrit Jensen's authorship, but the attribution is questionable (see text).

BOUGHTON HOUSE,
THE DUKE OF BUCCLEUCH

a number of more conventional pieces in the Royal Collections which can safely be ascribed to Jensen. One of these is a glazed marquetry cabinet currently installed at Kensington Palace. This has been substantially altered in the interior, but can nevertheless plausibly be associated with a bill of 1693 for 'a glass case of fine Markatree upon a Cabonett with doors'.[46] If it is not the exact cabinet, it is certainly representative of the type. William III's writing desk, formerly at Kensington Palace but now in the Private Closet at Hampton Court (6:16), is another more conventional piece which probably came from Jensen's workshops.

Like many top cabinet-makers, Jensen was also a dealer in glass and this line of business provided him with some of his most profitable work. In the King's Bedchamber at Hampton Court is an extraordinary pier glass measuring 13ft. (4m) from top to bottom, supplied by Jensen in 1699 (6.13).[47] The main plate is over 4ft. (1.2m) high, bordered with engraved glass and scalloped dark blue glass slips. Similar blue glass slips border the upper plates and form the Royal crown and cipher in the 'cresting'. Gilt roses conceal the heads of screws used to fix the slips through the main plate.

Early in Queen Anne's reign Jensen was busy supplying furniture for St James's and Kensington Palaces, including a number of substantial carved and gilded pier tables (6:27). These make an interesting comparison with those supplied by the Pelletiers to Hampton Court (6:28). Both are of the pillar leg and cross-stretcher type, which is typical of the period, but the treatment of certain elements is both distinctive and different.[48] Pelletier's Ionic capitals are angled at forty-five degrees to the frame, whereas Jensen's are more or less aligned with the face of the frieze. Both makers employed highly stylised stretchers, but Jensen's have a characteristic 'step', rising towards the central finial. On Pelletier's tables the finial is omitted in favour of a small platform, presumably to accommodate a porcelain vase. Here are two workshops or makers, working in the same stylistic idiom, producing furniture of the same type and form, but exhibiting decided preferences in the manner of handling particular elements of the design.

Numerous pieces attributed to Jensen survive outside the Royal Collections, but few are documented. One of the most securely attributed examples is shown in 6:29. This is one of several strong boxes supplied to Colonel James Grahme in the 1680s and is probably the 'Strong Box upon a frame [*illegible*] With Iron Work' invoiced in July 1688 for the sum of £12.[49] It is made in the form of a scriptor, with a fall-front enclosing small drawers. The 'frame' or stand is clearly an afterthought, but the box still has its long iron bolts which pass through the carcase from top to bottom, allowing it to be secured to the floor.

Despite being supplied by an illustrious maker, the strong box is of very ordinary quality, and this is illustrative of the great range and variety of Jensen's output. The lack of a homogenous workshop style suggests that by the 1690s Jensen was no mere artisan. His premises in St Martin's Lane are unlikely to have afforded sufficient space to produce even a fraction of his recorded output, nor to support his country house at Hammersmith or his estates in Kent. Rather, he was a man with many and varied business interests, commissioning work from numerous workshops, employing specialists where needed and perhaps sourcing work abroad if he could not find its equivalent in England. This makes the work of modern furniture historians very difficult, for with an output so diverse, analogies between one piece and another are far to seek, and attributions based on stylistic or technical similarities must be treated with caution.

The war against France

The wars waged against Louis XIV (1689-97, 1702-13) were the most expensive yet undertaken by an English monarch. With hindsight, the results probably justified the expenditure, for victory against France secured the international recognition of William III and Queen Anne, curtailed French power in Europe, and finally saw the emergence of Great Britain (as it now was after the Union with Scotland in 1707) as a first-class world power. But to the merchants and tradesmen of London the wars must have seemed long, bloody and excessively burdensome. Seaborne trade, the lifeblood of England's economy, was badly hit, as both sides did their utmost to ruin the other's shipping (English merchants reckoned that between 1702 and 1708 1,100 of their ships had been

46. PRO LC 9/280, f. 111.
47. PRO LC 9/281, f. 23.
48. These tables and others are discussed in Murdoch (1998). Dr Murdoch suggests that Jensen's tables might have been produced by the Pelletier workshop, but for the reason given in the text I think this is doubtful.
49. Cumbria Record Office, Levens Hall Archive, Box C.1.

Plate 6:27. Pier table, carved and gilded deal with marble top, c.1702-3. This table bears Queen Anne's crown and cipher, and was probably one of pair supplied by Gerrit Jensen for St James's Palace in 1702-03. Note the distinctive stepped stretcher and central urn.
WINDSOR CASTLE,
THE ROYAL COLLECTION, ©2002
HER MAJESTY QUEEN ELIZABETH II

Plate 6:28. Pier table, carved and gilded deal with marble top, 1701. This is one of a pair supplied by Jean Pelletier for the New Gallery at Hampton Court Palace, at a cost of £35 each, not including the marble. Note the stretcher design, which appears to be characteristic of Pelletier, and the distinctly angled capitals to the legs.   BUCKINGHAM PALACE,
THE ROYAL COLLECTION, ©2002
HER MAJESTY QUEEN ELIZABETH II

lost to enemy action, together with cargoes worth many millions of pounds). Scarcity and price inflation were the inevitable consequence of such losses and this was on top of the usual wartime price rises caused by increases in marine insurance, seamen's wages and general profiteering.

Furniture makers were surprisingly vulnerable to these commercial pressures because of their dependence on imported raw materials. Importations of French walnut, the mainstay of the fine furniture trade, were stopped by the prohibition of all trade with France in 1689 and again in 1704.[50] Even in the years of peace between 1697 and 1702 French goods were subject to punitive additional duties. Although customs returns for the years prior to 1698 do not survive, the effect of these measures thereafter is very clear. The value of walnut importations from France in peacetime between 1698 and 1702 totalled £2,819.8s.0d., whereas between 1703 and 1712 no walnut at all was imported from France and supplies from other countries fell far short of the amount needed to make good the shortfall.[51]

It may be significant that furniture makers supplying the Royal Palaces, particularly Thomas Roberts and Gerrit Jensen, continually stressed the use of 'French', 'Grenoble' or 'best' walnut during these years.[52] Before the war any mention of French walnut would have been redundant, since its use was taken for granted, but it now became a matter of some importance. Whether Roberts was really able to obtain French walnut at this time is a matter of conjecture, but it was clearly important to be able to claim so. Other makers, particularly in the provincial towns, may have found it difficult to obtain any walnut at all, and it is certainly true that much case furniture made during this period was made with native veneers such as ash, elm, maple and yew. Although severe, the shortage was nevertheless brief, for on the signing of peace in 1713 trade with France was resumed and supplies of French walnut were soon more plentiful. Between 1713 and 1720 they were more or less at their pre-war level, averaging around £350 per annum, and this was augmented by importations from Holland, Spain, Portugal and Italy.

A more substantive problem arose from the imposition of wartime import duties on imported timber. The *Book of Rates* (1660) imposed a common duty of five per cent by value on all imported goods. With the outbreak of war in 1689 duties began to rise inexorably to offset military expenditure, and timber was not exempt from this trend. In December 1690 a ten per cent additional duty was imposed on all 'Deal Timber... Boards, Wainscot... and other Wood' imported from Europe.[53] In 1699 another five per cent general duty was imposed,[54] so that by 1700 imported wainscots and deals, the staples of the furniture trades, paid a total of twenty per cent import duty.[55] When war recommenced in 1702 duties rose further. Two Acts of 1703 and 1704 effectively doubled the duty payable on imported timber to a minimum of forty per cent.[56]

The effect of these increases is revealed in the prices paid for deals and wainscot in London. In 1660, standard Norway deals (usually 11ft. x 11in. x 1¼in. (3.35m x 279.4mm x 31.75mm) cost around £5 per 120, or 1d. per superficial foot.[57] By 1710 the average price had risen to between £6 and £8 per 120, or between 1.2d and 1.6d per foot. Similarly, in 1660 wainscots averaged about 20d. each, and by 1710 nearer 30d. These increases of pence and fractions of pence may seem trivial but, when one considers that a busy furniture workshop consumed thousands of feet of timber annually, price rises of this magnitude added greatly to its costs. It would not be surprising, therefore, if furniture makers modified their working methods to minimise the effects of such inflation, and one possible indication of this is the widespread adoption of thinner dustboards from about 1700-1710 onwards. This phenomenon is discussed in more detail in Chapter Seven.

Some furniture makers actually gained from the war. Joiners who specialised in japanned ware, together with the japanners themselves and their dependent trades, all capitalised on the contraction of overseas trade which substantially reduced importations of lacquered ware from China. The consequent scarcity of lacquered goods offered English japanners a prime commercial opportunity which they seized with alacrity. The peace, when it came, was most unwelcome, since it resulted in an immediate resumption of East Indian imports. The japanners were not alone in their discomfiture and from 1697 onwards there was a concerted campaign led by the English cloth manufacturers and traders to have the East India trade curtailed, restricted or even abolished. Their case was plainly stated in a petition, *A True Relation of the Rise and Progress of the East-Indian Com-*

50. 1 William and Mary *ca*p. 34; 3 and 4 Anne cap. 13.51. With the exception of one shipment worth £1330, captured from a French prize, the yearly average imported from elsewhere in Europe was £128.
52. For instance, in 1706 Thomas Roberts supplied 'two Arm Chair frames made of best french wallnut tree carved arched railes corner arms and polished' [PRO LC 5/41, f. 268].
53. 2 William & Mary, Sess. 2, *cap.* 4.
54. 9 and 10 William and Mary, *cap.* 22.
55. These duties are summarised in Carkesse (1702).
56. 2 and 3 Anne *cap.* 9; 3 & 4 Anne *cap.* 5.
57. The superficial foot measured 12in. x 12in. x 1in. (304.8mm x 304.8mm x 25.4mm).

Plate 6:29. Strong box on a frame,
supplied by Gerrit Jensen to Colonel
James Grahme in 1688. Walnut
veneers on oak and deal. This is a rare
example of a modest, workmanlike
piece supplied by a royal cabinet-
maker to a non-noble patron. All the
fittings are original.   LEVENS HALL

pany; 'during the great part of the late War, the East-India Trade was under some Discouragement, and while it was so, our English Manufactures flourished very much...'.[58] Another broadsheet published in 1700 pointed out that 'In the Two Years last past there have been more Ships sent to the East-Indies than in Seven Years before'.[59]

The japanners found plenty of ammunition here for their lobby against lacquered goods, and were further encouraged by the words of John Polloxfen, whose lengthy polemic against the East India Company, *A Discourse of Trade, Coyn and Paper Credit,* was first published in 1697:

> ... the *Cabinets, China, Lacquered and Japan Ware,* and several other sorts of Goods that come ready made, are too costly to the Nation, a great hindrance to the imploy of our own People, and a prodigal unprofitable Expence.[60]

It was against this general groundswell of opinion against the Company, which served to unite disaffected parties of all kinds, that the Joiners' and japanners' petitions of 1701 were formulated. But, as we have already seen in Chapter Five, the petitions were unsuccessful and competition from the Orient was now a fact of life for England's furniture makers. Given the enormous future growth of the furniture industry in the eighteenth century, their objections seem to have had no real foundation.

58. *A true Relation of the Rise and Progress of the East India Company* (c.1700)
59 England's Almanack (1700). Between December 1690 and December 1697 52 English ships sailed for the East Indies, and the same number between February 1698 and March 1700.
60. Polloxfen (1697), p. 126.

Chapter Seven
CASE FURNITURE
1689-1714

Plate 7:1. Detail from 7:5 showing
the central door of the cabinet.

Later floral marquetry

Bills from Gerrit Jensen and others in the Lord Chamberlain's accounts show that 'flower'd' furniture continued to be fashionable into the 1690s, and this is borne out by the large quantity of floral marquetry clock cases made even into the early years of the eighteenth century. The difficulty with dating floral marquetry case furniture from this period is that there is nothing in its carcase or drawer construction to distinguish it from earlier pieces. First-phase construction remained the norm until after 1700. In some cases the marquetry, while not obviously different in style, has a rather 'late' feel to it – rather stiff, two-dimensional and cramped (7:1 and 7:2). Many such pieces try to impress by the sheer quantity of decoration, rather than its quality.

In other cases the marquetry is clearly different, for in the late 1680s a new, less figurative style began to develop. The designs were essentially two-dimensional, with an emphasis on symmetry rather than variety (7:3). Foliage and flowers were heavily stylised, with shading and perspective kept to a minimum or entirely absent. A rare dated example of this style of marquetry, made in 1688, is shown in 7:4 and 7:5. Close examination shows that this marquetry was produced in a slightly different way from earlier floral marquetry. The six drawers flanking the cupboards are of equal size and the marquetry panels are identical (7:6). Consequently, all the parts, including the ground, could be cut in a packet. Each panel contains four woods – walnut for the ground, padouk, ebony and holly – so that, in theory, four complete versions of the design could have been made at a single cutting, sufficient to decorate four cabinets (indeed, another cabinet of identical design is known, dated 1698).[1] The savings in time and money are obvious and it is worth questioning whether aesthetic or commercial considerations were more important in the emergence of this style.

Arabesque marquetry

The two-dimensional style of decoration described above might be seen as a half-way house between floral marquetry and another type of marquetry variously called 'seaweed', 'endive' or 'arabesque', which is one of the most easily recognisable traits of the 'William and Mary' style. Arabesque marquetry eschews the naturalistic effect of floral marquetry in favour of dense, two-

1. Edwards (1954), I, p.167, figs 12 and 13.

Plate 7:2. Chest of drawers (1690-1710), walnut and
marquetry. This is typical of later floral marquetry work The
careful drawing and naturalistic style of the early pieces has
been replaced by rather stiff and cramped designs and the
quality of execution leaves much to be desired. Handles and
escutcheons are replacements and the reversed top moulding
suggests this might once have been on a stand.   SOTHEBY'S

Plate 7:3. Chest of drawers (1685-1700), walnut and
marquetry. A new style of marquetry introduced from the mid-
1680s relied for its effect on stylised, two-dimensional foliage
executed in strong, contrasting colours. Handles and
escutcheons probably replaced, but in the appropriate style.
SOTHEBY'S

Plate 7:4. Cabinet (1688), walnut and marquetry. The date 1688 is inlaid into the doors. The stand to this cabinet has been lost and replaced by a chest of drawers. This two-dimensional style of marquetry mimics the marquetry in metal recently introduced from France.

TOPSHAM MUSEUM, VICTORIA AND ALBERT MUSEUM

Plate 7:5. 7:4 (open). Note that the marquetry on the six smaller drawers is identical, as is that on the four larger ones. This enabled the marqueteur to cut the veneers in packets, thereby saving both labour and money. The trio of initials on the central door is unusual and is more commonly found on provincial or vernacular furniture. They probably commemorate a marriage. The metalware is probably original.

Plate 7:6. Detail of 7:4. Four woods are used in the marquetry – a plain, straight-grained walnut for the background (pale brown), padouk (red) and ebony (black) for the foliage, and holly (white) for the tendrils. The original effect would have been very striking. Note the white/black/white stringing, commonly found throughout the period 1680-1710.

Plate 7:7. Chest of drawers with strongbox (1690-1710). Marquetry of rosewood and holly with princeswood mouldings. This chest was purpose-made to accommodate the strong box. The quality of the marquetry is superb and the use of both rosewood and princeswood makes this an expensive chest of drawers. The colours are now muted, but would originally have been white (holly) on purple-red (rosewood). The drawer handles are replaced.
LYME PARK, NATIONAL TRUST PHOTO-GRAPHIC LIBRARY/ANDREAS VON EINSIEDEL

Plate 7:8. Detail of 7:6. Side of the chest in 7:6, showing the marquetry divided into four identical quarters. These could be cut simultaneously in one packet.

dimensional patterns developed out of highly stylised foliate scrollwork. No attempt was made to imitate the natural colouring and shading of floral marquetry; instead, most designs were of two contrasting colours, either light on dark or the reverse.

Some authorities sub-divide the various types of arabesque marquetry according to their various styles – 'seaweed', 'endive', etc.,[2] - but such distinctions tend to be rather subjective. They also ignore a fundamental point, which is that all these different styles were produced by the same technique, which was different from that used for floral marquetry. Whereas in floral marquetry all the elements of a design were cut and assembled piece by piece, arabesque marquetry was cut in a single operation. For instance, look at the chest in 7:7 and 7:8, which is veneered with marquetry of holly and rosewood. The side of the chest is veneered in four identical quarters which can be sawn simultaneously by placing four veneers of holly and four veneers of rosewood in a packet (7:8). Furthermore, since there are a total of eight veneers, there will actually be eight identical versions of the design, four in holly and four in rosewood. By combining the ground from one and the pattern from the other, two matching chests can be produced, one a light pattern on a dark ground, and the other with a dark pattern on a light ground. This is sometimes known as *partie* and *contre-partie*. Whether one terms it 'seaweed', 'endive' or 'arabesque', the important point is that all were produced by this method, and therefore in this chapter one term – arabesque – will be used for all. The most common contemporary term, which occurs in early eighteenth century inventories, was 'filigree'.

2. Symonds (1929), pp. 60-61. Symonds even detected another style of this marquetry, which he called 'Persian'.

Plate7:9. Cabinet (1690-1700), one of a pair, attributed to Gerrit Jensen. Marquetry of walnut and holly on an oak and deal carcase. Although undocumented, these cabinets can plausibly be attributed to Gerrit Jensen. The quality is outstanding. The scrolled legs stand was probably the most popular type at this date, and was gradually superseded by the pillar leg from c.1690 onwards.

Plate 7:11. Detail of 7:9, showing the base of the long drawer in the stand. The drawer bottom is raised and secured by mitred slips rebated into the drawer sides. This sophisticated construction has been employed to prevent the drawer bottom binding on the lower frame rail in use.

Plate 7:10. 7:9 (open) showing the drawer fronts in *partie* and *contre-partie* marquetry. The metalware is original.

English arabesque marquetry is particularly associated with the work of Gerrit Jensen (fl.1667-1715). Jensen's bills reveal that he made a distinction between floral marquetry, which he called 'inlaid' or 'flower'd', and 'markatree', by which he implied arabesque marquetry. The distinction might be based on the different methods of production described above. He first used the term 'markatree' in a bill of 1686, for 'a Table Stands and glasse of Markatree... £35.00.00',[3] and continued to produce both 'flower'd' and 'markatree' work until after 1700.

A number of arabesque marquetry pieces of case furniture attributed to Jensen are extant, some of which have been discussed in Chapter Six. Stylistic similarities between some of Jensen's documented work and a pair of cabinets at Chatsworth House, Derbyshire, suggest that these too were supplied by Gerrit Jensen. One of the pair is shown in 7:9-7:11) The quality of both materials and workmanship is superlative and they are certainly the finest surviving examples of their type. Although there are no bills relating to the cabinets, Jensen was much involved with furnishing at Chatsworth between 1688 and 1698,[4] and the style of the piece is consistent with these dates. The carcase is of wainscot throughout and the marquetry is of walnut and holly. The drawers are also entirely of wainscot and through-dovetailed. The metal fittings are all gilt and are of the most advanced and expensive type. The cabinet sits on its stand in the conventional manner and this is raised on scrolled legs veneered on every face. Finally, the feet are carved as compressed acanthus scrolls and were probably gilt originally.

The construction of the cabinet, although exemplary in all respects, is conventional English first-phase work and very different from the bureau discussed in Chapter Six. The drawer in the stand, however, incorporates an important modification to improve its working. The drawer bottom is raised well above the base and secured

Plate 7:12. Cabinet on stand (1690-1710), princeswood and marquetry on a deal carcase. This is a high quality London-made piece, but of standard design and execution. Note that the marquetry, although of fine quality, is laid in reserves separated by oyster-cut veneers, suggesting that these could have been bought in from a specialist marqueteur. The leafy, interlocked borders to the panels and drawers is typical of the 1690s and early 1700s.
FAIRFAX HOUSE, YORK

by a narrow oak strip around all four sides (7:11). This was done because the drawer is a very wide one and the drawer bottom was therefore liable to sag and rub on the carcase rail in use. The oak strips acted as runners, keeping friction to a minimum. This construction is found only rarely before 1700 (it was used on the library scriptor at Ham House) but, as we shall see, variations of it became increasingly common thereafter.

Compared with the Chatsworth cabinets most other London cabinet-work seems decidedly second-rate. Nevertheless, cabinets such as that in 7:12 were by no means cheap. The use of princeswood veneers is a sure indication of first-class manufacture and this is endorsed by the delicacy and accuracy of the marquetry. But, unlike the Chatsworth cabinets, of which every inch is decorated, the marquetry on this cabinet is confined to shaped reserves in the conventional manner. The construction is also conventional, with a first-phase carcase, dust-boards and drawers. Both style and construction suggest a date of manufacture between c.1690 and c.1705.

An intriguing chest of drawers which recently came to light might also be attributed to Jensen

3. PRO LC 9/278, f. 45.
4. Beard and Gilbert (1986), pp. 486-7.

201

Plate 7:13. Chest of drawers (1690-1710), walnut and marquetry. The top of this chest is inlaid with a royal crown, suggesting it might have been made for William III or Queen Anne. The form is conventional but the marquetry is unusually delicate. The metalware is replaced and the chest probably once stood on a stand.

SOTHEBY'S

(7:13).[5] The top is centred by a royal crown, which is specific to the English sovereign, and the quality, while not outstanding, is good. Jensen was not above supplying fairly mundane household furniture when asked, such as the 'chest of Drawers upon balls' made for the royal household in 1697.[6]

We have seen that Jensen also followed French precedent in producing marquetry in metal, a technique popularly associated with the work of André Charles Boulle, and now commonly called *Boulle*. A table and a pair of stands attributed to Jensen at Drayton House are among the earliest English examples of this technique, dating from before 1688 (cf. 9:14 and 15), but not until the 1690s does metal marquetry furniture appear regularly in the Lord Chamberlain's accounts. The difficulties concerning the authorship of some metal marquetry pieces attributed to Jensen have already been discussed (above, page 190), but there is little doubt that he was among its foremost practitioners in England, since he is one of the few makers whose bills for this type of work survive. The cost of this type of furniture was probably much greater than marquetry in wood and must have restricted its production to a few specialised makers with a very select clientele.

There is a common belief that arabesque marquetry went out of fashion rather rapidly after 1700,[7] but Jensen's bills record numerous items of 'markatree' and 'mettle' supplied to the Royal Palaces in Queen Anne's reign.[8] As we shall see, the carcase work of surviving arabesque marquetry case furniture spans the transition from first- to second-phase construction, indicating production extending until at least 1715 or later, and longcase clocks continued to be made with arabesque marquetry cases into the 1720s.

Second-phase cabinet construction

First-phase cabinet construction had a number of technical weaknesses, most of which were associated with the proper functioning of drawers and dustboards. The rebated flush-bottomed drawer, supported across its whole width by the dustboard, often gave trouble, because even a small degree of warping in either the drawer bottom or the dustboard was sufficient to impede the smooth running of the drawer. If the drawer was to function efficiently for any length of time, it had to be accurately made and with good materials, both of which added to the cost of production. In the case of the best quality furniture, cost was not perhaps the major consideration, but as the demand for cabinet-made furniture became more widespread, particularly among the aspiring but penny-wise middle classes, so cost increasingly influenced the cabinet-maker's approach to construction.

One of the most common tricks to avoid the problem of drawer binding was to raise the drawer bottom clear of the dustboard and we have seen how the maker of the Chatsworth cabinet achieved this in a particularly neat manner. A similar method of construction has been used on the large drawers of the scriptor in 7:14. This bears the trade label of John Guilbaud, who worked at the Crowne and Looking Glasse in Long Acre between 1693 and 1712 (7:15). The carcase and drawer construction is standard first-phase work, with the exception of the two long drawers in the base. These have raised bottoms with deal runner strips glued on all four sides (7:16); the fact that raised bottoms are not used on the two short drawers immediately above indicates that the raised bottom is intended specifically to counteract the tendency of long drawers to rub or drag in use. Despite the care given to this particular detail, the general standard of workmanship is not high. There is an abundance of over-cut dovetails, mis-judged scribe lines and glue over-runs, all suggesting that the maker was working in a hurry.

5. This was sold at Sotheby's London, 7 November 1997, Lot 16.
6. PRO LC 11/5, f. 42.
7. Symonds (1929), p. 61.
8. PRO LC 9/281, 282.

Some cabinet-makers cheated by simply cutting the rebate for the drawer bottom deeper than the thickness of the bottom boards, thus raising them clear of the dustboards. The cabinet shown in 7:4 has drawers constructed in this way (7:17). One obvious drawback of this method of construction is that the drawer does not have any runners, so that the whole weight of the drawer and its contents is borne by the narrow rebated edges of the drawer. In heavy use the wear must have been very rapid. A better, and indeed simpler, way to achieve the same end was to nail or glue the bottom up to the drawer sides and then to add runner strips down each side

Plate 7:15. Detail of 7:14. Trade label of John Guilbaud, who worked at the Crowne and Looking Glasse in Long Acre between 1693 and 1712.

Plate 7:16. Detail of 7:4, showing the base of a large drawer, raised and rebated into the drawer sides with deal runner slips added. This modification was carried out only on the two long drawers, indicating that its purpose was to overcome friction or binding when the drawer was loaded. The second runner slip at the base of the picture is a later addition.

Plate 7:14. Scriptor (c.1690-1710) bearing the trade label of John Guilbaud. Walnut on a deal and oak carcase. By 1690 the scriptor-on-stand was becoming outmoded, to be replaced by the scriptor-on-chest. This is a transitional piece, having essentially first-phase construction but with slight modifications to the drawer and carcase. The metalware is mostly original and the feet are replaced.   DAVID O'BRIEN/LAWRENCE'S FINE ART

Plate 7:17. Detail of 7:4, showing the drawer bottom slightly raised to reduce friction. This is a crude and only partly effective solution, since the whole weight of the drawer rests on the narrow edges of the drawer sides.

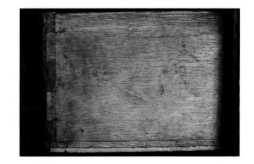

Plate 7:18. Detail of 7:19, showing the raised drawer bottom and added runners. This was the standard 'second phase' drawer construction generally adopted in London and elsewhere from c.1700 onwards. Note the lapped dovetails, made necessary in this case by the fact that the drawer front is not veneered.

Plate 7:19. Specimen cabinet (1704), oak and deal. Made by the Cambridge joiner John Austen for John Francis Vigani, first Professor of Chemistry at Cambridge University. This is a very accomplished piece, no different in materials, style or technique from contemporary London wainscot furniture. Metalware and feet are original.

QUEENS' COLLEGE, CAMBRIDGE, BY PERMISSION OF THE PRESIDENT AND FELLOWS

9. Bowett (1994).

Plate 7:20. Cabinet on chest (c.1710), walnut and marquetry on a deal carcase. This was made for Edward Dryden of Canons Ashby, Northamptonshire, and is probably the 'large inlaid Cabinet, wᵗʰ Chest of Drawers under it' recorded in the principal bedchamber in the 1717 inventory.   CANONS ASHBY, THE NATIONAL TRUST

Plate 7:21. 7:20 (open). The cabinet has been restored but the metalware appears to be original. It has a 'first-phase' carcase with 'second-phase' drawers in the lower part. Note that the interior arrangement is essentially unchanged from 17th century examples – within a few years the central cupboard was abandoned and the layout changed (cf. 7:60).

(7:18). This was the solution adopted by John Austen, a Cambridge joiner, who made the cabinet in 7:19 in 1704.⁹ Although this is the earliest known *documented* piece on which this construction occurs, it is unlikely to have been the first and one might plausibly suggest a date of c.1700 for its general introduction. By c.1710 this 'second-phase' drawer construction was standard practice among London's furniture makers. However, the construction of small drawers for the interior of cabinets and scriptors remained unchanged.

It is quite common to find second-phase drawers combined with first-phase carcases. The cabinet in 7:20 and 7:21 is at Canons Ashby, Northamptonshire. Two closely-spaced inventories of 1708 and 1717 show that the cabinet was supplied to Sir Edward Dryden, owner of Canons Ashby, between those dates. The maker is unknown, but the

Plate 7:22. Detail of 7:20 showing the drawer construction of the Canons Ashby cabinet. 'Second-phase' construction is distinguished by having three separate components visible on the drawer side – the side itself, the drawer bottom and the runner. Through dovetails are still the norm, however. Note the slip of oak on the top edge of the drawer front. This is a common conceit to disguise the use of deal for the drawer front proper.

piece is probably of London manufacture and it is known that Dryden bought other furniture from London makers.[10] The drawers in the lower carcase are all of second-phase type (7:22), although the carcase itself is conventional first-phase work. A similar combination of second-phase drawers and first-phase carcase occurs on the chest in 7:23. Judged solely on external appearance, this chest might date from the 1680s, but the second-phase construction suggests a date after 1700.

Documented examples of hybrid first-phase carcases with second-phase drawers can be found as late as 1717 (7:55), but before this time many London makers were taking advantage of the new drawer construction to make changes to the dustboards as well. Because the weight of the drawer was transferred via the runners to the sides of the carcase, the dustboards could be made thinner. Instead of having dustboards of equal thickness extending right to the back of the carcase, cabinet-makers began to install a separate front rail, usually about ½in. (12.5mm) thick and about 2½in. (63.5mm) deep, and behind that used thinner boards to make up the rest of the dustboard. The top of the dustboard was made flush with the rail, but on the underside there was a palpable 'step' where the rail met the thinner board. The usual method of constructing stepped dustboards was to plough a groove in the carcase side wide enough to accept the dustboards and then to widen it at the front to accept the front rail (7:24). Alternatively, the whole groove was ploughed to the thickness of the rail and the narrower boards were then glued and wedged in place (7:25 and 7:26).

After about 1710 the combination of second-phase drawers together with stepped dustboards is so ubiquitous that it constitutes a true 'second-phase' of London cabinet-work. Judged by these criteria, once can see that many late seventeenth century furniture types were carried over into the early years of the eighteenth (7:26).

There are also other, less obvious details which are usually indicative of second-phase work. Whereas most first-phase drawers have square-topped sides, level with the top of the drawer front, the sides of second-phase drawers are often rounded off and set down slightly from the drawer

10. Jackson-Stops (1985).

Plate 7:23. Chest of drawers (1700-20), olivewood on a deal carcase. Judged by its external appearance alone, this chest might date from the 1670s or 1680s, but it has a first-phase carcase with second-phase drawers. Similar construction can be found on documented London-made furniture up to about 1720 (cf. 7:20 and 7:55). The metalware is not original, and is of a style popular before 1690.
PRIVATE COLLECTION

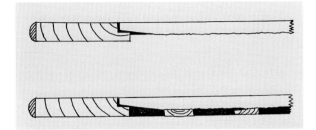

Plate 7:24. Second-phase dustboard and rail construction (1700-35). The most common method was to plough a groove to the thickness of the dustboard and then widen it to accept the rail (top). The alternative was to plough the entire groove to the thickness of the front rail and wedge the dustboards in place (bottom).

Plate 7:25. Detail from 7:26 showing wedged dustboards.

Plate 7:26. Scriptor (1710-30), walnut on a deal carcase. This piece has second-phase construction throughout, suggesting it was made rather later than its external appearance might suggest. The metalware and feet are not original.
NUNNINGTON HALL,
THE NATIONAL TRUST/VICTORIA AND ALBERT MUSEUM

Plate 7:27. Modified second-phase drawer (c.1715-30). This has lapped dovetails, commonly used on second phase drawers in the 1720s. Note also the rounded tops to the drawer sides, which are also slightly stepped down from the drawer front. From a labelled desk-and-bookcase by John Gatehouse.
TEMPLE NEWSAM HOUSE,
LEEDS CITY ART GALLERIES

front. Some makers also preferred to use lapped rather than through dovetails on the drawer front (7:27). Although lapped dovetails were commonly employed for drawers in furniture made of solid timber (cf. 7:18), they were rarely used for veneered furniture until after 1700, and then not commonly until after c.1720.

Plate 7:29. Featherbanded drawer (c.1690-1710). From the Guilbaud scriptor shown in 7:14. This became the most common type of drawer edge banding after 1700.

Plate 7:28. Double-bead rail moulding. This was commonly used from c.1700 until after 1730, although apparently never as popular as the half-round. In this case the moulding is in solid timber, run in the long grain. On veneered furniture it was more usual to apply the moulding in short, cross-grained sections.

The second-phase features discussed so far are internal and made no difference to the external appearance of case furniture. One obvious external change to occur around 1700 was the adoption of the double-bead rail or carcase moulding (7:28). There are no documented examples of this moulding on English case furniture prior to 1700, and this seems a reasonable date *post quem* for this style of moulding, which continued popular into the 1730s. The single half round was not completely superseded, however, and occurs on documented case furniture well into the 1720s.

Another external indicator of eighteenth century date is the use of featherbanded drawer edgings (7:29). Most late seventeenth century drawers were finished either with a plain band of light coloured wood (usually holly or sycamore) or with a crossband of walnut or olive. Fine quality furniture sometimes employed decorative drawer edgings, of which the most common was an interlocked and shaded leaf design, running around the drawer fronts. This was the device used on most arabesque marquetry case furniture from the 1690s onwards (cf. 7:20 and 31). It seems probable that the featherband was a modification of this design, simplified to make production easier and cheaper. While it is difficult to be specific about the date of its introduction, it is very unlikely to have been common before 1700. As a general rule, featherbanded drawers occur only occasionally in combination with first-phase construction, and this again points to an early eighteenth rather than late seventeenth century date.

One final point to note regarding second-phase construction is the transference of the cabinet base moulding from the cabinet to the lower carcase or stand, a development which preceded full second-phase construction by some years. On the scriptor by John Guilbaud, discussed above, the base moulding is no longer integral to the upper case, but fixed instead to the top of the lower carcase. Similarly, the scriptor in 7:30, which has standard first-phase carcase and drawer construction, also has the base moulding for the upper case attached to the lower carcase. This became almost universal practice by about 1710. The change might relate to the gradual

Plate 7:30. Scriptor (1690-1710). Princeswood on deal and wainscot. This has first-phase construction throughout with the exception that the base moulding of the upper carcase is no longer integral to it, being fixed instead to the lower case. This became standard 18th century practice.   W.R. HARVEY & CO.

obsolescence of the cabinet-on-stand and its replacement by the cabinet-on-chest. Notionally, the cabinet and its stand were separate pieces of furniture, so that the base moulding naturally belonged to the cabinet and not the stand or table on which it stood. By 1690 this concept was fading fast and the cabinet or scriptor began increasingly to be unified with a lower case of drawers. Some specimens might be Carolean, but the majority are probably later, since documentary references to cabinets and scriptors 'upon a Chest of Drawers' do not become common until the 1690s.[11]

Many surviving scriptors and cabinets on chests are marriages, because the original stands proved both flimsy and impractical in the long term. Hence it was quite normal for a scriptor to be removed from its stand and mounted on a chest of drawers. While many of these marriages are recent, others are of longer duration. A remarkable bill from the London cabinet-maker John Gumley (later cabinet-maker to George I) describes the creation of such a marriage in 1695:

	£	s	d
ffor Crapen of a new worken of a Woolt Scrutore and putten in severall peeces	00-	12-	00
Ffor new vernishen of the Scrutore	00-	10-	00
ffor taken of the loocks and new Clennen of them and maken a new Key to them	00-	05-	00
ffor new Drops and Skuchons and Butons of Brass lackquered	00-	05-	00
for Linnen the Scrutore with Green Cloth and binding itt round	00-	03-	00
Ffor maken a new Chest to ye Scrutore	02-	00-	00[12]

Roughly translated, this relates how Gumley first scraped, repaired and re-varnished the scriptor, then removed and cleaned the locks. He supplied new handles and escutcheons of lacquered brass and lined the fall with cloth. Finally he made a new chest of drawers on which the scriptor could be placed. The redundant stand was then made into a table:

ffor maken of a table of the frame of a woolt Scrutore and vernish itt	00-	15-	00

Another scriptor, already on a chest of drawers, was converted to a cabinet by the simple expedient of cutting the fall vertically in half:

ffor new Crapen of a Scrutore on a Chest of Drawers and new woorken of itt and putten in severall peeces and Cutten the doors to make it a Cabinett and fineeren the side of the doors and maken two large drawers	02-	00-	00
ffor new vernishen the Cabinett on the Chest of Drawers	01-	02-	00

Conversions of this sort are quite common and can usually be detected by discrepancies in the design of the fall, which originally was in one piece and not two. 7:31 shows an obvious example. Additionally, the interior arrangement of cabinets and scriptors was different; scriptors always had an open shelf below the central cupboard in which papers could be placed when the fall was shut. They also usually had a row of pigeon-holes directly beneath the frieze. On cabinets these spaces were generally occupied by drawers. In the above cited case it appears that Gumley made two new drawers for the converted scriptor, perhaps to fit where the pigeon-holes have been removed.

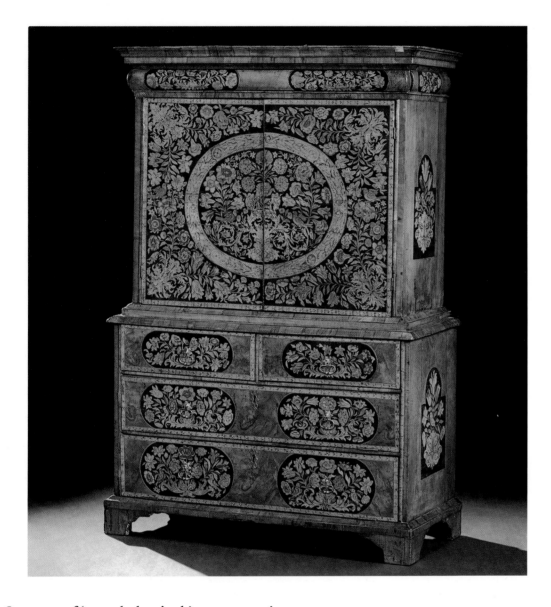

Plate 7:31. Converted scriptor (1690-1710), walnut and marquetry. The fall of this scriptor has been cut in half and hinged at the sides to create a cabinet. Not all conversion are this obvious. Note the crowded style of marquetry and leafy, interlocked drawer banding, both indicative of a late date. SOTHEBY'S

Summary of 'second-phase' cabinet construction, 1700-30

Carcase:	as first-phase.
Interior:	small divisions in cabinets as first-phase.
Dustboards:	'stepped' construction, with ½in. (12.5mm) front rail and thinner dustboards, usually rebated into the rear edge of the rail. First-phase full thickness dustboards occasionally found as late as c.1720.
Drawers:	small interior drawers as first-phase. Larger external drawers have through or (less commonly) lapped dovetails. Bottoms are raised, glued up to the sides, and runners added. Drawer sides frequently rounded on the top edge and stepped down from the drawer front. Drawer fronts often featherbanded around the edges.
Mouldings:	Main carcase mouldings as first-phase, except that on two-part carcases the base moulding nominally belonging to the upper case is attached to the lower case. Rail mouldings either half-round or double-bead.
Feet:	Bun or 'ball'.

Plate 7:32. Bureau (c.1672), attributed to Pierre Gole. Brass and pewter marquetry on an oak carcase. The top was originally hinged twice to fold back against the upper drawers, while the long upper drawer is sham, with a fall front. 					BOUGHTON HOUSE, THE DUKE OF BUCCLEUCH

Plate 7:33. Bureau table (1690-1720), burr maple with rosewood crossbanding and pewter stringing. The top folds back and the 'drawer' front lets down to reveal a writing surface, fitted with small drawers at the back. The bright yellow colour of the maple was probably achieved by staining with nitric acid. 							RANKIN TAYLOR ANTIQUES

Plate 7:34. Bureau table (1700-30), walnut. A very pleasing example, simple but functional and well made. The handles are not original. 				BENINGBOROUGH HALL, THE NATIONAL TRUST

Bureau tables and desks

Modern parlance has reversed the original meanings of 'desk' and 'bureau'. The modern bureau has a sloping front which opens to reveal a fitted interior and writing surface, and the modern desk is a flat-topped writing table with drawers beneath. In the late seventeenth century a desk was a box or board with a sloping surface, either for reading and writing, whereas a bureau was a flat-topped table, usually with drawers under.[13]

Bureaux were originally conceived in France towards the end of the seventeenth century[14] and seem to have been developed from the conventional 'triad' tables. Contemporary illustrations show them placed against a pier, usually with a looking-glass over, but not necessarily with stands *en suite*.[15] One of the earliest English references occurs in a bill of Gerrit Jensen, whose furniture was much influenced by French models. In January 1688 he supplied 'a little Bewre Wallnuttree' to Colonel James Grahme of Levens Hall, Westmorland, for the sum of £4.[16] Among the furniture supplied by Jensen to the Duchess of Somerset in April 1690 were 'a Glass in a black Japan frame and a Table to fall Like a Bewro and Stands £16'. The following year he supplied her with 'a fine Markatree Bewro and Guilt pillars, a pare of Stands and Glass of the same £30.'[17]

The wording of these bills throws an interesting light on the early form of the bureau and on its use. In both cases the bureau is associated with a looking glass and candlestands, which suggests that it was an alternative to the conventional triad. The 'Guilt pillars' reveal that some examples stood on pillar legs in the manner of a French *bureau Mazarin*. The phrase 'to fall Like a Bewro' is intriguing and the most plausible interpretation is that it referred to a hinged fall-front, of the kind now called a 'secretaire' drawer. The bureau in 7:32, attributed to the Parisian cabinet-maker Pierre Gole, has such a drawer, and this may have been the model for Jensen's various 'Bewros'.[18] Most English bureaux are modest by comparison, but numerous examples with fall-front drawers survive. Some, like that in 7:33, have a kneehole, and others, like that in 7:34, do not. Unlike later Georgian models, the secretaire does not draw out. Instead the top hinges back half-way to allow the sitter room to work.

Another new type of furniture which seems to have emerged during the 1690s was the purpose-made writing table with folding top. In October 1690 Gerrit Jensen supplied three folding tables for Queen Mary's use at Kensington Palace, one of 'Cinamont wood' (*Cinnamomum camphora* – camphorwood), one of 'Markatree' and one 'flowred'.[19] These are described as each having six 'pillars' or legs, and probably looked like the table in 7:35. This type of table survives in considerable numbers, and in varying qualities. When not in use the table stands closed against a wall. The top folds forward to rest on the two middle pillars which swing out on gates to support

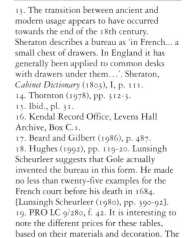

13. The transition between ancient and modern usage appears to have occurred towards the end of the 18th century. Sheraton describes a bureau as 'in French... a small chest of drawers. In England it has generally been applied to common desks with drawers under them...'. Sheraton, *Cabinet Dictionary* (1803), I, p. 111.
14. Thornton (1978), pp. 312-3.
15. Ibid., pl. 31.
16. Kendal Record Office, Levens Hall Archive, Box C.1.
17. Beard and Gilbert (1986), p. 487.
18. Hughes (1992), pp. 119-20. Lunsingh Scheurleer suggests that Gole actually invented the bureau in this form. He made no less than twenty-five examples for the French court before his death in 1684. [Lunsingh Scheurleer (1980), pp. 390-92].
19. PRO LC 9/280, f. 42. It is interesting to note the different prices for these tables, based on their materials and decoration. The camphorwood table was cheapest, at £4.10s. The Markatree table cost £6.15s., and the 'flowred' version was the dearest at £9 exactly.

Plate 7:35. Writing table (1690-1700), marquetry of walnut and holly. This is a high quality example of a common type. The pillar legs suggest an early date, and the marquetry is comparable to pieces attributed to Jensen.
CLANDON PARK, COUNTRY LIFE

Plate 7:36. Writing table (1690-1710), walnut. This is a joiner-made piece, in solid walnut, but in a fashionable style. It is fitted with drawers to each end.
FAIRFAX HOUSE, YORK

Plate 7:37. Writing table (open). The baize-lined top lifts to reveal a shallow well for papers.

20 .'For a Desk writing Table to stand under ye Cabonett... £6.o.o.'. PRO LC 9/280, f. 44.

it. In contrast with the sophistication of 7:35, the next example is probably joiner-made, pre-dominantly of solid walnut, and with the top constructed in the manner of a parquet floor (7:36). It has drawers at each end and compartments for papers inside the top (7:37). The rather fussy and etiolated turning of the pillars might suggest an early date, perhaps 1695, whereas the more robust faceted pillars of the example in 7:38 are more typical of the period after 1700.

A slightly different form of writing furniture was known as a 'Desk writing Table'. Several were supplied by Gerrit Jensen to the various royal palaces,[20] and the wording of his bills suggests a hybrid, somehow combining the functions of a table and a slope-topped box or desk. Hitherto, most desks were by definition portable, usually a box with a sloping lid enclosing a well, sometimes fitted with small drawers or pigeon-holes. Many thousands of these survive, usually of oak, and in a vernacular context they continued to be made and used well into the eighteenth century. The 'desk writing table', on the other hand, was more or less static and was perhaps similar to the examples shown in 7:39 and 7:40. In contrast to the portable desk, this is fixed to a gated frame in the same way as conventional folding tables. Instead of opening upwards, as is the case with most portable desks, the fall is hinged at the base, and folds down to make a flat surface or 'table'. Note that the fall folds on top of the carcase sides and not within them. This is a constructional link with the portable desk-box from which the desk-table was derived and distinguishes these first models from later examples, on which the fall closes within the carcase sides.

Plate 7:38. Writing table (1700-1715) walnut. Another joiner-made piece (note the solid construction and exposed joints), but probably a few years later in date. The faceted pillar legs are commonly found after 1700, and the beaded lower edge to the carcase below the drawer is an early eighteenth century introduction. SOTHEBY'S

Plate 7:40. Detail of 7:39. CHRISTIE'S

Plate 7:39. Desk-table (1690-1710), walnut and marquetry. This is a very typical example, with high quality marquetry, although the twist-turned legs strike a slightly archaic note. Note the overhung desk with shallow slope to the fall and the pen drawer to one side. CHRISTIE'S

Plate 7:41. Desk-table (1700-20), walnut. This is a rare type, although eminently practical. The top is hinged and ratcheted so that it can be used sloping or flat. Indicators of early 18th century date include the featherbanded top, the ogee edge moulding, double bead carcase mouldings, beaded lower edge to the carcase, faceted pillar legs and stylised scroll feet. The concave stretcher allows room for the feet (cf. 7:46). CHRISTIE'S

Plate 7:42. Bureau table (1700-20), red japanning on a deal ground. This ingenious piece functions both as a writing table and as a chest of drawers. The folding top is leather lined and has a built-in adjustable reading slope. This is a rare type, perhaps because difficult and expensive to make, but other examples are known. MALLETT

A variant form of desk-table is shown in 7:41. In this case the flat top is hinged to rise and is supported by a ratchet behind. Several design features suggest a date after 1700 and perhaps as late as 1720. The double bead carcase mouldings are unlikely to date from before 1700 and the faceted pillar leg and stylised scroll feet are both typically post-1700 features. The cockbeaded lower edge of the carcase is also an eighteenth century feature found, for instance, on contemporary card tables. Finally, the standard seventeenth century ovolo edge moulding to the top has been superseded by an eighteenth century ogee.

The forward-hinged gateleg frame which is a feature of most of these desk-tables is not the easiest to use and is wasteful of space, since the structure of the lower frame inhibits its use for further storage. An ingenious solution was contrived by the maker of the japanned bureau in 7:42, but a neater solution was to support the fall on sliding lopers concealed within the carcase. The desk in 7:43 is an early example of this form. The arabesque marquetry, overhung top and pillar leg all suggest an early date, perhaps a few years either side of 1700. Somewhat later in date is the well-known desk in 7:44, remarkable chiefly for the inscription on the fall, which relates that it was made from the timber of a huge walnut tree blown down in the great storm of 1703. This provides a neat *terminus post quem* for the desk and, allowing for seasoning, it is unlikely to have been made before c.1705. However, a number of design details suggest even this is probably too early. The fall is set within the carcase sides, rather than on top of them (this feature is discussed further in the context of desk-and-bookcases below, page 219) The profile of the waist moulding, with its concave upper surface instead of the usual ogee, is not commonly found until the 1720s. Similarly, the dropped lappet in the centre of the lower carcase rail is found on early cabriole-leg chairs and tables of about 1715-30. A similar date might be proposed for the desk in 7:45.

Plate 7:43. Desk (1690-1710), walnut and marquetry. This is an exquisite piece, with a wonderful patina. The overhung top and architectural pillar legs both suggest that this an early example of the type. CHRISTIE'S

Plate 7:44. Desk (after 1703, perhaps 1710-20), walnut. The faceted pillar leg is one of the most popular early 18th century forms. Note that this piece and the next have their fall enclosed between the carcase sides, unlike 7:42-3 and 7:46. This was a common-sense development which had probably occurred by about 1710. PARTRIDGE FINE ART

Plate 7:45. Desk (1715-30), walnut. Like the previous example, this has a dropped centre to the lower carcase rail. This is a feature which occurs on cabriole leg chairs and tables after about 1715. Note also the featherbanded drawers and double-bead carcase mouldings. CHRISTIE'S

7:46. Desk-with-drawers (1695-1715), walnut and marquetry. The shallow, overhung fall, arabesque marquetry and first-phase construction all point to an early date. The handles and feet are not original.   MONTACUTE HOUSE, THE NATIONAL TRUST

The origins of the desk-and-bookcase

The abundance of second-phase scriptors is testament to their continuing popularity after 1700 – scriptors or 'scrutores' are listed among the stock-in-trade of London cabinet-makers well into the 1720s. Nevertheless, the conversions described in John Gumley's bill, quoted above, suggest that the fall-front scriptor was not a particularly convenient form of furniture for casual or everyday use. The extraordinarily good interior condition of many scriptors and cabinets is evidence that their many small drawers and pigeon-holes often saw little use, and from 1700 onwards their status as the pre-eminent product of the cabinet-maker's workshop was in decline. The introduction of bureaux-tables and desk-tables during the 1690s indicates that alternative and less ponderous types of writing furniture were becoming favoured for small apartments, while for principal rooms an entirely new form of furniture was emerging. The desk-and-bookcase (now commonly called a bureau bookcase) combined the functions of cabinet, scriptor and pier glass in one and, since it became one of the most popular and prestigious of all eighteenth century furniture types, it is worth spending time discussing its origins and early development.

The desk-and-bookcase was essentially a conjunction of three separate pieces of furniture – a chest of drawers, a desk and a bookcase. In the same way that the bureau-table was conceived as a pier table with drawers under, so the desk with drawers developed from the desk-table on stand. The earliest documentary reference to a desk in this form occurs in the inventory of Dyrham Park, where 'a writing Desk wth Drawers' was recorded in the Family Parlor in 1710.[21] This article was not in the room when the previous inventory was taken in 1703, which suggests that it was only recently acquired.[22] Interestingly, the notion of the desk-with-drawers as a combination of two distinct parts was still alive a century later, when Sheraton referred to 'common desks with drawers under them'.[23]

The Dyrham Park desk does not survive, but we can make a number of reasonable assumptions about these first desks-with-drawers. First, we would expect them to have first-phase carcase and drawer construction. Second, their surface decoration, where present, should be consistent with a

21. Walton (1986), p. 56.
22. Gloucestershire Record Office, E254.
23. Sheraton (1803), I, p. 111

date of about 1700. Third, their form should exhibit some traces of their hybrid conception. Based on these criteria, the example in 7:46 seems a worthy candidate. It has a first-phase carcase and drawers arranged around the kneehole. The topmost long drawer is sham and the space it encloses is a well accessible only from inside the desk. This interior well became a standard feature of most English desks well into the 1730s. The japanned desk in 7:47 is probably of a similar date and shares the early-type fall which closes on to the carcase sides, not between them. This method of closure was rather insecure, since the fall could easily be forced by a tool inserted from the side, and it was probably for this reason that it became more usual to close the fall within the carcase sides (7:48-49). This subsequently became standard eighteenth century practice. This desk, as well as having a later type of fall, has a first-phase carcase with modified first-phase drawers, having raised bottoms and runner strips all round, suggesting a probable date of 1700-1710.

On all these examples the 'desk' appears separate, over-hanging the base by a good margin, as if added as an afterthought. The width of the overhang is determined by the thickness of the boards used for the desk sides, which are often simply nailed or rebated to the top of the lower carcase. This is an astonishingly crude method of assembly, soon abandoned in favour of a one-piece carcase on which the desk sides are formed by extending the carcase sides upwards. On most of

Plate 7:47. Black japanned desk-with-drawers (1695-1715). This is virtually identical to the previous example, save for the decoration. The standardisation of design argues a high degree of consensus about how a desk-with-drawers should be made.   SOTHEBY'S

Plate 7:48. Desk-with-drawers (1700-1710), walnut and marquetry on a deal carcase. A first-phase carcase with transitional drawers, having raised bottoms with rebated slips all round. The fall now closes within the carcase sides, making the desk more secure. The handles and feet are replaced.   CAVENDISH FINE ARTS

Plate 7:49. The same desk open, showing the typically simple interior arrangement.

these early models the shallow angle of the fall corresponds with those on contemporary desk-tables, and the simple layout of the interior, lacking the later central cupboard, is typical (7:49-50).

It seems an obvious step to set a bookcase on top of the desk-with-drawers to create a combined desk-and-bookcase, but the documentary evidence suggests that the complete ensemble was some years in the making. One of Gerrit Jensen's bills for 1691 describes a 'Desk writeing Table to stand under ye Cabonett' made for Queen Mary at Whitehall, and this is the first documentary record of a desk being associated with a cabinet above it.[24] Another, made in 1694, was described as a writing table with 'a cabinet to set over it... with Doors finely inlayed with Mettel.[25] In 1698 Jensen was paid for 'new varnishing and mending the Desk and bookcase' which stood in the Gallery at Kensington Palace, and this is the first time the phrase 'desk and bookcase' occurs in the Lord Chamberlain's accounts.[26] The bill also makes clear that the whole article was decorated with 'markatree'. This might well have been a fully-fledged desk-and-bookcase, but the reference must be treated with caution, since there is no mention of any form of lower carcase. For the first unequivocal reference to a fully formed desk-and-bookcase in the modern sense, with a full lower carcase fitted with drawers, we must wait until an entry in the *Spectator* of March 1711. This advertised the stock in trade of Thomas Pistor, deceased, among which were 'Three fine japan'd and walnut cabinetts, one Indian scrutore, one wainscott Desk and Bookcase on Drawers...'.[27]

At some point between 1698 and 1711, then, the desk-and-bookcase entered the repertoire of London cabinet-makers. Gerrit Jensen made several for the Royal Household from 1710 onwards and in April 1714 John Gumley advertised in *The Lover* a varied selection of furniture, including 'Desk and Book-Cases'.[28] He supplied one such, 'a Wallnuttree Desk & Bookcase with a glass Door' costing £12, for the Princess's Dressing Room at St James's Palace in 1716.[29]

Genuinely early examples of the complete desk-and-bookcase are rare, although one sees numerous 'William and Mary' examples in sale catalogues. Like the contemporary desk-with-

24. PRO LC 9/280, f. 44.
25. PRO LC 9/280.
26. PRO LC 11/5, f. 141.
27. Beard and Gilbert (1986), p. 700.
28. PRO LC 9/284, f. 62; Beard and Gilbert (1986), p. 379.
29. PRO LC 9/286, f. 14.

Plate 7:50. Desk-with-drawers (1700-15), walnut. A similar piece, to 7.49 with figured veneers rather than marquetry. The enclosed fall, featherbanded drawers and cockbeaded edge to the kneehole all suggest an early 18th century date. Handles, escutcheons and feet are not original.
NORMAN ADAMS LTD.

Plate 7:51. Desk-and-bookcase (1700-1715), walnut and marquetry. These are very rare. The handles and escutcheons are replaced and the feet are missing.

Plate 7:52. Desk-and-bookcase (1700-1715), walnut. Note the absence of a moulding between the bookcase and the desk, and the lack of candleslides. The desk has the early shallow fall closing on to the desk sides. Metalware and feet are replaced. NORMAN ADAMS LTD.

drawers, the first desks-and-bookcases are likely to be those with first-phase carcase and drawer construction. Some are decorated with arabesque marquetry (7:51), others with figured walnut veneers (7:52). The early type enclosed fall is particularly uncommon and was probably a short-lived type.

The construction of these early models gives them a rather thrown-together look. There is often little or no moulding between the bookcase and the desk top and the overhung desk appears to perch precariously on the drawers below. It has already been remarked that the overhung desk was an inherently weak construction. Far better to make the carcase in one piece, with the sides of the

7:53. Black japanned desk-and-bookcase (1713). A fine expression of the English high baroque style, signed by its maker, W. Price, and dated 1713. It demonstrates the rapid development of the type, which twenty years earlier was unknown. This is the earliest documented example of the double arched cornice. Features to note include the enclosed fall; the bookcase located within a moulding fixed to the top of the desk; the flush-sided construction with waist moulding. As with all other desks-and-bookcases prior to about 1725, the bookcase mirrors are set proud of the doors within a bold projecting moulding. Handles, escutcheons and feet are not original.   SOTHEBY'S

7:54. Japanned cabinet on chest (1710-30). Another example of the double arched cornice, which was one of the most popular baroque forms. This cornice entailed a great deal more work than the standard flat version and therefore represents a more expensive option. Although notionally derived from architectural sources, it was probably devised by cabinet-makers to accentuate the newly fashionable arched mirror plates.   SOTHEBY'S

Plate 8:19. Daniel Marot, *Second Livre d'Appartements,* Plate 6 (1703). Note the similarities between the middle design and the Burley chairs.

Plate 8:18. Elbow chair (c.1702). Walnut frame with original velvet covers. This is a chair of the finest quality, made for the State Bedroom at Burley-on-the-Hill, Rutland. Compare the fore-rail with that shown in Marot's design (8:19).   SOTHEBY'S

Plate 8:20. Elbow chair (1695-1705).
Walnut frame, upholstery not original.
This is one of a set (now dispersed)
from Rushbrooke Hall, Suffolk. A high
quality 'corner horsebone' chair with
both the arm supports and legs 'cut
through' into three scrolls each.
TREASURER'S HOUSE, YORK,
THE NATIONAL TRUST

A similar suite of chairs was formerly at Rushbrooke Hall, Suffolk (8:20). The powerfully moulded legs and arm supports are cut through, a feature which recurs on both upholstered and caned chairs. The general form is very similar to the two previous examples, and the design of the fore-rail suggests a date a few years either side of 1700.

Splendid though they are, the Drayton, Burley and Rushbrooke chairs are all eclipsed by the chair in 8:21, which was made by Thomas Roberts in 1702. This is Queen Anne's coronation throne, described in the Lord Chamberlain's warrants as 'a Rich Chair of State the top of the back Carv'd with a Lyon and Unicorn and Sheilds [sic], Cypher and Crown and Scepters in the Lower parts Carv'd rich all gilt'.[17] It was made *en suite* with a footstool and originally covered with a blue and gold silk brocade, which cost a staggering £72.0.0. The frames, by comparison, cost £17.0.0. for the chair and £3.0.0. for the stool.[18]

So far as State or 'parade' furniture is concerned, the Coronation throne represents the zenith of the horsebone chair's development. Although the type continued to evolve until after 1710 (cf. 8:67-77), it is significant that Roberts submitted no bills for horsebone chairs after 1704, concentrating instead on new forms, of which the most important was the 'cross-frame' or cross-stretchered chair.

17. PRO LC/5 44, f. 157.
18. Ibid. The chair is discussed in Coleridge (1967), p. 67; Beard (1997), p. 141; Bowett, 'Horsebone' (1999), p. 266.

Plate 8:21. Chair of State (1702), supplied by Thomas Roberts for the Coronation of Queen Anne. This regal expression of baroque chair design constitutes the high water mark of the English horsebone chair. Although the type continued to evolve until after 1710, it rapidly lost ground in fashionable circles to the new 'cross-stretcher' chair.   HATFIELD HOUSE, THE MARQUIS OF SALISBURY

Plate 8:22. Chair of State (c.1697-1702). Walnut, with original upholstery. This important chair, one of a pair, introduces several innovations in English chair design. Both back and seat are 'false', i.e., removable, and located within moulded and carved frames. The legs are conceived as classical pillars and the stretchers or 'cross-frames' are an entirely new type.

HARDWICK HALL, THE NATIONAL TRUST

Cross-stretchers and pillar legs

In contrast to the horsebone chair, whose lineage extends back to the late 1670s, the 'cross-frame' or cross-stretcher chair was an entirely new introduction of the 1690s. This is made explicit in Thomas Roberts' first bill for such a chair, submitted in 1694: 'for one elbow chair carved rich made of a new fashion with a cross frame & false back & seat with mouldings carved round the back and seate with a handsome rail carved on top of the back Japann'd black... £2.15.00.'.[19]

A chair similar to this description is shown in 8:22, together with one of five surviving stools *en suite* (8:23). The chair is one of a pair, perhaps made to accompany a State bed supplied by Francis Lapiere to the Duke of Devonshire in 1697. The attribution is not certain, however, and the chairs might conceivably relate to bills for other seat furniture supplied by Thomas Roberts in 1702.[20]

19. PRO LC/9 280, f. 189.
20. Beard (1996), p. 133, figs. 108-9; Bowett (2000), pp. 344-5; Beard and Gilbert (1986), p. 753.
21. PRO LC/9 280, f. 376.
22. PRO, LC/9 282, f. 101.

The splayed back, which is such a notable feature of the chair, occurs in another of Roberts' bills for 1696: 'for a large handsome chair of State the back made to spread out and the Elbows to turn on the corner'.[21] A similarly splayed back can be seen on Queen Anne's coronation throne (8:21) and another chair with a back 'to spread out at Top' is recorded in one of Roberts' bills of 1702.[22]

The moulded frames to the seat and back, enclosing 'false' or removable upholstery, are also novel features, but our primary concern is with the cross-stretcher and pillar leg, both seen here for the first time. The stretcher is a typical early pattern, consisting of four flat quadrant arcs with moulded upper surfaces and centred by a turned finial. The pillar leg is likewise an early model, strongly architectural in form, with a gadrooned capital and tapered, stop-fluted shaft. The same leg and cross-frame can be seen on the desk and chair in Plate 4 of Marot's *Nouveau Livre Da Partements* (1703, 8:24) and an enriched version of it occurs on a couch bearing the cipher of the Duke of Leeds, which was probably made for his house at Kiveton, Yorkshire, about 1700 (8:25).[23]

Plate 8:23. Stool (c.1697-1702) *en suite* with the Chair of State in 8:22. Curved 'quadrant' stretchers appear to be an early form, in contrast with the complex curves of later examples.

Plate 8:24. Daniel Marot, *Nouveaux Livre Da Partements* (1703), Plate 4. This depicts William III's library at Het Loo, and shows a desk and chair with pillar legs and curved quadrant stretchers.

Plate 8:25. Couch (c.1700). Giltwood frame with original cut velvet upholstery, attributed to Philip Guibert. This was made for Thomas Osborne, Duke of Leeds, probably for his house at Kiveton, Yorkshire (built 1697-1705). Although unusually elaborate, both the pillar legs and quadrant stretchers are of an early form.   TEMPLE NEWSAM HOUSE, LEEDS CITY ART GALLERIES

Plate 8:27. Detail of 8:26, showing the fluted shaft and capital of the leg and the pierced and carved stretcher.

Plate 8:26. Chair (1695-1705). Japanned beechwood frame, original upholstery and fringes. This is one of a pair at Drumlanrig Castle. As with the previous example, the form of the leg and stretcher is early, although the latter is unusually decorated.   DRUMLANRIG CASTLE, THE DUKE OF BUCCLEUCH

Plate 8:28. Elbow chair (1695-1795). Original silk upholstery and fringes. Turned pillar legs were less tied to architectural forms, resulting in some fanciful and decorative conceptions. Note that the out-turned arm terminals conform to those found on contemporary horsebone chairs.

BOUGHTON HOUSE,
THE DUKE OF BUCCLEUCH

Plate 8:29. Detail of 8:28. This shouldered baluster or 'peg-top' rear leg is common to the majority of early pillar leg chairs.

8:26 and 8:27 show a chair of similar date with an unusually ornate stretcher. This is perhaps similar to the type described in a bill submitted by Thomas Roberts in 1696: 'for six square stooles the feet and cross frames carved handsome in Scroles & Japand black... £16.0.0.'.[24]

It was cheaper, of course, to turn the leg than to cut and carve it. On the lathe architectural formality soon gave way to turner's fancy, which accounts for the exaggerated and sometimes bizarre forms seen on some chairs of this type (8:28). In contrast to the fore-legs, the back legs of most early pillar leg chairs are relatively plain, the most common being an inverted 'shouldered' baluster (8:29). Antique dealers sometimes call this a 'peg-top' leg. On later examples this tended to become a baluster proper, without the shoulder between bulb and shaft.

23. Gilbert (1978), II. p. 264-8.
24. PRO LC/9 280, f. 378.

Plate 8:30. Stool (c.1704). Carved and gilt wood, upholstery not original. This stool is part of a suite reputedly installed at Warwick Castle in anticipation of a visit by Queen Anne. Even at this early date the pillar leg has become stylised, and the stretchers increasingly complex. WARWICK CASTLE

Plate 8:31 Detail of 8:30. Note the delicacy of the cutting and the hatched ground, comparable to the detailing of contemporary pier tables supplied to the Royal Palaces by Gerrit Jensen and the Pelletiers.

25. Thornton (1977), p.139.
26. Ibid. One of the chairs with this bed is French, but the rest of the suite appears to be English, probably supplied by Thomas Roberts.
27. PRO LC/9 282, f. 49.
28. PRO LC/9 282, f. 39.

From c.1700 onwards the pillar leg tended to become increasingly stylised, much in the manner of contemporary pier tables. 8:30 shows a stool from a suite at Warwick Castle, reputedly installed in anticipation of a visit by Queen Anne in 1704.[25] The leg (8:31) is less architectural than earlier versions, becoming rather 'weighted' towards the top; the slightly waisted profile with leaf-clasped base occurs on pier tables by both Jensen and the Pelletiers. Also significant is the increasing complexity of the stretcher, shaped in both horizontal and vertical axes. The changing profile of the pillar and the increasingly complex stretcher are both clues to dating which can be confirmed by reference to documented examples (8:32).

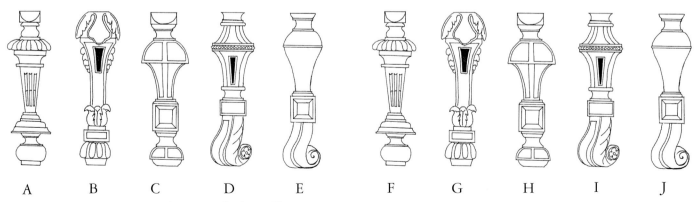

A   B   C   D   E   F   G   H   I   J

Plate 8:32. Pillar leg profiles, 1695-1714. Pillar leg chairs survive much more commonly from after 1700 than before. Leg designs from B onwards all post-date 1700, while the scrolled-foot versions from D onwards cannot realistically be dated prior to 1705.

'French' feet and moulded frames

Alongside the two dominant forms of horsebone and pillar legs were a number of less common leg and stretcher designs, of which that shown in 8:33 is an example. This chair is one of a pair surviving at Hampton Court Palace, almost certainly supplied by Thomas Roberts shortly after 1700. The scrolled leg derives from contemporary French models and the same leg occurs on the stools and chairs made *en suite* with William III's State Bed of 1699 (6:12).[26] One of this suite is almost certainly French and perhaps served as the model for the rest. It is suggestive that among Roberts' bills for the year 1700 is one for chairs with 'French' feet.[27] Could this be a 'French' foot? Possibly, but in absence of better evidence it is perhaps better merely to call it 'scrolled'.

A common feature of several sets of chairs and stools with this type of scrolled leg is the moulded frame enclosing removable upholstery. References to moulded frames occur in several of Roberts' bills after 1700, such as the 'two Arm'd Chair frames made of the best Wallnuttree the frames made moulding work with Carv'd Corner Elbows... £3.10.0.' (1704).[28] As well as the chairs and stools already discussed (8:22 and 8:23), Hardwick Hall contains several sets of stools with moulded frames which are worth discussing. 8:34 is one of six long stool or 'banketts' supplied by

Plate 8:33. Chair (c.1702), attributed to Thomas Roberts. Walnut frame with original upholstery. The leg and stretcher configuration on this chair is taken directly from French models. The style seems to have been briefly popular in England in the years immediately after 1700.

THE ROYAL COLLECTION, ©2002 HER MAJESTY
QUEEN ELIZABETH II

Plate 8:34. Long stool or bankette
(1702), supplied by Thomas Roberts to
the Duke of Devonshire. The drop-in
seat is contained within a moulded
walnut frame with carved 'corners and
middles'.

HARDWICK HALL, THE NATIONAL TRUST

29. Beard and Gilbert (1986), p. 753. This
attribution seems reasonably secure.
Roberts' bill describes '6 Banketts of
wallnuttree all carved with Mouldings
round the seats'.
30. Murdoch (1997), p. 737.
31. PRO 9/281.
32. Beard and Gilbert (1986), p. 753.
33 The first reference to this feature occurs
in 1703: 'For three Wallnuttree elbow
Chairs Carved and arched fore Rails and
Backs...' PRO LC 9/281, f. 201.

Plate 8:35. Long stool or bankette (c.1702). Carved and gilt wood with
later upholstery. Perhaps supplied by Thomas Roberts.

HARDWICK HALL, THE NATIONAL TRUST

Roberts to the Duke of Devonshire in 1702, combining delicately moulded scrolled legs with
addorsed and pierced central stretchers.[29] 8:35 is a more elaborate example, perhaps also by Roberts.
The decoration of the rails on all these stools, with their reserves of shallow carving separated by
lengths of plain moulding, is of a type also found on contemporary mirror and picture frames and
known at the time by the wonderfully descriptive phrase 'corners and middles'.[30]

Stylistic affinities with examples of Roberts' work at Hardwick and Hampton Court might
suggest a similar attribution for a large suite of furniture at Penshurst Place (8:36 and 8:37). These
pieces combine moulded rails and scrolled legs with a flat, French-style stretcher. The whole suite
exhibits the highest degree of luxury; all the show-wood is gilt, and the frames are carved along
their entire length. The form of the day bed roughly corresponds to a description given in one of
Roberts' bills for 'one long couch frame richly carved round the back and seat finely gilt' (1702).[31]
It has been suggested that the entire suite might have been a royal commission, acquired by the
Earl of Leicester after William III's death.[32] The scrolled-over back occurs on other day beds of this
date, but the extraordinary shell cresting is apparently unique. The
date is probably 1700-05.

The most obvious difference between late seventeenth and early
eighteenth century upholstered chairs is in the shape of the back.
With a very few exceptions, seventeenth century upholstered chairs
had rectangular backs with square tops and these continued to be
made in the early years of the next century. Within a few years,
however, the square back gave way almost entirely to the shaped or
arched back. This transition, which is amply documented in
Roberts' bills,[33] is an important dating criterion for English seat
furniture.

The change from square to arched backs is embodied in the
back-chairs of the Penshurst suite (8:37). The back is arched both
top and bottom, as is the lower edge of the seat rails. Of a similar
date is the chair in 8:38, one of a pair at Dyrham Park. The general
shape and proportions are late seventeenth century, but the gentle
arch to the top suggests a post-1700 date. This hypothesis is
strengthened by their association with an entry in the 1703
inventory of Dyrham, which records '2: Elbow velvet Chairs wth

Plate 8:36. Daybed (1700-05). Carved and gilt wood frame, original upholstery. The moulded seat rails, scrolled leg and flat stretcher all occur on furniture supplied by or attributed to Thomas Roberts, which raises the distinct possibility that this extraordinary daybed is also by Roberts. Note the dropped wooden 'aprons' beneath the seat rails; this is probably the earliest manifestation of this new feature, which became increasingly popular from this time onwards.

PENSHURST PLACE, THE LORD DE L'ISLE

Plate 8:37. Chair (1700-05). Carved and gilt wood frame, original upholstery. This is one of six chairs *en suite* with the day bed. Note the shaping of the back, a revolutionary new feature introduced at the beginning of the 18th century (compare with 8:33).

PENSHURST PLACE, THE LORD DE L'ISLE

Plate 8:38. Elbow chair (c.1703). Walnut frame with later upholstery. This is one of a pair, probably the '2: Velvet Chairs wth Gold ffringe & covers' recorded in the Ante Roome below Stairs at Dyrham Park in 1703. The combination of out-turned 'French' feet and undulating cross-stretcher is highly unusual. Note the slight arch to the back.

DYRHAM PARK, THE NATIONAL TRUST

Gold Fringe' in the Ante Room below Stairs.[34] Since the room in question was not completed until 1702, it is likely that the chairs were brand new at this date.

A slightly later suite of chairs at Dyrham was installed in the Best Bed Chamber between 1703 and 1710 (8:39).[35] The chairs retain their original red and yellow velvet upholstery, matching the hangings of the state bed. The backs are shaped both top and bottom, bearing close comparison with the Penshurst suite. The 'in-line' horsebone legs and fore-rails are perhaps a little old-fahioned by this date, but the side stretchers are a new type, direct descendants of the shaft-and-ball stretcher of the 1690s, now simplified into a tapered shaft only.

Contemporary with the newly-fashionable arched back was the arched fore-rail. Many of Thomas Roberts' between 1700 and 1710 specifically mention this feature, e.g. 'for six square stoole frames wallnuttree feet and arched railes carved and pollished' (1703).[36] The simple arched rail shown in 8:40 is one of the most common designs, but variations on the theme are legion, and can be found on both upholstered and caned furniture. Like the arched back, the arched fore-rail is an important diagnostic feature, indicating an early eighteenth century date.

Plate 8:39. Elbow chair (c.1705). Walnut frame and original velvet upholstery. This is one of a set of chairs *en suite* with a State Bed, installed at Dyrham between 1703 and 1710. Although the 'in-line' horsebone frames are somewhat old-fashioned, the shaping of the backs clearly distinguishes these chairs from late 17th century models. The plain tapered stretchers are another indicator of 18th century date, since they are not found on any documented 17th century chairs. DYRHAM PARK, THE NATIONAL TRUST

Plate 8:40. Stool (1700-1710). Japanned beechwood frame with later upholstery. This is a common model, with a prominent arched fore-rail declaring its post-1700 manufacture. CHRISTIE'S

Plate 8:41. Easy chair (1695-1705). Walnut frame with original red velvet upholstery and fringes. This type of easy chair, with square 'cheeks', was introduced at the end of the 1680s, and was the prototype for the ubiquitous Georgian 'wing' chair. The corner horsebone legs and scrolled fore-rail of this example suggest a date after 1690.   KNOLE, THE NATIONAL TRUST

Plate 8:42. Easy chair (1700-1705). Japanned frame with old green velvet upholstery. This is one of a pair at Boughton House. The 'scrolled cheeks' and arms suggest a date a few years later than the previous example.
                    BOUGHTON HOUSE, THE DUKE OF BUCCLEUCH

Easy chairs and the origins of the sofa

Among the new upholstered seating forms to emerge in the 1690s, the most significant were the 'easy chair' and the 'sofa'. The ancestry of easy chairs extends back to Carolean sleeping chairs like those at Ham House, but at that time they were rather exceptional. Even in the 1690s easy chairs were not common, and usually took the form of a standard elbow chair with rectangular wings or 'cheeks' added. Thomas Roberts supplied such a chair in 1689: 'for one Easey Elbow Chair of Wallnutt carved and cheeks framed down the sides'.[37] Several examples answering this description survive at Holyroodhouse, Edinburgh, and at Knole (8:41). From about 1700 these began to acquire arched backs and the cheeks were also often curved, as in the example in 8:42, one of a pair

34. Walton (1986), pp. 36-37.
35. Bowett Horsebone (1999), pp. 266-7.
36. PRO LC/5 44, f. 202.
37. PRO LC/9 279, f. 75.

Plate 8:43. Easy chair (1705-10). Walnut frame with original upholstery. This chair was discovered at Chastleton House, Oxfordshire. The dilapidated upholstery is original and the pattern of the silk damask top cover has allowed the chair to be dated after 1705. The inverted scroll leg is a common pattern, as is the double-arched fore-rail. Note the tapered stretchers.

VICTORIA & ALBERT MUSEUM

at Boughton House. A year or two later in date is the example in 8:43, formerly at Chastleton House, Oxfordshire. The form corresponds to a type described by Thomas Roberts, having an 'arch back and Scrowle cheeks',[38] and the fragments of original silk upholstery date the chair to after c.1705-06.[39] The inverted-scroll legs are turned 'on the corner' and the powerfully moulded fore-rail rises to a double arched centre. The latter was a popular design for both upholstered and caned chairs and this example serves as a useful reference for unprovenanced chairs having similar fore-rails.

Although bills for individual easy chairs are not uncommon, it became usual to include easy chairs in a suite, together with a set of back-chairs and a State bed (indeed, inventory evidence reveals that easy chairs were originally bedroom furniture, and only later translated to the drawing room). In some cases, a sofa was also introduced. Like many other furnishing innovations, the sofa or 'saffaw' was introduced into England from France, but it was ultimately of Islamic origin. A contemporary French commentator described it as 'un éspece de lit de repos de la maniere des Turcs'.[40]

The word sofa first occurs in the Royal Household accounts for 1697, when Philip Guibert supplied 'a fine black soffa of a new fashion, filled up with fine hair, and its cushion filled up with down, the frieze and cheeks all moulded and fringed... £14. 0. 0.'.[41] The sofa differed from the conventional couch in having a very high back and (usually) enclosed sides or 'cheeks'. The upholstery, which on conventional chairs and couches essentially followed the rectilinear outline of the frame, was extravagantly moulded and fringed.

Thomas Roberts was among several English makers who quickly incorporated the sofa into their repertoires. In 1701 he supplied two 'saffaws' with carved frames to the Duchess of Monmouth,[42] and in 1704 he supplied to St James's Palace 'a large Sopha made of French Wallnuttree Pollished, and arch back and Scrowle Cheeks and Elbows... £4.5.0.'.[43] (The difference in price between Roberts' and Guibert's sofa is accounted for by the fact that Roberts' bill was for the frame only.) In 1706 he supplied Queen Anne with a pair of 'Settees... made of best Wallnuttree carv'd feet cross frames Scrowled cheeks roling arms and pollished... £9.0.0.'.[44] The terms sofa and settee appear to be synonymous.

No documented sofas of the 1690s are known, but one of the earliest examples is that in 8:44, made for Thomas Coningsby of Hampton Court, near Leominster, about 1700. It has the early form of pillar leg and quadrant stretcher, and a double arched back with scrolled cheeks and 'rolling' arms. The sides are straight but slightly splayed from back to front. 8:45 is a few years later in date. Its fore-rail compares closely with the Chastleton chair, the back is arched and both the arms and the cheeks are rolled. The date is perhaps about 1705-15.[45] The extraordinary height of the back was a relatively short-lived phenomenon and most early Georgian sofas are considerably lower.

38. PRO LC/9 282, f. 35.
39. Thornton 'Upholstered evidence' (1974), p. 18.
40. Thornton (1978), p. 212.
41. PRO, LC 11/5, f. 88.
42. DEFM, p. 753.
43. PRO LC/9 282, f. 112.
44. PRO LC/9 283, f. 112.
45. Similar examples are illustrated in DEF, III, p. 74, fig. 7 and p. 76, fig. 11.

252

Plate 8:44. Sofa (1695-1705). Walnut frame with original upholstery. This is probably the earliest surviving English sofa. It was made for Hampton Court, near Leominster, the home of Thomas Coningsby. The pillar leg and quadrant stretchers are both early forms introduced in the 1690s, although the shaping of the back suggests a date close to 1700.
VICTORIA & ALBERT MUSEUM

Plate 8:45. Sofa (1705-15). Japanned frame with modern upholstery. This sofa, at Penshurst in Kent, has the double-arched fore-rail and tapered stretchers typical of the decade or so after 1700. The rounded back and 'rolled' cheeks and arms both suggest a date close to 1710.   PENSHURST PLACE, THE LORD DE L'ISLE

Plate 8:46. Pair of chairs (1709).
Japanned frame with later upholstery.
These are from a set of ten supplied by
John Burroughs to Stoneleigh Abbey,
Warwickshire. They are the earliest
documented English back-chairs
having fully raked back legs. They are
also the earliest documented examples
having scrolled 'Braganza' feet.
CHRISTIE'S

46. Details of John Burroughs' career can be
found in Beard and Gilbert (1986), p. 133.
However, the entry conflates the careers of
father and son, since John Burroughs senior
died in or before 1683 [G.L. 8046 , Minutes of
the Joiners' Company, 6 Feb. 1783].
47. Christie's, Stoneleigh Abbey sale, 15
October 1981, lots 100 and 101. The sale
catalogue described the chairs as 'William
and Mary' and suggested that Burroughs'
1709 bill was 'too late'. However, there seems
no reason to doubt that these are the chairs
delivered by Burroughs. Not only do they
match the description in the bill, but their
design is entirely consistent with the date.
48. Bowett Horsebone (1999), pp. 269-70.
49. PRO LC/9 284, f. 189. For a further
discussion of the introduction of the raked
back leg see Bowett, Horsebone (1999), pp.
269-70.
50. Hatfield House, Bills 476.

The scrolled foot and raked back leg

Although initially associated with cross-stretcher designs, the pillar leg also came to be made with a conventional H stretcher. The example in 8:46 is one of a set of ten supplied by John Burroughs to the Hon. Mr. Leigh of Stoneleigh Abbey, Warwickshire, in 1709.[46] Burroughs' bill ran as follows:

10 chear frames japaned with gold	10 0	0
2 dozen ½ of curled hare to stuff		
the ten chears	1 2	6
Sowe backing & lining to the chears	- 12	0
guert web	- 10	0
for Princes metall nales used	1 10	0
box (?) & making up 10 chears	1 5	0

The frames retain their black and gold japanning, but the original damask covers were replaced with leather in 1740.[47]

Burroughs' chairs are worth looking at in some detail, because they embody some key stylistic and structural developments which occurred about this time. The arched back with its pierced cresting is mirrored in the rising fore-rail, and both these designs can be found on contemporary cane chairs (cf. 8:67-69). The shaping of the seat rail we have seen on other upholstered chairs and sofas after 1700 (cf. 8:37, 39 and 47), although Burroughs' are perhaps the earliest documented examples. The fore-leg is an even more stylised version of that found on the Warwick stools, and the feet are of particular interest. They take the form of a moulded three-lobed scroll, which many authorities call a 'Spanish' or 'Braganza' foot. Neither of these terms is contemporary and both are misnomers. There is scant evidence that this design originated in Spain and the association with Charles II's queen, Catherine of Braganza, is entirely spurious. Although the three-lobed foot occurs in various forms in the seventeenth century (3:41 and 3:44), the 'Braganza' version shown here is not found on English chairs before 1700. Indeed, John Burroughs' chairs are the earliest documented examples known at the time of writing and represent a realistic date *post quem* for this design.

Finally, and perhaps most importantly, Burroughs' chairs are among the first documented English chairs with fully raked back legs, i.e., raked from the seat down, rather than just in the lower section or 'heel'. It is widely believed that late seventeenth century English chairs can be distinguished from their Continental counterparts by their raked back legs. In fact, with the exception of some sleeping chairs, whose adjustable inclined backs demand radical frame geometry, raked legs do not occur on seventeenth century English chairs. Rather, it was merely the lowest section or 'heel' below the stretcher which was raked or 'compassed', and the main shank of the leg was vertical. The fully raked back leg, raked from the seat rail downwards, was an eighteenth century introduction.[48] The first documentary record of this feature occurs in one of Thomas Roberts' bills for 1708, when he supplied '12 fine Carved Wallnuttree Cain Chaires with Spreading back feet' for Her Majesty's warship the *Royal Anne,* and this tallies closely with their appearance on John Burroughs' chairs in 1709.[49]

All the significant developments described above can be seen on a suite of seat furniture supplied to the Marquis of Salisbury by the upholsterer Thomas How in 1711. The suite comprises a state bed, two easy chairs and eight back chairs. How's bill describes the easy chairs as '2 very handsom Easy Chares with Carveid Sides & Cross Stretchors richly Carveid & gilt with gold' (8:47).[50] They epitomise the high baroque extravagance of the most luxurious late Queen Anne seat furniture – the frame shaped in every line and plane, the upholstery sumptuously padded, moulded and fringed, and the woodwork highly wrought and richly gilt. The stretchers are shaped in all dimensions, pierced through with scrolls and decorated on every surface with shallow relief carving. The leg, sharply tapered and compressed, faceted and pierced, is only just recognisable as a descendant of its architecturally derived forebears, and the richly detailed scroll foot was by this time the very acme of fashionable design.

Plate 8:47. Easy chair (1711). Carved and gilt frame with modern upholstery. This splendid chair is one of a pair supplied by the London upholsterer Thomas How in 1711. The extravagant shaping, highly stylised pillar legs, complex stretcher and scrolled feet are all hallmarks of the high baroque style popular towards the end of Queen Anne's reign. HATFIELD HOUSE, THE MARQUIS OF SALISBURY

Plate 8:48. Chair (1711). Carved and gilt frame with modern upholstery. This is one of eight chairs supplied by Thomas How *en suite* with 8:47. The extreme rake and height of the back necessitate a strongly raked back leg.

Plate 8:49. Chair (1710-15). Carved and gilt frame with original red velvet cover. This is one of a set of four surviving chairs from Hampton Court, Leominster.　MALLET & SON (ANTIQUES) LTD.

The six back-chairs *en suite* differ in one significant respect (8:48). Whereas the easy chairs, with their relatively upright posture, have vertical back legs with raked heels, the steeply inclined back-chairs have fully raked back legs. This strongly suggests that the introduction of the raked back leg was a matter of practical necessity rather than style. Nevertheless, the exaggerated rake found on some examples of this type leads one to suspect that functionality was soon subsumed by fashion (8:49-51).

One consequence of adopting the raked back leg was that the crossing point of the stretchers had to be moved forward. Ordinarily the crossing point was mid-way between front and back legs, but with raked legs the true mid-point was so far back as to make it almost invisible from a frontal view. Hence short extensions were added to the stretchers so as to move the crossing point forward, bringing it approximately under the centre of the seat (8:52).

Plate 8:50. Chair (1710-20). Walnut frame with original silk needlework cover. This chair is one of large set *en suite* with a State bed made for Sir Richard Onslow, who was Speaker of the House of Commons between 1708 and 1715. The shaping of the seat rails is typical of English chairs made during this period.

CLANDON PARK, THE NATIONAL TRUST

Plate 8:51. Chair (1710-20). Walnut frame with modern upholstery. Like the previous example, this has a highly stylised pillar leg, faceted, fluted and gadrooned. The stretcher design is unusual.   NORMAN ADAMS LTD.

Plate 8:52. Detail of 8:48, showing the asymmetric stretcher design made necessary by the raked back legs.

Plate 8:54. Easy chair (1714) Walnut frame with original cover. This was made *en suite* with the State bed in 8:53. The form is unusually restrained, but the round back and 'rolling' arms and sides are typical of the period 1710-20.
THE ROYAL COLLECTION, ©2002 HER MAJESTY QUEEN ELIZABETH II

Plate 8:53. State bed (1714), supplied by Richard Roberts for Queen Anne's use at Windsor.
THE ROYAL COLLECTION, ©2002 HER MAJESTY QUEEN ELIZABETH II

In 1714 Richard Roberts succeeded to Thomas Roberts' post as chairmaker to the royal household.[51] One of his first jobs was to supply a new State bed, a chair and eight stools for Queen Anne's bedchamber at Windsor. By the time the commission was complete in the summer of 1714, Anne was dead. The bed, chair and stools were nevertheless delivered and were later removed to Hampton Court Palace, where they remain (8:53 and 8:54). The chair is still covered in its original red and white figured velvet, now much faded. Notwithstanding the rolled arms and flared seat, the design is modest, with few of the baroque flourishes of many contemporary easy chairs. The broad-arched top and the simple baluster shaped legs occur on numerous undocumented examples, such as the settee and back chair in 8:55 and 8:56. This is part of a large suite formerly at Burley-on-the-Hill and now at Dudmaston in Shropshire. The magnificent needlework covers are reputed to have been worked by the Duchess of Nottingham and her daughters. They are much restored and lack the fringes and other trimmings usually applied to such chairs, but are none the less stunning in their design and colouring. The shape of the back, broader and rounder than hitherto, and similar to the Hampton Court example, is one which remained fashionable for a number of years. Several bills submitted by both Richard Roberts and the upholsterer Thomas Phill in 1716 contain references to chairs with 'compass' or 'round' backs, which almost certainly refer to this form.[52]

51. The precise relationship between Thomas and Richard Roberts is still unclear. It is assumed that Richard was Thomas' son and supplied the Royal Household with seat furniture until his presumed death in 1729. DEFM, p. 752-3.

52. For example: 'for a wallnuttree round back Easy Chair frame carvbed and pollished… £3.10.0.'. PRO LC/9 286, f. 30.

Plate 8:55. Sofa (1715-20). Walnut frame with original (?) woollen needlework cover. This sofa was originally installed at Burley-on-the-Hill. Once again the rounded back suggests a relatively late date, as do the turned baluster legs (compare with 8:54). DUDMASTON, THE NATIONAL TRUST

Plate 8:56. Chair (1715-20). Walnut frame with needlework cover, *en suite* with the sofa in 8:55. A fine example of a 'late' cross-stretcher chair.

Plate 8:57. Caned chair (1699).
Walnut. This extravagant chair
exhibits some curious archaisms in its
twist-turned back, but the pierced
horsebone legs and carved fore-rail are
very much *à la mode*. The arms in the
cresting are those of the Cann family,
and the date 1699 is carved into the
tops of the rear posts.
PARTRIDGE FINE ART

Caned chairs after 1700

It is now time to retrace our steps to describe the development of caned chairs between 1700 and
1714. In many cases the cane chairs follow an identical path to that already described for
upholstered ones – arched tops and fore-rails, scrolled feet and raked legs – and the corroboration
afforded by documented examples suggests that the chronology proposed thus far is essentially
reliable. However, some elements of caned chair design differ markedly from those of upholstered
ones, so that it is worth discussing them separately and in detail.

The oval-backed caned chair was a short-lived phenomenon and few English examples can
confidently be dated much after 1700. The probable explanation for this is that the oval shape
limited the height to which the chair back could be extended, so that as fashion demanded taller
chairs, oval backs quickly lost favour. Compare, for example, the chair in 8:10, which is 40in. tall
(102cm) with the chair in 8:64, which at 66in. (168cm) is over 2ft. (61cm) higher. The trend
towards taller chairs was well under way by the time the chair in 8:57 was made. This finely carved
example exhibits some curious archaisms. It bears the arms of the Cann family and is dated 1699
on the tops of the rear posts. The cut-through leg and arm supports and the scrolling fore-rail are

Plate 8:58. Caned chair (1695-1705). Japanned beechwood. The height of the back has caused the maker to insert additional turnings in the rear posts. The position of the arms, set half-way along the seat rails, is unusual.

TREASURER'S HOUSE, YORK, THE NATIONAL TRUST

Plate 8:59. Chair (1700-1705). Japanned beechwood, with modern upholstery. This superb chair, one of a large set, has two features which probably place it a few years after 1700. The first is the C-scroll crest rail and the second is the tapered stretcher profile.

DRUMLANRIG CASTLE, THE DUKE OF BUCCLEUCH

in the latest style, but the twist-turned rear posts date back twenty years and more.

The same statuesque proportions are possessed by 8:58 and 8:59. Because of the higher backs, the banister turnings are noticeably more extended than on earlier examples. The fore-rails are exactly comparable to those on contemporary upholstered chairs (cf. 8:19 and 8:20), while the C-scroll crest rail of 8:59 is one of the most common post-1700 designs. The 'prototype' can be found on the Hardwick state chairs, which might date from 1697 (above, 8:22, but most examples have structural or stylistic attributes which place them later. Indeed, this crest rail was still fashionable, albeit in a simplified form, in 1709 (cf. 8:64).

Plate 8:60. Caned chair (1700-05). Painted beechwood. This chair and the next example embody several important developments in cane chair design which took place immediately after 1700. The rear posts (in this case square-cut, not turned) are simplified into an extended baluster-and-shaft. The crest and fore-rails are carved with addorsed C-scrolls, giving an upward emphasis to both. Most important of all, the seat frame carries a continuous moulding on its forward edge, and the legs are dowelled into it from below.
VICTORIA & ALBERT MUSEUM

Plate 8:61. Caned chair (1700-05). Painted beechwood. This is so similar to the previous example as to suggest a common maker. BURTON AGNES HALL

The chair in 8:60 is a rare survivor. Underneath the modern green and white paint is its original blue, white and gold finish. The quality of carving and ornament is exceptional and suggests a commission of significant status. The delicate ornamentation implies a decorative rather than practical role and its condition attests to relatively little use. A similar example is shown in 8:61, although in this case the japanning has not survived.

The similarities between these two chairs extend beyond their surface decoration. They both have design features in common which introduce some of the main developments in banister-back chairs after 1700. Compared with the compressed, heavily ringed style of 1690, the profiles of the banisters are noticeably more open and extended. The height of the backs is exaggerated by the narrow caned centre panel, an effect deliberately enhanced by allowing the cane to intrude into the top and bottom cross-rails. The paired C-scrolls of the cresting have the effect of drawing the eye upwards, while the shape of the lower cross-rail exerts a pull in the opposite direction, giving shape and movement to what is still essentially a rectangular form. The fore-rail mimics the crest, again creating an upward stress in its centre. A very similar chair recorded by the late Benno Forman is dated 1703, giving us a good probable date for these two.[53]

Both chairs also have a novel feature in the moulded edge to the seat rails, which demanded a new and unfamiliar method of construction. Instead of the seat rails being tenoned into the tops of the

53. Forman (1988), p. 282, fig. 151.

Plate 8:62. Caned chair (1705-1715). Walnut. This is a crudely made-example, incorporating an archaic 'boyes and crownes' top rail with an up-to-date moulded seat frame.
HADDON HALL

Plate 8:63. Caned chair (1705-15) Walnut. This is another rather crude interpretation of fashionable models. The carving is Carolean in style, but the arched fore-rail and moulded seat frame suggest a date after 1700.
MONTACUTE HOUSE,
THE NATIONAL TRUST

fore-legs, the front and sides of the seat were framed up as a unit, either with half-lapped or mortise and tenon joints, and the legs were then tenoned or dowelled up into its corners. This allowed the outer edge of the seat rails to carry a continuous moulding in imitation of the moulded rails employed on some contemporary upholstered furniture. Compared with the traditional seat construction this method appears structurally unsound, because of the weak joint between seat and fore-leg, but it was certainly popular and, judging by the number of surviving examples, surprisingly strong.

As one might expect, many chairmakers continued to use earlier designs and motifs in com bination with more up-to-date features. The example in 8:62 has moulded seat rails and extended banister profiles, both of which point to a date after 1700, but the 'boyes and crownes' crest rails hark back to the 1690s, and the stretcher turning is a very old-fashioned ball-and-ring. 8:63 shows a crudely made chair whose style of carving has a decidedly Carolean look. However, the extended banisters and moulded seat rails point to an early eighteenth century date, as do the arched back and fore-rail.

Variations in banister turnings and in crest and fore-rail design, though significant, had relatively little impact on the overall structure of caned chairs. The same cannot be said of two innovations which were of paramount importance in the development of English chairs – the superimposed crest rail and the raked back leg.

Plate 8:64. Chair (1709). Walnut, seat and back originally caned. This superb chair was supplied by Charles Hopson for the use of Henry Compton, Bishop of London. It is a fine expression of English baroque chair design and embodies a number of crucial stylistic and technical developments. This front view shows the extended column rear posts which typify late banister-back chairs and it has a superimposed top rail, the first time that this method of construction appears on a documented English chair.   St Paul's Cathedral

Plate 8:65. Side view of 8:64, showing the strongly raked rear leg. This is the first documented example of an English caned chair with a fully raked rear leg.

Plate 8:66. Detail of 8:64, showing the back of the crest rail. The carver's initials RT are stamped twice and the fact that they are upside-down indicates that they were stamped before the chair was assembled.

54. Bowett 'Bishop Compton's elbow chair' (1999).

Prior to 1700 English chairs were invariably made with crest rails set between the rear posts. This was true even in exceptional cases, such as the Hardwick Hall state chairs (8:22), where the design of the back eliminated any visual distinction between the crest rail and posts. By 1710, however, it had become usual to set the crest rail on top of the rear posts and this apparently innocuous development introduced a fundamental change to the structure of English chairs for the first time since the Restoration. Henceforth, almost all English chairs, of whatever style or period, would be made in this way until the early nineteenth century.

With hindsight one can see that the adoption of the superimposed crest rail was a natural consequence of the fashion for shaped tops to chairs. So long as the back panel remained rectangular the crest rail was able to sit comfortably between the rear posts, even if the toprail carried a carved cresting. But if the back panel itself was shaped and extended upward into the area normally occupied by the crest rail, then the structure of the back was compromised and another solution had to be found. This, at least, is one possible explanation of the genesis of the superimposed crest rail.

The introduction of the raked back leg in relation to upholstered chairs has already been mentioned. In the case of caned chairs it is closely linked, both chronologically and structurally, to the superimposed crest rail. The superimposed rail not only heightened chairs still further, but added weight where it would most affect the balance of the chair. Raking the leg brought the

Plate 8:67. Caned chair (1710-20). Walnut. A fine late 'banister-back' chair, with columnar rear posts, a superimposed crest-rail, moulded face to the back panel, moulded seat frame and raked back legs. The fore-leg is late manifestation of the horsebone. Note also the turned underarms supports, which were introduced from about 1700 onwards.   HADDON HALL

Plate 8:68. Caned chair (1710-20). Painted beech or walnut. Similar in many respects to the previous example, this has fore-legs which are recognisably a late version of the horsebone. Note also the distinctive medial stretcher, placed asymmetrically towards the front of the chair.   BURTON AGNES HALL

Plate 8:69. Caned chair (1710-20). Walnut. This has the plain tapered stretchers introduced after 1700 and a late, highly stylised pillar leg.
CHASTLETON HOUSE, THE NATIONAL TRUST

centre of gravity back within practical bounds and solved the problem of instability which afflicted many caned chairs made a few years either side of 1700.

The splendid chair in 8:64-66 embodies these two crucial developments in English chair design in what is the earliest documented example known at the time of writing. It was supplied in 1709 for Henry Compton, Bishop of London, by Charles Hopson, a noted London joiner who was at this time also Lord Mayor of London.[54] It is very close in date to Thomas Roberts' first bill for chairs with 'spreading back feet' (1708) and was made in the same year as John Burroughs' back chairs which also have raked back legs (8:46). It might be argued that the references in Roberts' bills could post-date the actual introduction of this feature by a year or two, but it is very difficult to place the introduction of either the superimposed crest rail or the raked back leg any earlier than about 1705. Even after this date neither feature was universally adopted, and chairs continued to be made with traditional in-set crest rails and straight back legs for some year to come.

The modern velvet padding on the Hopson chair disguises the fact that the caned back panel is enclosed by a moulded frame, of the sort which was by now virtually universal. Equally noteworthy

Plate 8:70. Caned chair (1710-20). Walnut. A rather crude chair, with plain fore-legs, but nevertheless embodying advanced structural features such as the superimposed top rail and raked rear leg.
RED LODGE, BRISTOL

Plate 8:71. Caned chair (1705-15). Walnut. A fine, high baroque chair, with raked rear legs but still with its crest rail between the rear posts.
RED LODGE, BRISTOL

are the banisters, which are purely classical in form, eschewing the fussy, multi-ringed style of earlier models. Both the moulded frame and slender, tapered banisters are common to the majority of late banister-back chairs, like those illustrated in 8:67-73.

The extraordinary variety of caned chairs produced in the latter half of Queen Anne's reign is testimony to the fertile virtuosity of English chairmakers. Equally remarkable is the degree to which that fertility is contained within a consistent overall structure. Stripped of their decorative differences, from c.1708 onwards most caned banister-back chairs have a moulded, shaped back and superimposed crest rail set on turned column posts. The seat rails are moulded, usually with a simple torus or astragal on their outer edge, and the rear legs are turned and raked. Occasional variations, such as the inset crest rail on 8:71, do not substantially affect the general pattern.

Plate 8:74. Caned chair (1710-20). Walnut. Chairs having 'moulding' backs occur reasonably frequently in Thomas Roberts' bills after 1710. This is an important development, because the traditional post-and-cross-rail construction of English chairs is here abandoned in favour of a unified design, an essential precursor to conventional 18th century construction. Note the highly stylised 'mushroom' knopped legs, similar to that found on contemporary cabinets-on-stands.

VICTORIA & ALBERT MUSEUM

Plate 8:75. Caned chair (1710-1720). Walnut. A similar chair to the previous example, but less elaborately decorated.

CHASTLETON HOUSE, THE NATIONAL TRUST

Plate 8:76. Caned chair (1710-20). Walnut. Another variation of the moulded back theme, incorporating a late 'horsebone' fore-leg.

CHASTLETON HOUSE, THE NATIONAL TRUST

Moulded backs and asymmetric stretchers

Thomas Roberts supplied banister-back chairs to the royal household until at least 1711 (although not for the State apartments),[55] and in the country at large they remained popular for many years – examples in mahogany are known. Among fashionable makers, however, the banister-back was on the way out after 1710. The final phase of caned chair design under the Stuarts was characterised by chairs with what Thomas Roberts called 'moulding backs'. In 1713, for instance, he supplied for Queen Anne's closet at Hampton Court '… 24 very fine wallnuttree Caned Chairs with moulding backs and seats… £27. 0. 0.'.[56] The term 'moulding back' probably described a chair with a framed back, moulded on the forward face of the posts and cross-rails (8:74). The structural and visual distinction between posts, central panel and cross-rails vanished and in its place was a design which combined all these elements into a single integrated panel. Early signs of the change can be

55. For example, at St James's Palace: 'For 6 bannister Back Chair frames for ye pages eating Room:£3.o.o.'. PRO LC/9 284, f.16.
56. PRO LC/9 285, f.22.

Plate 8:77. Caned elbow chair (1710-20). Walnut. This example has an asymmetric stretcher, carved and placed horizontally. This curious arrangement occurs quite commonly on chairs of this period.

TREASURER'S HOUSE, YORK, THE NATIONAL TRUST

Plate 8:78. Caned elbow chair. (1715-20). Walnut. This is a very late example of a cross-stretcher chair. The truncated, raised top to the back occurs on fashionable chairs made from c.1714 onwards, so this is very unlikely to predate 1715.

HADDON HALL

detected as far back as 1700, from which time many banister-back chairs had their caned panels enclosed in moulded frames. The crucial step was the adoption of the superimposed crest rail, which allowed the rail to be conceived as a continuation of the rear posts rather than as a cross-member between two uprights.

As well as the moulded back, the chair in 8:74 has scrolled feet and raked back legs. The raked legs are shared by all the chairs in 8:75-80 and some examples also have an asymmetric medial stretcher (8:77 and 8:80), placed well forward of the mid-point between front and back legs. This asymmetric arrangement has already been noted with respect to cross-frame chairs and in those cases it seems to have occurred as a consequences of the introduction of the raked back leg. In the case of conventional H stretchers the problem was not so pressing, since the decorative role of the medial stretcher was subordinate to that of the fore-rail. Thus neither Bishop Compton's chair

Plate 8:79. Caned elbow chair (1715-20). Walnut. The flared shoulders to the back also occur on early cabriole-leg chairs of c.1715-20, suggesting a comparable date for this example. The front stretcher is an ill-conceived replacement.   HADDON HALL.

Plate 8:80. Caned chair (c.1715). Walnut. This is probably a survivor of several sets of caned chairs recorded at Canons Ashby in 1717. Note the flat, asymmetric stretcher and the stylised ionic capitals on the fore-legs.

CANONS ASHBY, THE NATIONAL TRUST

(8:64), nor John Burroughs' chairs (8:46, all made in 1709), have asymmetric stretchers. It is unlikely, therefore, that the asymmetric medial stretcher was introduced for H-stretchered chairs before about 1710, and it is probable that for several years thereafter symmetric and asymmetric stretchers were produced concurrently. Indeed, the symmetrical version is found on documented chairs as late as 1716, but by this date it was probably a *retardataire* feature.[57] The asymmetric stretcher, by contrast, can be found on the earliest cabriole leg chairs of 1715-20, and remained a standard feature of English chairmaking for the rest of the eighteenth century.

The many moulded back chairs share leg, fore-rail and stretcher designs with late banister-back chairs and therefore the likelihood is that they are contemporary. A similar overlap occurs between some moulded back designs and early cabriole leg chairs. Thus the raised, truncated top to the

57. A chair of this type made for the Parish Clerks' Company in 1716 is illustrated in Graham (1994).

chair in 8:78 is also found on both wooden and upholstered cabriole leg chairs made between c.1715 and 1725, and the flared shoulders of the chairs in 8:79 and 8:80 are equally common on both late pillar-leg and early cabriole leg chairs. However, at the time of writing no English cabriole-leg chairs are known to have been made before 1714, and so the history of their introduction and development must be reserved for the next volume of this work.

Dutch banister-back chairs

Just as the oval-backed, twist-turned chair was made in both England and Holland, so banister-backed versions were also common to both countries. Many hundreds of Dutch examples are now in English collections and as a consequence there is some confusion as to which are Dutch and which English. However, as with the twist-turned versions, the Dutch chairs have a number of distinctive stylistic and structural attributes which set them apart from their English counterparts. One of the commonest Dutch models is shown in 8:81. The carving is typically fine and detailed, and quite unlike contemporary English work. The double-baluster turning profile is also typical and is not found on English examples. The most significant differences are below the seat, where

Plate 8:81. Caned chair (c.1830). Walnut. This superb chair is Dutch, made in the style of about 1700. The quality of construction and carving is exemplary and better than most genuine examples. This is not a fake, but a copy, one of a set bought to furnish an 'Elizabethan' interior recreated at Levens Hall, probably between 1820 and 1850. LEVENS HALL

the combination of scrolled legs and scrolled cross-stretchers sets them apart from English models. The leg itself is a common Dutch form, usually terminating either in a scrolled toe or in a carved paw.

The presence of considerable numbers of these Dutch chairs in English collections requires some explanation. There is no evidence that they were imported into England in the late seventeenth or early eighteenth centuries. Indeed, the trade in caned chairs seems to have been all the other way. The 'Dutch' chairs mentioned in English inventories were invariably described as having 'matted bottoms', i.e. rushed seats, and these were probably of the ladder-back type. Caned and carved chairs, of the type discussed above, begin to appear in watercolours of English interiors from the 1820s onwards and it is probable, therefore, that they were imported to furnish nineteenth century 'Elizabethan' and 'Carolean' interiors. J.C. Loudon's *Cottage, Farm and Villa Architecture* (1835) contains several pages of text and illustrations on 'Elizabethan' villa furniture, in which a 'richly carved Dutch chair' of the banister-back type is illustrated.[58] He further relates that 'Wilkinson of Oxford Street, and Hanson of John Street, have extensive collections of Elizabethan and Dutch furniture and carvings,...'.[59] By the time Percy Macquoid came to write his pioneering work, *The Age of Walnut* (1905), these Dutch chairs had quietly been absorbed into the English canon. Several examples are illustrated in his book and the mistake has been perpetuated in many subsequent texts.[60]

Chairs with carved backs

There is one numerous group of chairs found in English collections whose design does not fit easily into the typologies proposed in the foregoing pages. This comprises chairs with banister backs and carved splats, of the sort often described as 'Anglo-Dutch' and more often than not attributed to the designs of Daniel Marot. 8:82-87 show a representative selection.

Some of these chairs are undoubtedly Dutch. Many, perhaps most, of these chairs are nineteenth century pastiches, made to fulfil the demand for 'antique' furniture prevalent from the 1820s onwards. The example in 8:83 is a case in point. The frame of this chair exhibits every sign of age, including old repairs, and might easily pass muster as being made c.1700. Fortunately, however, it retains all its original upholstery and this, from the top cover to the scrim, stuffing and webbing, is entirely nineteenth century. The chair is English, and probably dates from c.1830. Because so little is known about these chairs, it is perhaps counter-productive to speculate further about their age and origins. Numerous examples are housed in collections in England and abroad and all should be looked at with a very sceptical eye.

58. Loudon (1829), pp. 130-31.
59. Ibid.
60. Macquoid (1905), pl. 1b, figs 9, 12, 13 and 60; Symonds (1921), fig. 20.

Plates 8:82-87. A selection of 'Anglo-Dutch' chairs. The variety of forms and styles is consistent only in being unlikely to be older than c.1820.

Plate 8:82.

Plate 8:83.

Plate 8:84.

Plate 8:85.

Plate 8:86.

Plate 8:87.

Chapter Nine

TABLES, STANDS AND LOOKING-GLASSES, 1689-1714

Dining Tables

There is little to say about dining tables in the reigns of William III and Queen Anne, since the gateleg form established during the early Restoration continued into the eighteenth century without significant modification. In 1694, for instance, Thomas Roberts supplied to the Royal Household an 'Oval table of Wainscott to fall down on both sides',[1] and this is the sort of table one

Gateleg table (1690-1720). Brazilwood. This is a rare example of brazilwood furniture. Note the narrow boards used for the top. The table would have been bright orange-red when new.

Plate 9:1. Gateleg table (1690-1720). Oak. Gateleg tables such as this were a perennially popular form, and are difficult to date with certainty. The ball, ring and pillar turnings suggest a date around the turn of the 17th and 18th centuries, and the opposed baluster stretchers are usually a sign of early 18th century date. The edge of the top is square, rather than ovolo-moulded in the Georgian manner, and there is a tongue-and-groove joint between the fixed and hinged leaves.   SOTHEBY'S

1. PRO LC 11/5, f. 177.
2. Walton (1986), pp. 34 and 56; Westman (1994), p. 9.

finds in inventories throughout the period. In 1710 the dining tables stored in the Sideboard Parlour at Dyrham Park were described as oval, and Francis Lapiere's Parlour in Pall Mall was also furnished with (among other things) 'one Oviall [sic] Wainscott Table'.[2]

Although twist-turned and ball-turned frames probably continued to be made, particularly in a vernacular context, dining tables of the 1690s and later tended to favour baluster or pillar-type turnings, more or less in step with developments in contemporary side tables and 'banister-back' chairs. Accurate dating of these workaday items is often difficult, if not impossible. The table in 9:1 might date from any time between 1690 and 1720, but the fussiness of the turnings suggests the earlier date might be closer. Similarly, the turnings of the small table in 9:2 have similarities with those on banister-back chairs and candlestands of the 1690s. 9:3 shows an unusual form, with complex turnings and stylised scroll feet; again, a date in the 1690s or early 1700s is probable.

Plate 9:2. Gateleg table (1690-1710). Oak. The turnings on this diminutive table bear some comparison with chair banister and stretcher designs around 1700.   PRIVATE COLLECTION

Plate 9:3. Gateleg table (1690-1710). Oak. This is a rare type; the turning is unusually rich and has some similarities with contemporary candlestands. The scrolled feet are perhaps rare precursors of the more common 'Spanish' foot introduced after c.1710.   SOTHEBY'S

We are on firmer ground with the table in 9:4. If analogies with contemporary chair design are sound, then the scrolled feet are unlikely to have been made before c.1710. The turning profile of the legs is also an early eighteenth century pattern (cf. 9:19 and 9:20 below), as is the opposed baluster stretcher design. We can propose a similar date for the next example, a diminutive gateleg in solid yew-tree (9:5). The tongue-and-groove joint between the leaves and the fixed top is an old-fashioned feature, but tables of this kind are unlikely to have been made by a metropolitan joiner.

Although oval tended to be the preferred shape for dining tables, many smaller examples are square or rectangular (9:6). This example has a common ball-and-baluster leg profile which is impossible to place with certainty, but the ovolo-moulded top with rule joints suggests an eighteenth rather than seventeenth century date. The small japanned table in 9:7 is an extraordinary rarity, whose extreme simplicity of form suggests a strong Chinese influence. It is very difficult to propose a date for this, since only the feet have any stylistic embellishment. They might be conceived as stylised scroll feet, or might have been taken direct from Chinese originals. Something very similar occurs on Chinese kang tables of the Ming and early Qing dynasties.[3] The date is probably 1700-1720.

3. Shixiang (1990), II, figs. B5-B12.

Plate 9:4. Gateleg table (1710-30). Oak. This is very definitely an 18th century form. The scrolled feet are unlikely to be earlier than 1710; the shouldered baluster and tapered supports bear comparison with the Dyrham Park tables (9:19 and 20) and the ogee arched end rails have beaded lower edges. The opposed baluster stretchers are an early 18th century introduction.

SOTHEBY'S

Plate 9:5 Gateleg table (1710-40). Yew-tree. Yew-tree furniture is highly sought-after and small, well-patinated examples such as this command high prices at auction. Note that the feet are made by adding a thickness of wood to the two outer faces of the leg. This is standard construction, both on metropolitan and provincial work.   PHILLIPS

Plate 9:6. Gateleg table (1710-40). Padouk top with plum wood base. The pear-shaped feet of this pretty table hark back to Carolean times, but the ovolo-moulded and rule-jointed top suggest a much later date.   EAST RIDDLESDEN HALL, THE NATIONAL TRUST

Plate 9:7. Gateleg table (1700-20). Japanned softwood. This is a rare survivor of uncertain date, but probably early 18th century. The extreme simplicity of form is reminiscent of Chinese furniture.   DRAYTON HOUSE, PRIVATE COLLECTION

Plate 9:8. Table, glass and stands (c.1690), Japanned softwood. This 'triad' is attributed to Gerrit Jensen. The design of the stands, with the tapered shaft and elliptical ball, is similar to other examples attributed to Jensen (cf. 9:11 and 15). The handles on the table are not original, and the mirror once had a cresting.   KNOLE, THE NATIONAL TRUST

Plate 9:9. Table and glass (1690-1700). Marquetry of holly and princeswood on a deal carcase. These fine quality pieces exemplify the 'William and Mary' style of triad. Because of its expense, the use of princeswood is always an indication of quality. One of a pair.

BENINGBROUGH HALL, NATIONAL TRUST PHOTOGRAPHIC LIBRARY/ANDREAS VON EINSIEDEL

Plate 9:10. Stand (1690-1710). Walnut. Because of its small size, this is unlikely to have been part of a 'triad', but was probably intended for informal use. The tapered and faceted lower shaft is typical of the period, superseding the ubiquitous twist-turned style of the Carolean era.

BENINGBOROUGH HALL, THE NATIONAL TRUST

Plate 9:11. Stand (1690-1700). Marquetry of walnut and holly, with princeswood and rosewood. This high quality example has been attributed to Gerrit Jensen on stylistic grounds, and Jensen is known to have supplied furniture to the house in which it rests.

LEVENS HALL

Plate 9:13. Stand (1700-1720). Carved and gilt gesso on softwood. This stand is superficially similar in form to the previous example, but the faceted lower shaft is comparable to the legs of dressing and other tables made after 1700. RED LODGE, BRISTOL

Tables and stands

At the beginning of the 1690s the scrolled leg was the most popular form of leg for tables with stands, although twist-turned examples probably represented a cheaper option. 9:8 shows a suite of table, stands and looking-glass probably supplied by Gerrit Jensen to the 6th Earl of Dorset in December 1690. The cost of this ensemble was £18.[4] A pair of tables of similar form, with mirrors *en suite,* are now at Beningborough Hall, Yorkshire (9:9). These are veneered with princeswood oysters and panels of arabesque marquetry The legs are 'in-line' rather than angled, which is not uncommon, and the fretting of the mirror is particularly rich.

The candlestands of the Knole suite are of a form introduced in the late 1680s, with a faceted, tapered lower shaft surmounted by a large compressed ball and turned upper section. Similar examples are not uncommon, occurring both singly and in pairs (9:10). 9:11 and 9:12 show a very fine and probably early example, veneered in arabesque marquetry with princeswood and rose-wood, while that in 9:13 is rather later. The form is essentially similar, but the faceted lower shaft has more in common with the pillar legs of tables made after c.1700 and the low relief decoration compares closely with that used on mirror frames and pier tables of about 1710-30.

Plate 9:12. Detail of 9:11. The marquetry is probably of walnut and holly, bordered with princeswood. When new, the contrast of colours would have been very striking.

4. The National Trust, Knole Guide Book, p. 21.

Plate 9:14. Table and stands (c.1688). Ebony and ebonised wood with pewter and brass. This triad is attributed to Gerrit Jensen and is the earliest documented English example of marquetry in metal. The pillar legs were an avant garde design at this date. The form of the stretcher, however, is entirely conventional.   DRAYTON HOUSE, PRIVATE COLLECTION

Plate 9:15. Stand (c.1688). The visual impact of this stand is diminished by the loss of metal marquetry on the feet, but it is nevertheless a highly important exemplar of the new 'pillar' style.

DRAYTON HOUSE, PRIVATE COLLECTION

Plate 9:16. Table (c.1690). Carved and gilt gesso on softwood. This was made for Ralph Montagu, probably by the carvers Jean and René Pelletier. The top bears the Earl's cipher, suggesting the table was made shortly after his creation in 1689. The quality of design and cutting is outstanding.   BOUGHTON HOUSE, COUNTRY LIFE

Contemporary with the new tapered pillar stand was a new form of table with pillar legs, rather than scrolled or turned. The earliest documented example of this form is shown in 9:14. This was almost certainly supplied to the 2nd Earl of Peterborough by Gerrit Jensen. A bill of March 1688 records that he charged £1 'for altaring the stands inlay'd with mettle' (9:15), which implies that the suite was made before this date.[5] This suite is also the earliest documented English example of marquetry in metal, of which Jensen was probably the foremost practitioner in England.

Pillar leg tables were indeed the coming thing. The table in 9:16 bears an earl's coronet and the cipher of Ralph Montagu, which dates it to after the creation of Montagu's earldom in 1689. The cutting of the gesso is particularly fine, and it is attributed to Jean and René Pelletier, Huguenot carvers whose talents, as we have seen, were much in demand at Court.[6] The legs are turned, with slight concavity to the shaft, and carved with fine detail. Similar leg profiles can be seen on a pair of marble topped tables at Hampton Court, supplied by Jean Pelletier in 1699 (9:17). The frames for these tables cost £3.5s. each, and the marble

Plate 9:17. Table (c.1699). Walnut frame with marble top. This is one of a pair supplied by Jean Pelletier to Hampton Court Palace. The form is very similar to the previous example, but much simpler, being essentially just joiners' and turners' work.

CROWN COPYRIGHT:
HISTORIC ROYAL PALACES

'Tables' or tops £8 the pair.[7] Recent work on the Pelletier firm suggests that although Pelletier's name heads the bill, the tables might have been produced by the Huguenot joiner Peter Rieusset, who worked for the Earl of Montagu at Boughton House.[8] This is certainly plausible, for there is no carver's work on the tables, and this class of furniture was generally produced by joiners.

In 9:16 and 9:17 the flat stretcher is fairly conventional, having bifurcated ends joined by a tie-bar, but later examples of the Pelletiers' work employ newly-fashionable cross-stretchers. The table in 9:18 is one of a pair made for the Earl's London house in 1699 – it is very similar in form and style to others supplied to the Royal Palaces around the same time (cf. 6:28).[9] Surviving bills at Boughton House reveal that Jean Pelletier charged £20 for carving and gilding each frame.[10] The difference between the last two tables, supplied by the same firm and at approximately the same

5. Jackson-Stops (1985), p. 168.
6. Murdoch (1997), p. 740.
7. PRO LC 9/281, f. 44.
8. Murdoch (1998), p. 736
9. Ibid., pp. 735-6.

Plate 9:18. Table (1699). Carved and gilt softwood with marble top. This table is one of a pair supplied by Jean Pelletier for Montagu House. The pillar leg, cross-stretcher form was by now the dominant type for 'parade' furniture and this example is comparable in style and quality to tables supplied by Pelletier to the Royal Palaces. The original carved and pierced 'apron' is missing.

BOUGHTON HOUSE, THE DUKE OF BUCCLEUCH

Plate 9:19. Table (1701). Walnut. The marble top for this table came from London, but the frame was produced by joiners on site at Dyrham. The shouldered baluster leg, which is used in an inverted form on contemporary cross-framed chairs, is seen here for the first time on a documented table. DYRHAM PARK, THE NATIONAL TRUST

Plate 9:20. Table (1701). Cedar. Another table made by the site joiners at Dyrham. The drawer escutcheon, if original, provides a useful date *post quem* for this style.

DYRHAM PARK, THE NATIONAL TRUST

date, is interesting. It suggests a distinction in form and style between 'parade' furniture for State apartments and furniture intended for daily use. Given the possibility that one of these tables was supplied by a sub-contracted joiner, the traditional art-historical approach of identifying the work of a particular maker or workshop by stylistic analogy alone becomes extremely difficult, if not impossible.

Two workmanlike tables at Dyrham Park make an interesting comparison with the Hampton Court example (9:19 and 9:20). Both were supplied in 1701, with the marble tops coming from London and the frames being made on site by the joiners Alexander Hunter and Jonathan Fisher.[11] There are some obvious differences between the two – 9:19 is of walnut and 9:20 of cedar, and both the style and the construction of the stretchers is different, but the similarities are also significant. In particular, the turning profile of the legs gives us a firm point of departure for this style, which recurs frequently on tables and stands of all kinds hereafter (cf. 9:4). The opposed-baluster stretcher turnings also bear comparison with those found on many contemporary chairs.

It was suggested in Chapter Eight that from about 1700 onwards both the pillar leg and the cross-stretcher became increasingly stylised and more complex in form. The trend is certainly borne out in the design of pier tables, such as those supplied by Gerrit Jensen in the early years of Queen Anne's reign (9:21). The heavily stylised legs, stepped and scrolled stretchers, rising strongly to a central finial, and deep aprons of controlled strapwork are quite different in style and execution from the florid style of the Carolean era and derive from flat pattern designs of the sort popularised by Bérain and Marot. One of the characteristic details of Jensen's tables (and no doubt of other makers) is the punched ground to the strapwork, which gives a matt surface to contrast with the burnished edges (9:22). Cross hatching produced a studded, scintillating surface, and other practitioners used a curious ribbed or rippled surface to similar effect. The same techniques can be seen on the carved crestings of contemporary pier glasses.

10. Murdoch (1998), p. 736.
11. Walton (1986), p. 35.

Plate 9:21. Table (1704). Carved and gilded softwood. This is a side view of one of the tables supplied by Gerrit Jensen to Kensington Palace in 1704 (cf. 5:7). The form is impressively solid and sculptural, as if made in gilded bronze rather than wood. The complex stretcher design is a feature of both pier tables and chairs in the years after 1700.   SOTHEBY'S

Plate 9:22. Detail of 9:21 showing the front apron with the crown and cipher of Queen Anne. The dropped apron, rigorously controlled in a frame of baroque strapwork, is another hallmark of pier tables after 1700. Note the punched ground, producing a matted effect, and the degrees of hatching and studding on different elements of the design. The contrast between matt and gloss areas would have been highlighted by burnishing, traces of which are still visible on some parts of the foliage.   SOTHEBY'S

Plate 9:23. Table (c.1700). Carved and gilded softwood. This table was made for Thomas Coningsby, of Hampton Court, Leominster. In place of the more usual pillar leg it employs a scroll of the type seen on chairs supplied by Thomas Roberts (cf. 8:33 and 8:36). Coningsby was a close associate of William III, and there are striking similarities between the furnishings of Coningsby's house and William's apartments at Hampton Court Palace.

PARTRIDGE FINE ART

12. 'Londⁿ, May 20 1713. This day ye peace between Engl^d and France was proclaim'd here by ye heralds as is usual in such cases to ye great joy and satisfactⁿ of all people… John Polloxfen Jun.'
13. This is illustrated in Edwards (1954), III, p. 280, fig. 18. Another example is in the collection at Wilton House.

There were, of course exceptions to the dominant pillar-leg form. 9:23 shows a table made for Lord Coningsby around 1700. The legs are larger versions of the scrolled 'French' leg which was briefly fashionable for chairs and stools at about this date. The table is otherwise conventional, with a gesso-cut top decorated with 'corners and middles' and a sinuous, moulded cross-stretcher. This type is uncommon, however, and the pillar leg remained the most popular form for 'parade' furniture until the end of Queen Anne's reign. The table in 9:24 has a scagliola top, inlaid with playing cards and a letter recording the peace of Utrecht, signed in May 1713.[12] 9:25 and 9:26 show similar tables with tops probably by the same maker. The frame of 9:26 is virtually identical to one in the Royal Collection, whose scagliola top bears the cipher of Queen Anne.[13]

Plate 9:24. Table (1713). Carved and gilded softwood. This table has a scagliola top, dated 1713. The profile of the legs approaches the 'mushroom' knopped style found on the stands of veneered case furniture at this date.

SALTRAM, THE NATIONAL TRUST

Plate 9:25. Table top (1713). Scagliola. This is one of a group of similar scagliola tops probably made by Italian specialists working in London.
SALTRAM, THE NATIONAL TRUST

Plate 9:26. Table (1705-15). Carved and silvered softwood. This beautiful table retains its original silvered finish. The legs and stretchers have some affinities with Jensen's work, and the scagliola top appears to be from the same workshop as that in 9:25.
PRIVATE COLLECTION

Plate 9:27. Table (1680-1700). Oak. This is a very traditional form of small table, suitable for most domestic uses. The ball-and-ring turning and moulded drawer fronts suggest a date in the last quarter of the 17th century.

MONTACUTE HOUSE, THE NATIONAL TRUST

Plate 9:28. Table (1700-1720). Elm. This joiner-made example makes passing reference to contemporary fashions. The shouldered baluster leg and waved peripheral stretcher suggest a date after 1700. Note the veneered face of the drawer. CHRISTIE'S

Plate 9:29. Dressing table (1710-30). Yew-tree. The knopped legs are a 'late' manifestation of the pillar leg, and the arched frieze relates clearly to the more fashionable veneered examples in the following illustrations. Note also the double-bead carcase moulding and the cockbeaded lower edge, both post-1700 features. PRIVATE COLLECTION

Plate 9:30. Dressing table (1710-30). Walnut veneers on a deal carcase. The three-part front, with two deep drawers flanking a 'kneehole', may derive from contemporary bureaux. Certainly this three-drawer form is not seen before c.1700. CHRISTIE'S

Dressing tables

In a domestic setting the formality of the triad was not always convenient, and indeed it is questionable whether this fashionable ensemble made much impact in English households below a certain level of means and status. The evidence of rural and vernacular inventories suggests that it did not, but small tables on their own were nevertheless common and must have served a variety of purposes. Tables of this kind, made of common woods by provincial joiners and carpenters, are still abundant, and are usually classified as 'country' furniture (9:27-29). However, from c.1700 onwards cabinet-made examples, veneered in walnut and other woods and possessing all the attributes of metropolitan design, begin to be much more numerous. The most common form of these has three drawers over a shaped frieze with central arched apron or 'kneehole' (9:30-32). Indeed, these are so common, and so similar in conception, that there was evidently a considerable degree of consensus about their design and function. This fact, and the fashionable drawer arrangement, makes it unlikely that the three-drawer table derived from vernacular precedents. One possible design source is the bureau table, which as we have seen became increasingly common from 1690 onwards. With its two deep drawers flanking the kneehole, the arrangement is essentially the same as the French 'bureau Mazarin', but translated into a much more modest form. Whether this hypothesis is true or not, it is noteworthy that this form of small three-drawer table made its appearance at the turn of the seventeenth and eighteenth centuries, and soon became a popular type. In the antiques trade such tables are commonly called 'lowboys', but the term is not contemporary. Some modern authorities prefer the term 'dressing table', which is as good as any, and at least reflects one of its probable functions.

It is difficult to place any surviving examples of the three-drawer table before c.1700. The earliest have attributes which place them in the first decades of the new century. On 9:30 both the

Plate 9:31. Dressing table (1710-30). Japanned on a deal carcase. A stylish example, having scroll feet and the new-style ogee moulding to the top.

THE GEFFRYE MUSEUM, LONDON

double-bead carcase mouldings and featherbanded drawers suggest a date after 1700. Similarly, the faceted pillar leg was probably the most common type made between 1700 and c.1720. The japanned example in 9:31 is of a similar date. The stylised scroll feet suggest perhaps c.1710 at the earliest, and this is borne out by the lapped dovetail drawer construction. The edge profile of the top is a new type, and should be compared with the standard quarter-round of 9:30. The same moulding occurs on 9:32, which has been signed and dated by the maker – *Henry Hill 1715.* The whimsical turning profile of the legs is accounted for by the fact that the legs are not original.

9:33 retains the seventeenth century ovolo edge moulding suggesting that the handles, which are in the style of c.1730, might not be original. On the other hand, one suspects that this 'William and Mary' style of table persisted rather longer than most authorities allow. There is a considerable overlap between turned-leg dressing tables and those with cabriole legs, and it would not be surprising to find turned-leg examples made well after 1720. This is certainly the case in North America, where turned leg tables persist into the 1730s. Similarly, chests on stands with turned legs could well be rather later than commonly thought. Most have second or even third-phase cabinet work, and examples in mahogany are not unknown.[14]

Plate 9:32. Dressing table (1715). Walnut on a deal carcase. This is signed by the maker, Henry Hill, and dated 1715. Note the new-style edge moulding to the top, replacing the conventional ovolo. This table offers a useful date *post quem* for this feature. The legs are replaced. SOTHEBY'S

Plate 9:33. Dressing table (1710-30). Walnut veneers on deal and oak. This table has the old style ovolo top moulding. Both this and the half-round carcase mouldings would have been old fashioned by 1730. The handles are of a style typical of the 1730s, and are probably replaced. PHILLIPS

Plate 9:34. Folding table (18th century). Oak. This is one of several tables of this type at Cotehele House, Cornwall. Once common, these are now rare. So-called 'French' and 'Spanish' folding tables were probably of a similar form, sometimes fitted with iron rather than wooden braces. COTEHELE, THE NATIONAL TRUST

The origins of the card table

'Tables' for cards, dice and other games were originally conceived simply as boards for playing on. Those with inlaid tops, such as for chess and backgammon, were made to fold to protect the surface when not in use, and so in the late sixteenth and early seventeenth centuries one finds frequent references to 'pairs' of playing tables. This usage was still current in 1660, when 'playing Tables of Wainscot, and all other sorts' were listed in the Book of Rates and valued 'the pair'.[15] The Lord Chamberlain's accounts make frequent references to 'French' and 'Spanish' tables which had folding legs supported by metal or wooden struts (9:34).[16] These were particularly useful on campaign, or whenever the court was mobile, but were also fit for any occasional use, including, one imagines, for gaming.[17] Games tables in the modern sense, as a complete article of furniture made specifically for the purpose, were uncommon before the late seventeenth century, and few survive.[18] The table in 9:35 is a rare example, probably dating from about 1675-80. The centre of the top is removable and is inlaid on the reverse for chess and draughts, while the well beneath is

14. Readers will have to wait until the second volume of this work for an exposition of 'third-phase' cabinet work.
15. 12 Charles II cap. 4. 'Coarse' playing tables of wainscot were rated at 5s. the pair. Fancier items were much more expensive and taxed according to their individual worth.
16. An example is illustrated in Thornton (1978), figures 212 and 213.
17. 'For a folding Spanish Table of Wallnuttree wrought Handsome and light... £2.10.0'. PRO LC 9/281, f. 24. This table was described as being 'For his Majesty's service in Progress'.
18. One notable exception is at Hardwick Hall, Derbyshire. This is a table of about 1580-1600, with a top inlaid for chess and draughts, with playing cards depicted at each corner. See Edwards (1954), III, p. 193, fig. 3.

inlaid for backgammon. Usually, the arrangements for gaming were more *ad hoc*. The frontispiece of the *Complete Gamester* (1674) depicts a backgammon board unfolded on a trestle or frame and card games being played at ordinary tables covered with cloth.[19]

Despite the great popularity of card games since the Restoration, there is scant evidence that purpose-made card tables were produced in numbers much before 1690. The emergence of the card table as a furniture type had therefore very little to do with card playing *per se* and was probably related to the changing use of established furniture forms. The rectangular folding table on pillars, introduced during the 1690s, lent itself to many uses other than writing, and it was a small step to line the top with baize to make it suitable for cards. In this guise it was essentially a modified pier table, designed to stand against the wall, perhaps with a mirror over, and to be brought out into the room when desired. One of the earliest references to this arrangement occurs in a bill of 1699, for furniture supplied by Gerrit Jensen to Thomas Coke, M.P. for Melbourne in Derbyshire. Among other items the bill lists a pier glass in black frame, and 'a folding Table black... £2.10.0'.[20] The two items are listed consecutively, which strongly suggests that one is intended to complement the other. The arrangement became more common over the next decade or two, which is yet another indication that the formality of the 'triad' was becoming inconvenient, at least in a domestic setting. The inventory of Francis Lapiere's London house in Pall Mall, taken after his death in 1715, records among the furnishings of the drawing room 'two Walnutt tree folding tables, 2 Peer glasses' (which sounds very like two card tables with pier glasses over), but no stands *en suite*.[21]

The first specific reference to card tables in the Lord Chamberlain's accounts does not occur until 1712, when Thomas Roberts submitted a bill 'for mending six Card Tables that was much Broake'.[22] This is certainly evidence that card tables were now installed at Court and that they suffered hard use, but their appearance is not described. The lack of any firmly documented examples of the type means that the dating of early card tables relies on stylistic analogies with

Plate 9:35. Games table (1675-90). Walnut and other woods on an oak and deal carcase. This is a rare survival of an early purpose-made games table. The centre of the top is removable, revealing a well with an inlaid games board. VICTORIA & ALBERT MUSEUM

Plate 9:36. Games table (1700-1715). Walnut on deal carcase. This is the standard type of early 18th century card table. Note the hollow moulding to the edge of the top, a feature common to many card tables throughout the 18th century.

BENINGBOROUGH HALL,
THE NATIONAL TRUST

other furniture forms. Yet their most distinctive attribute, the half-round shape, is unprecedented, and must be considered a true innovation, rather than an adaptation of an existing type. At a time when conventional pier tables were uniformly rectangular, the half-round shape is startlingly novel, but it is less so when perceived as a circular or oval table folded. As with contemporary dining tables, the round or oval shape lent itself to conviviality, and could accommodate an even or odd number of people. The popular game of *Ombre*, for instance, was a three-handed card game, and it is possible that the 'ombre tables' which feature commonly in advertisements and trade cards of the early eighteenth century were of this circular type. A French drawing of c.1700 depicts the Dauphin's card table, circular in form and on pillar legs, covered with a cloth.[23] Perhaps tables like this were the prototypes for the English version.

The examples in 9:36-40 are so essentially similar that it is difficult to separate them by any meaningful criteria. All have half-round tops with supporting gates to the rear. The edges are moulded hollow to allow the fingers some purchase when opening the table. The friezes are shaped

19. Illustrated in Edwards (1954), III, p. 193, fig. 2.
20. B.L., Coke Papers, Add. Mss. 69975. I am grateful to David Dewing for drawing this bill to my attention.
21. Westman (1994), p. 10.
22. PRO LC 9/284, f. 62.
23. Illustrated in Thornton (1978), fig. 223.

Plate 9:37. Card table (1700-1715). Black japanning on a deal carcase. A rather fussier example than the previous one, but probably of a similar date.　　　　SOTHEBY'S

and most have a cockbead applied to the lower edge (9:40). The legs are turned and usually faceted. The rather fussy turnings of 9:37, together with the lack of a cockbead on the frieze, might suggest an early date, but on the other hand the double-bead moulding is unlikely to date from before 1700. Stylised scroll feet are fairly common (9:38) and probably indicate a date of c.1710 or later.

The fact that some tables have three drawers tends to support the notion that these could be 'ombre' tables. The gates are hinged on wooden pins, rather than the later type of knuckle-joint, and the action is rather fragile. Few of these tables seem to have retained their original gates and many have also suffered damage to the legs and stretchers, so that none should be allowed to pass muster without careful scrutiny.

Plate 9:38. Card table (1710-1730). Walnut on a deal carcase. The scrolled feet probably indicate a date after 1710 and the type was still popular twenty years later. SOTHEBY'S

Plate 9:39. Card table (1710-30). Walnut on a deal carcase. Similar to the previous example, with minor variations. In familiar English style, the overall form is standard, but the variations in detail are legion. BENINGBOROUGH HALL, THE NATIONAL TRUST

Plate 9:40. Detail of 9:37, showing the manner in which the cockbead is crudely cut and pinned to the carcase. The purpose of the bead was to protect the edge of the veneers – no documented examples of this practice have so far been recorded.

Plate 9:41. Card table (1710-30). A wonderfully original example, showing the brilliance of the japanning preserved inside the folding top. The baize appears to be original and the manner of finishing the edge with gimp and gilt pins is typical. One of a pair. PRIVATE COLLECTION

Plate 9:42. Trade card of Phillip Hunt (1689-94). This is noteworthy for the half-round shape of the mirror cresting, compared with the lower, flatter arch of the 1670s and 1680s. Equally interesting is the marquetry and oyster-veneered cabinet depicted in the glass. Clearly, twist-turned stands were still fashionable at this date.

Cushion-frame mirrors

9:42 shows the trade card of Phillip Hunt, depicting a cushion-framed mirror beneath a half-round fret-cut or inlaid cresting. The cresting bears the royal crown with lion and unicorn over the cipher of William and Mary, which suggests that the card was printed between 1689 and 1694. It is worth noting the floral marquetry on the mirror frame, and also the cabinet reflected in the glass, which still has floral marquetry on the doors and stands on a twist-turned frame. Our primary interest, however, is in the style of the cresting, which by this date has grown from the low, depressed arch of the 1670s into a full semicircle. This is the beginning of a process of seemingly inexorable upward growth which culminated in the towering pier glasses of the late Queen Anne and early Georgian eras.

Small cushion-framed mirrors remain popular well into the early years of the eighteenth century and there is probably little to distinguish those of c.1690 from those of 1710. The two very similar examples shown in 9:43 and 9:44 are typical of their kind. The naïvely rendered fret-cutting has a particular charm and suggests these are not the products of a metropolitan workshop. By way of contrast, the next example is very much more sophisticated, the frets carefully drawn and accurately cut, and the marquetry is of fine quality (9:45).

Plate 9:43. Mirror (1685-1710). Walnut on a deal carcase. This lobed shape of cresting is found on examples from the late 1680s, but might persist for many years after. TENNANTS

Plate 9:44. Mirror (1690-1710) Walnut on a deal carcase. A very similar example to the previous one, but this time with a half-round cresting. TENNANTS

Plate 9:45. Mirror (1690-1710) Walnut and marquetry on a deal carcase. A fine example of arabesque or 'filigree' marquetry, notable for its fluid style. Most arabesque marquetry is more controlled in its design. SOTHEBY'S

Plate 9:46. Mirror (1690-1710). Black japanning on a deal carcase. A high quality example. Note the way the design is carefully reconciled at the corners.   SOTHEBY'S

Plate 9:47. Mirror (1715-30). Red japanning on a deal carcase. In the first years of the 18th century the proportions of mirrors changed noticeably, becoming taller and narrower, with slimmer frames. The cresting is a simplified version of that found on pier glasses of the late Queen Anne/early Georgian period.   SOTHEBY'S

24. Walton (1986); Gloucestershire Record Office, E254.
25. *Nouvelles Cheminées* (1703), *Nouveaux Livre de Cheminées a la Hollondoise, Nouvelles Cheminées a Panneaux de Glace a la Maniere de France* (both 1712).

Mirrors of 'Japan' occur very commonly in inventories, although it is often difficult to tell whether these were of genuine oriental lacquer or English japanning. 9:46 is noteworthy on several counts, not least because of the fine quality of the japanning. Compared with preceding examples, the frame is noticeably slimmer in relation to the plate, and the plate is itself more 'portrait' oriented. Both these features indicate a relatively late date, perhaps after 1700. The same development can be observed in the design of large mirrors and pier glasses between 1700 and 1710 (see below). At the same time, the symmetry of the semi-circular cresting gave way to more complex shapes, again matching developments in contemporary pier glasses (9:47).

Overmantel mirrors

Another type of mirror which makes an increasingly common appearance in inventories is the fireplace overmantel mirror. Thus in the Gilt Leather Parlor at Dyrham Park in 1710 there was a 'looking Glass & two Glass Sconses ov[r] y[e] Chimney'. There were similar mirrors in eighteen of the principal rooms, both upstairs and down, all having been installed since the previous inventory was taken in 1703.[24] Some of these are still *in situ*. Most are rectangular (9:48), but that in the 'Great Room above Stairs' has an arched central plate, which was absolutely *à la mode* in the first decade after 1700. A similar mirror survives at Hampton Court Palace, its three plates bordered with slips of blue glass fixed with metal rosettes (9:49). Some idea of the importance attached to overmantel mirrors at this time can be gauged from the fact that Daniel Marot devoted three books of engravings solely to fireplaces and their overmantels (9:50).[25]

Later examples are less formal in their symmetry. The mirror in

Plate 9:48. Overmantel mirror (1700-1710). This is a survivor of numerous overmantel mirrors installed at Dyrham in the first decade of the 18th century. The three-plate division is typical.

DYRHAM PARK, THE NATIONAL TRUST

Plate 9:49. Overmantel Mirror (c.1700). This was probably supplied by Gerrit Jensen. The arched central plate appears in many Marot engravings, and was clearly a highly fashionable form. Blue glass borders appear on other mirrors supplied by Jensen for the King's Apartments. HAMPTON COURT PALACE, CROWN COPYRIGHT: HISTORIC ROYAL PALACES

Plate 9:50. Daniel Marot, design for an overmantel from *Nouveaux Livre de Cheminées a la Hollondoise* (1712). Here the mirror and overmantel painting are depicted *en suite*. Note the side elevation on the right of the plate. The projecting chimneybreast is a typically Continental type. Compare with 9:52.

Plate 9:51. Overmantel mirror
(c.1710). This was installed as part of
Edward Dryden's renovations at
Canons Ashby, Northamptonshire. The
mirror is carefully fitted to the
panelling and is angled downwards
into the room.

CANON'S ASHBY, THE NATIONAL TRUST

the Right Hand Parlour at Canons Ashby, which dates from the remodelling of 1710, has flanking
plates shaped in ogee curves (9:51); a very similar one was installed at Burley-on-the-Hill at about
the same time.[26] Some inventories mention both looking glasses and paintings on the chimney-
piece. Some were entirely separate, but others were made as an integrated unit, with the painting
specially commissioned to fit the space. 9:52 shows a fine example, with engraved plates and *verre
églomisé* borders.

One of the most consistent features of these early overmantels is the three-plate construction.
Although one can see how this was necessary in the case of mirrors with central arched plates, it
was also used for plain rectangular examples. Since the plates are neither large nor extravagantly
shaped, it is probable that the convention arose from the quasi-architectural design of the arched
overmantels and was perpetuated by customary usage. (It was probably also the case, however, that
three small plates were cheaper than one large one.)

Verre églomisé

The term *verre églomisé* describes a type of decoration on glass, particularly mirror glass, which
became highly fashionable at the turn of the seventeenth and eighteenth centuries. The decoration
was applied to the back of the mirror plate in the following manner. First, the area to be decorated
was backed with metal foil – usually gold or silver leaf – and the design then drawn or inscribed
into the foil. Areas of foil not wanted were scraped away and the background was then painted in
colours. From the front the finished design appeared as gold or silver decoration on a coloured
ground.

The technique is an ancient one and the term *verre églomisé* is not contemporary. It was
apparently coined in the mid-eighteenth century after a French printseller and collector, Jean-
Baptiste Glomy.[27] It is not certain when the technique was first used in England. *The Dictionary of
English Furniture* cites two newspaper advertisements which might refer to it. The first, in the
London Gazette of May 1691, claims that painting on glass 'is continued at Mr. Winches a Glass-
Painter in Bread Street near Cheapside, where any gentleman may be accommodated in any
anneal'd Draughts or Effigies whatever'.[28] The second comes from the *Postman*, in which an

26. This is illustrated in Edwards (1954), II,
p. 328, fig 45. It is bordered with engraved
glass slips and bears the monogram and
coronet of the Earl of Nottingham.
27. Child (1990) p. 16.
28. Edwards, (1954) II, p. 322.

Plate 9:52. Overmantel mirror (1710-20). A fine example of mirror and painting *en suite.* The shouldered shape of the mirror
might suggest a date after 1710. The butted edges of the plates are decorated by cutting, thus making a decorative feature out
of the otherwise unsightly join. Compare with the Marot design shown in 9:50.   CARLTON HOBBS

advertiser claimed that he 'makes and sells all sorts of works enamelled and of glass, different postures of all kinds, animals, Plants, Trees, Flowers and Fruit, together with all manner of Representations to the Life. In short whatever can be desired or thought on either in Glass or enamelled in the Fire, without using anything besides his hand or the matter'.[29] One wonders, however, whether the paintings referred to are not merely reverse painted glass plates, and the annealing or enamelling does not sound much like any technique used in *verre églomisé.* More plausible accounts are found at the beginning of the eighteenth century. The term 'Mosaic work', which occurs in a bill of furniture made as a gift from Queen Anne to the Emperor of Morocco in 1704, might be a contemporary description of *verre églomisé.* The bill, submitted by the cabinet-maker Philip Arbuthnot, describes 'two large sconces with Double Branches finely gilded being three foot deep scolloped diamond cutt and Engraved. Embellished with crimson and gold Mosaic worke with Flowers on the Bodyes of the glass'.[30] Something similar is described in one of Gerrit Jensen's bills for a mirror supplied to the 5th Earl of Salisbury: 'a large looking glass, the frame drawn with scarlet and silver, the mouldings gilt'.[31]

The evidence, such as it is, suggests that *verre églomisé* was perhaps introduced in the 1690s. If so, it was rare, and does not occur on any firmly dated English mirrors made before 1700 (none of the glasses at Hampton Court Palace has *verre églomisé* borders). Thereafter it became increasingly common, and the majority of extant examples probably date from the period 1710-30.

The development of the pier glass

Pier glass is the term used to describe a mirror fixed to the wall or 'pier' between two windows. In this sense many of the mirrors already discussed in this and previous chapters are pier glasses, but the term is usually more strictly applied and implies that the mirror is more or less a permanent fixture. This is less an aesthetic issue than a physical one, because as mirror plates grew larger it became increasingly impractical to treat them as movable objects, or to hang them by conventional means.[32] The sheer weight of glass meant that either the frames had to be made much stronger, which added to the overall weight and bulk, or the glass had to be secured to the wall itself. Some of the mirrors at Hampton Court Palace illustrate the problem. Those in the King's Eating Room retain the form of the conventional cushion-framed rectangular mirror, but they are actually fixed to the wall (6:11). The glass in the Great Bedchamber, installed in 1699, takes this process a stage further, since it has no frame at all, save for the moulded edge of the panelling (6:13). It is interesting that, although the entire pier is glazed from the dado upwards, the design of the mirror is intended to mimic a conventional frame and cresting, with a crown suspended from a blue glass 'ribbon' above it. Both this and the previous example are also significant in that the distinction between the mirror plate and its cresting is merely notional. In both cases the cresting is itself mirrored, and this was the first step towards discarding the division between plate and cresting altogether.

It was about the time that the Hampton Court mirrors were supplied that the term 'pier glass' became current, and the bill for furniture supplied by Gerrit Jensen to Thomas Coke M.P., already quoted in part above, contains an early use of the term. In June 1699 year Jensen charged Coke £8 'For 3 Glasses in a black fra[me] for a peer', and a further £18 for '2 peere glasses black frames' supplied in July.[33]

It was not unusual for cabinet-makers also to deal in glass. Apart from the many mirrors supplied to his various patrons, Jensen also supplied window glass when required, as at Chatsworth in 1688.[34] John Gumley was rather different, in that he was not only a cabinet maker but a manufacturer of mirror plates. In 1704 he was admitted a freeman of the Company of Looking Glass Sellers as a 'Looking Glass Grinder', and by 1705 he and others had established a glass manufactory at Lambeth.[35] A petition of that year stated that the manufacture of looking glasses in England had so improved 'that they serve not only for the Furniture and Ornament of her Majesty's Dominions at Home, but are likewise held in great esteem in Foreign Parts; the Venetians themselves buying of these Plates and preferring them to their own'.[36] Gumley claimed to have reduced the cost of production by twenty per cent, while simultaneously improving the quality and increasing the size of plates.

29. Ibid.
30. PRO LC 9/282, f.3. For details of Arbuthnot's career see Beard and Gilbert (1986), pp. 16-17.
31. Hatfield House, Bills 475.
32. The great increase in the size of mirror plates from 1700 onwards could be linked to the repeal of the 20% excise duty on mirror plates in 1699.
33. B.L., Add. MSS 69975, Coke Papers.
34. Beard and Gilbert (1986), pp. 486-7.
35. Beard and Gilbert (1986), p. 379.
36. Quoted in Edwards (1954), II, p. 322.
37. Beard and Gilbert (1986), p. 380.
38. I am grateful to Peter Day for drawing my attention to this entry. It is quoted in Beard and Gilbert (1986), p. 380, but the date is wrongly given as 1703.

Plate 9:53. Pier glass (1703). This is one of a pair supplied by John Gumley to the Duke of Devonshire in 1703. The form is still essentially 17th century, with a rectangular plate within a 'frame' and surmounted by a cresting.

Plate 9:54. Detail of 9:53. It is mystery why Gumley should have been permitted to deface a mirror of this importance with his signature.

A famous pair of mirrors made for Chatsworth bear John Gumley's name and the date 1703 (9:53 and 9:54). These are essentially seventeenth century in form, with a rectangular plate and separate cresting, but here again the cresting is mirrored The Chatsworth account books record that these cost £200 the pair, and a further £16 for carriage from London.[37]

A few years later in date is another pair of mirrors, also at Chatsworth (9:55). These might well relate to an entry in the Chatsworth accounts for 1705: 'Pd Gilbert Ball Carriage for 2 large Looking glasses & frames 2 other large Cases with furniture chair frames £6.10s'.[38] The mirrors are English, probably supplied by either John Gumley or Gerrit Jensen, but they owe a great deal to contemporary French designs. The cresting, in particular, is a development of that on the French mirrors at Boughton (6:21).

Plate 9:55. Pier glass (c.1705). Perhaps supplied by John Gumley (see text). This is one of a pair, richly decorated with *verre églomisé* within carved and gilded borders. Only two years later in date than 9:53, but clearly moving towards the 18th century conception of the pier glass as an integrated whole.

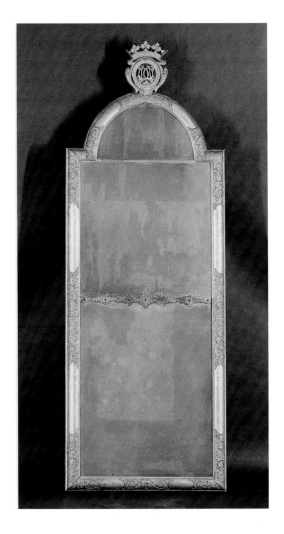

Plate 9:56. Pier glass (c.1710). This bears the cipher of the 2nd Duke of Queensbury, who died in 1711. The frame is decorated with 'corners and middles', and has a broad ovolo section in the 17th century manner. The narrow proportions are decidedly 18th century, however, and the half-round top echoes the doors of cabinets and desks-and-bookcases. Additionally, the main plate and the 'cresting' are now contained within a single frame.
SOTHEBY'S

Plate 9:57. Pier glass (c.1710). This is one of several supplied to Burley-on-the-Hill by Richard Robinson and Thomas Howcraft. Among the additional embellishments billed by the makers were £3 for 'sholoping ye end glasses and cutting ye scroops', and £2.10s. for the 'ten gilt Rosoars [roses]'. Note the way the divisions between the plates are covered by engraved glass slips.
CHRISTOPHER GIBBS

9:55 is important in illustrating a preliminary step towards the fully integrated pier glass. Thus the main plate, the *églomisé* 'frame' and the *églomisé* cresting are all of glass, and the latter is contained within a carved wooden frame which rises in steps and scrolls to a central coronet. The next step was to eliminate the distinction between main plate and cresting altogether, and enclose both parts within the same outer frame. It is difficult to state with any certainly when this development took place, but it had certainly occurred by the time the mirrors in 9:56 and 9:57 were made. The first of these is topped with the cipher of James, 2nd Duke of Queensbury, who died in 1711. The mirror is composed of three plates, the divisions concealed by decorative glass slips 'scolloped and diamond cut'. The frame has a simple ovolo section and is decorated with 'corners and middles' in the manner of contemporary picture frames. The date is perhaps c.1705-10.

The second was made for Daniel Finch, 2nd Earl of Nottingham and Winchilsea (1647-1730). It is one of several made for Burley-on-the-Hill by Richard Robinson and Thomas Howcraft in 1711. This partnership exemplifies the close link between the makers of mirror plates and cabinet-makers, for Robinson was a looking-glass maker who worked in Beaufort Street, off the Strand, and Howcraft was a cabinet-maker and glass seller with premises in Cornhill and Long Acre.[39] Since Robinson had declared he was leaving off trade in April 1710 and Howcraft was declared bankrupt in July 1711, it is probable that this mirror was among the last of their products, perhaps manufactured in 1710. To minimise risk of breakage all the mirrors ordered by the Earl were sent from London to Burley in sections, to be assembled and mounted *in situ*.[40] Despite its simple form, this mirror cost £82.1s.6d. This was partly due to its size, over 10ft. (305cm) high, but also to the decoration, since the engraving of the borders was a highly skilled and delicate operation – the cipher and coronet alone cost £6.10s.

39. For further details see Beard and Gilbert (1986), pp. 455 and 759-60.
40. Finch (1901), p. 77.

Plate 9:58. Pier glass (1710-1730). This is one of a pair, *en suite,* with the card table in 9:41. The ovolo-section frame remained popular until at least 1730, although the shaping of the mirror-head perhaps suggests a date between 1710 and 1720.

PRIVATE COLLECTION

Plate 9:59. Pier glass (1710-20). The glass borders are decorated with gilt 'corners and middles', and the design of the cresting bears comparison with the aprons of contemporary pier tables.

SOTHEBY'S

41. *Nouveaux* [sic] *Livre de Boites de Pendules: Second Livre d'Orlogeries.* Neither of these was included in the 1703 edition of Marot's work, but both appear in the second edition of 1712. Both contain at least one plate dated 1706.

The simple arched head of both these mirrors is also found on the doors of contemporary cabinets (cf. 7:54) and of desks-and-bookcases. It might also be significant that it was between 1700 and 1710 that the break-arch dial was introduced for English bracket and long-case clocks. That the style was highly fashionable both here and on the Continent is indicated by the prevalence of break-arch designs in Marot's engravings of clock cases, published in 1712.[41]

The simple semi-circular mirror head seems to have been fairly short lived, at least so far as pier glasses were concerned. William Price's desk-and-bookcase (7:53) shows that by 1713 mirrors with shaped or shouldered heads had been introduced, and there is a strong correlation between the shape of bookcase mirrors and the shape of pier glasses. 9:58 shows one of a pair, *en suite* with the card table shown in 9:41. The shaping of the mirrors is similar to those on Price's desk-and-book case, as so, presumably, is the date.

Truly grand pier glasses required further ornamentation with carved crestings and these, with their combination of formal strapwork and foliage, owe much to the aprons on contemporary pier tables. 9:59 shows what is probably an early example of the type, which retains the 'corners and middles' style of ornamentation to the glass borders. Another example, perhaps slightly later in date, bears the pheon crest of John Sidney, 6th Earl of Leicester (9:60). This is a glass of the highest quality, the plates both bevelled and engraved, and the borders decorated with finely detailed *verre églomisé.* The shape of the plates, with sharp re-entrants at the corners, is very similar to numerous other examples, of which one is shown here (9:61). This bear the arms of Sir Gregory Page who was created baronet in 1714. Sir Gregory died in 1720, which gives us a close dating for the mirror.

Plate 9:60. Pier glass (1710-20). This superb glass was made for the 6th Earl of Leicester. Numerous examples survive of a similar form with *verre églomisé* borders, but most lack the finely carved cresting. Cresting apart, the similarities between this and 9:61 are compelling. PENSHURST PLACE, THE LORD DE L'ISLE

Plate 9:61. Pier glass (1714-20). This bears the arms of Sir Gregory Page, created baronet in 1714. MALLET AND SONS (ANTIQUES) LTD.

This stylistic development of pier glasses over this period has been described here as a fairly logical and consistent process, but the reality was undoubtedly more complex. Glasses with rectangular main plates and separate crestings, more or less in the seventeenth century manner, were still made for the Royal Palaces in George I's reign.[42] For domestic interiors the rectangular plate and arched cresting was a much cheaper option than the multi-plate, arched and shouldered designs of the noble pier glass. Examples of these simple, essentially seventeenth century forms can be seen in depictions of domestic interiors as late as the 1720s.[43]

42. See, for example, Edwards (1954), II, p. 323, fig. 31 and p. 324, fig. 37.
43. See, for example, the watercolours of Dr. William Stukeley (1727-9), reproduced in Francesca Scoones, 'Dr William Stukeley's House at Grantham', *The Georgian Group Journal*, IX (1999), pp. 158-165.

GLOSSARY OF FURNITURE WOODS

This glossary is by no means comprehensive. It discusses only the more important furniture woods mentioned in the text.

Ash *(Fraxinus excelsior)*

Ash is a common native tree. The timber is usually pale and straight grained, with pronounced early wood growth rings. It is strong and elastic, but not particularly durable, and is prone to worm. Although not usually considered a fashionable furniture timber, ash had a particular role in seventeenth century furniture as a substitute for olivewood. Because olivewood was rarely straight-grained enough to be used for table legs or candlestand shafts, ash, suitably stained and varnished, was used instead.

Some ash has a variegated brown heartwood closely resembling olivewood; this is now known as Olive ash, but in the late seventeenth century it was sometimes called Green Ebony. 'Some Ash is curiously cambleted and veined; I say, so differently from other timber, that our skilled cabinet-makers prize it equally with Ebony, and give it the name of Green Ebony, which their customers pay well for... But to bring it to that curious lustre, so as it is hardly to be distinguished from the most curiously diapered Olive, they varnish their work with China varnish'. Olive ash was used as a veneer in its own right, or in conjunction with olive wood.

Burr ash can be highly decorative and is occasionally found as a primary veneer on late seventeenth and early eighteenth century furniture. 'The truth is, the Bruscum or Molluscum, to be frequently found in this wood, is nothing inferior to that of Maple... being altogether as exquisitely diapered, and waved like the lines of Agate'. Stalker and Parker record that burr ash was also stained with *aqua fortis* (nitric acid) in combination with various metals to produce spectacularly coloured veneers in yellow, blue and green.

Barberry *(Berberis vulgaris)*

Barberry is a small shrub native to much of Europe. The wood is hard and fine-textured, and bright yellow in colour. Medullary rays are prominent on both tangential and quartered surfaces. Its primary commercial use was as the source of the dye, berberine.

Barberry is one of the woods described by John Evelyn as providing yellow timber for the use of 'inlayers', and recent research at the Rijksmuseum has revealed that it was extensively used in Dutch floral marquetry. Although similar work on English marquetry remains to be done, it is highly likely that barberry was also used by English marqueteurs.

Brazil wood *(Caesalpinia* spp.)

The name brazil wood derives from the French *braise,* a live or glowing coal, which aptly describes its vivid colour. The wood has been highly sought after since medieval times as a source of bright red dye. The first importations came from Asia, but the discovery of the Americas opened new areas of supply, of which the most important, Brazil, was named after the wood.

Brazil wood trees are small and the wood is hard, heavy and often difficult to work. The most sought-after timber was bright orange-red in colour, sometimes with streaks of black or brown. The best known variety came from northern Brazil and was often known as Pernambuco wood, from the port whence it was exported to Europe. Because Brazil was a Portuguese colony, and English vessels were therefore unable to trade there directly, the English tended to use varieties of West Indian brazil wood, commonly called Braziletto or Jamaica wood *(Caesalpinia echinata).* Although primarily a dyewood, Evelyn described brazil wood as one of the red woods used in floral marquetry. In addition, small pieces of furniture were occasionally made from it. In 1661-2 Thomas Malin supplied 'Two tables and Two pairs of stands of Jamaica Wood' to the Royal Household for £18.

Cedar *(Coniferae)*

Seventeenth century furniture makers gave the name cedar to any wood with an aromatic, cedary scent. While there is little evidence that the true cedars *(Cedrus* spp.) were ever much used in English furniture, a number of cedar-scented woods were commonly imported from North America and the West Indies. The most important of these was Eastern red cedar *(Juniperus* spp.), a reddish brown, fairly dense, straight-grained and fine-textured softwood which is easy to work and has an intense cedar aroma. It was imported primarily from Bermuda and Virginia and was used for furniture and panelling, both in the solid and as a veneer.

Northern white cedar *(Chamaecyparis thyoides)* is paler, lighter in weight and less scented, but nevertheless is a fine furniture wood. It is indigenous to the northern colonies of North America and was occasionally used in seventeenth century English furniture. So too was another North American cedar, *Thuya occidentalis.*

Several species of scented juniper grow in the West Indies, but the most important West Indian cedar was Cedrela (Cedrela spp.), now commonly called Havana or cigar-box cedar. This is a reddish-brown hardwood related to mahogany and, while not commonly imported in the seventeenth century, there are isolated examples of its use.

Cedar is quoted frequently in late seventeenth century inventories, but less commonly in the early eighteenth. There is some evidence to suggest that the increase in import duties from c.1690 onwards inhibited importations, a situation which was remedied by the Naval Stores Act of 1721, which abolished import duties on all West Indian and North American woods.

Cocus wood *(Brya ebenus)*

Cocus is a common West Indian tree, rarely growing higher than 40ft. (10m) or thicker than 10in. (250mm) The wood is very hard and heavy, with a dark, chocolate-brown heartwood and a prominent white sapwood. It is not the easiest wood to work, but turns beautifully and takes a very high polish. It is sometimes called Jamaica ebony, or granadillo, although the latter name is also applied to other woods.

Cocus wood was exported from Jamaica in large quantities from the 1660s onwards and was widely used by English cabinet-makers both as a veneer and in the solid. It was most typically used for oyster veneering, and is characteristic of early cabinets made between c.1660 and c.1675. Despite its abundance, cocus wood furniture is rarely mentioned in contemporary bills or inventories, probably because it was usually called 'ebony'. One notable exception is the probate inventory of Edward Traherne (1675), which records cocus wood worth £36 in his cellar.

In furniture history books, and among the antiques trade at large, cocus wood is usually wrongly identified as lignum vitae or laburnum.

Deal *(Coniferae)*

The word deal comes from the Dutch/German word *deel,* meaning a part. From late medieval times it was used as a generic term to describe coniferous (softwood) timber sawn into planks and boards. By extension, it also came to imply panelling, furniture or objects made from such timber, as in 'a deal table'.

Contrary to popular belief, deal was not a cheap, locally available material, since conifers were not abundant in England before the nineteenth century. The main sources of deal in the seventeenth century were Norway, Sweden and the Baltic states. The types of deal were distinguished either by place of origin – Christiana, Swinsund, Drammen, etc. – or colour. Red deal usually implied Scots pine *(Pinus sylvestris)* or Larch *(Larix decidua).* White deal implied Norway spruce *(Picea abies)* and Silver fir *(Abies alba).* 'Spruce' deals were deals imported from Prussia.

Red deal was a good general-purpose softwood, much used for general joinery, panelling and cheaper furniture. For cabinet-making the lighter, less resinous, white deal was preferred. Both varieties can be found on late seventeenth century cabinet work.

North American softwoods were known and occasionally imported in the seventeenth and early eighteenth centuries, but large scale importations were inhibited by the cost of shipping across the Atlantic.

Ebony *(Diospyros* spp.)

The French term for a cabinet-maker – *ébéniste* – testifies to the esteem in which this wood was held in the seventeenth century. There are numerous species of ebony, which grow throughout Asia and parts of Africa. The trees are generally small, with the bole rarely exceeding 2ft. (0.6m) in diameter. The wood is very hard, heavy and very fine textured, but is apt to split and can be difficult to work. It finishes beautifully, however, with a deep lustre which fully justifies the trouble taken.

Most ebonies are more or less variegated, ranging in colour from white to grey, yellow, brown and black. The truly jet-black ebony is not particularly common, which made it all the more sought after, and it was this wood that was particularly prized by seventeenth century cabinet-makers. English cabinet-makers were less prolific in their use of ebony than their Continental counterparts, but the wood was nevertheless an important addition to their repertoire. It was particularly favoured for early pendulum clock-cases, and was also commonly used as a ground for floral marquetry.

Because of its high price (between £20 and £40 per ton), English work in solid ebony is rare, except for small mouldings on clock hoods and cabinets. For the same reason, much that appears to be ebony is actually a cheaper wood dyed black. A hard, close-textured wood such as pear was ideal for the purpose, and numerous contemporary receipts for counterfeiting ebony survive. Cocus wood (q.v.) or Jamaica ebony was also commonly used in lieu of true ebony.

Elm *(Ulmus* spp.)

Like ash, elm is a common native tree not usually regarded as a first-class cabinet wood. In the solid it is unsuitable for high class cabinet-work, being coarse, fractious and apt to warp, but some cuts, especially burrs, are very beautiful. Many surviving examples, such as the Duke of Lauderdale's scriptor at Ham House, have been stained a bright golden yellow, probably with nitric acid. The same treatment, washed over with lampblack, produces a spectacular mottled effect which the antiques trade calls 'mulberry'.

Fustic *(Chlorophora tinctoria)*

John Evelyn described fustic as one of the natural yellow woods used by 'inlayers'. The tree is widespread in the West Indies and Central America, and produces substantial timber suitable for many uses. Its primary commercial importance, however, was as a dyewood, producing a range of yellow, khaki and drab colours, and it was shipped to Europe in large quantities throughout the seventeenth and eighteenth centuries.

The wood is moderately hard and heavy, the texture neither fine nor coarse, and when first cut it is a bright golden yellow. However, the colour soon fades to brown or russet, and for this reason it is not easily identified on historic furniture. It is highly likely that fustic was used in floral marquetry, but this has yet to be confirmed by microscopic analysis.

It is worth noting that fustic is a member of the mulberry family *(Moracae)*, and was sometimes known as 'dyer's mulberry'. This could well be the source of the common but mistaken belief that mulberry wood was used in cabinet-making. Celia Fiennes records that the hall at Chippenham Park in Cambridgeshire was 'wanscoated with Wallnut tree the pannells and rims round with Mulberry tree that is a lemon coullour'. Since true mulberry wood is not yellow but brown or tan, it is possible that she was describing fustic.

Holly *(Ilex aquifolium)*

A great deal more information is wanted on the use of holly in furniture making. The tree is common throughout the British Isles, and produces hard, compact and fine textured wood, almost chalk-white in colour. Like maple and sycamore (q.v.), holly takes stains easily, and was used in floral marquetry for much the same purposes. Because these three woods are so similar in appearance and uses it is virtually impossible to distinguish between them except under a microscope.

Laburnum *(Laburnum* spp.)

Laburnum is only included here because it is so frequently cited by the antiques trade. There is no evidence that laburnum was much, if ever, used in seventeenth or eighteenth century cabinet-making. Veneers casually identified as such usually turn out to be cocus or princeswood.

Lignum vitae *(Guaiacum* spp.)

Lignum vitae is a small West Indian tree, rarely growing much more than 1ft. (30cm) in diameter or 30ft. (9m) in height. The timber is exceptionally hard, heavy and tough, and its pores are saturated with natural oils. The heartwood is dark bronze-green, more or less variegated with black and brown, surrounded by a light-coloured sapwood.

In the seventeenth century lignum vitae (literally, 'the wood of life') was regarded as a drug, not a cabinet wood. It was thought to be effective against many ills, including venereal disease, for which reason it commanded a good price in Europe. Because of its hardness and self-lubricating quality it had many quasi-industrial uses, of which the most important was for pulleys and sheaves in the rigging of sailing ships.

Lignum was much used by turners, most notably for the large wassail bowls so sought after by collectors of treen, but it was not suitable for cabinet-work because of its oiliness and difficulty of working. Consequently, references to lignum vitae cabinets etc., in furniture history books are unlikely to be accurate. Several 'lignum vitae' cabinets recently analysed have proved to be cocus wood (q.v.).

Maple and Sycamore *(Acer* spp.)

The field maple *(Acer campestris)* is England's only native maple, and was once more common than it is now. It is typically a hedgerow tree and, although rarely very large, it produces timber sufficient for many general purposes. The wood is moderately hard and close-textured, pale brown or cream in colour, and generally even grained and easy to work.

Maple is a versatile wood, but was most typically used for turnery and domestic ware. Most famously, maple was used for the silver-mounted mazers or ceremonial drinking bowls made in England since early mediaeval times (in this context it is worth noting that the Welsh name for maple is *masarnen)*.

In cabinet-making its employment was more limited. It is most commonly seen as a primary veneer in burr form. Well-figured timber was highly prized and John Evelyn devoted considerable space to its decorative qualities: 'Above all, notable for these extravagant damaskings and characters, is the Maple'. The figure was often further enhanced by the use of stains, spectacular examples of which can be seen on the furniture of John Coxed and others. It is probable that maple was also used in floral marquetry in the same way as holly (q.v.) and sycamore, but until more detailed research has been carried out on marquetry woods this will remain conjectural.

Sycamore *(Acer pseudoplatanus)* is now so common that it is difficult to believe it was once rare. A native of central Europe, it is not mentioned in any English source until Turner's *Herbal* of 1551; Gerard *(Herball,* 1597) considered it a rarity. It was extensively planted in the seventeenth century, and by the 1660s was sufficiently common to be described by Evelyn as 'excellent for trenchers, cart and plough timber, being light, tough and not much inferior to ash itself'.

The wood is pale, creamy and even-textured, quite strong and easily worked, but not durable. Being larger, faster growing and more prolific than its native cousin, sycamore has largely replaced field maple for most traditional uses, although for fine cabinet-work the harder, denser maple is still superior. Together with holly and maple, sycamore was widely used in floral marquetry, either as a natural cream or white, or stained in colours to represent flowers and foliage. Sycamore/maple was also used for the pale, off-white banding and stringing found on late seventeenth century cabinet-work.

Mulberry *(Morus* spp.)

This is a nonsense term used in the antiques trade to describe maple, elm or ash veneers which have been stained with nitric acid and lampblack to produce a spectacular mottled or 'tortoiseshell' effect. There is no historical evidence for the use of mulberry in fine cabinet-making, although there is no reason why it could not be used for treen or novelty items. See fustic, above.

Oak *(Quercus* spp.)

Seventeenth and eighteenth century furniture makers recognised a clear distinction between native-grown oak and imported European oak or wainscot (q.v.). English oak was prized for its toughness and durability, and was the timber of choice for ship and house building, general joinery and vernacular furniture. These same qualities made much of it unsuitable for cabinet-work or fine joinery, since it was frequently cross-grained, difficult to work, knotty, and prone to shrink and warp. Much English oak also has a high tannin content, which causes corrosion in iron and steel fittings and makes it generally darker than its Continental counterpart. The difference in quality between native oak and wainscot was reflected in their market price, typically 1d.-2d. per foot for English oak and 3d.-4d. for wainscot. Nevertheless, for provincial cabinet-makers and joiners who either could not obtain or could not afford wainscot, native oak was an invaluable resource.

Olive *(Olea europa)*

Olivewood is one of the most important late seventeenth century cabinet woods. The tree is a native of southern Europe and the shores of the Mediterranean, and its fruit and oil are hugely important to the economy of that region. The tree is generally small, twisted and knotty, and does not immediately strike one as a first-class cabinet wood. However, it makes up in figure what it lacks in stature and stability, and for this reason was highly sought after. Olivewood is moderately heavy, hard and fine textured, and takes a high finish. The wood is often mistaken for walnut, particularly under three centuries of patination, but olive has a finer texture, with a more marked contrast between the light, tan-coloured background and its dark, sharply demarcated wavy figuring.

Because of its crooked growth and small size it was rarely used in the solid, being most commonly cut into 'oyster' veneers or short, straight-grained sections. Where straight, solid timber was needed, for the legs of tables and stands for instance, another wood, usually ash (q.v.), was used as a substitute.

Because olivewood was essentially a by-product of olive oil production it was relatively cheap and, because of its small size, it cost little to transport by sea. The Customs returns show that in the 1690s olivewood cost around £10 per ton, which was similar to walnut and very much cheaper than princeswood. Olivewood furniture was therefore well within the reach of the 'middling sort' of people – merchants, tradesmen, members of the professions – and this is borne out by the evidence of contemporary London inventories.

Padouk *(Pterocarpus* spp.)

The padouk family of trees is widespread throughout India, Burma, south-east Asia and parts of West Africa. Most are large timber trees, up to 3ft. (1m) in diameter and over 100ft. (30m) high. The wood is heavy, hard and durable, rather coarse textured, but takes a fine finish. It ranges in colour from straw yellow to pink and blood red, often streaked with darker veins.

Padouk was first imported as a dyewood, with one species in particular – red sanders *(P. santalinum)* – being highly valued. Other species were recognised as suitable for furniture making, and from about 1670 onwards padouk was commonly used in marquetry for its natural reds and pinks. The colour is fugitive, however, and has usually faded to a brown or grey. Solid padouk furniture is also found but was more common in the eighteenth century when the timber was imported in greater quantities.

Because of its colour, padouk was originally known as rosewood. This should not be confused with the modern rosewoods, which are members of the *Dalbergia* family.

Princeswood *(Dalbergia cearensis)*

There is some confusion over the true identity of princeswood. Some early authorities identify it as Spanish elm *(Cordia gerascanthus),* a common tree in the West Indies and northern South America. Sir Hans Sloane (1707) described this as 'a very large and stately Tree, affording very broad Boards to make Tables or Cabinets of... making a pleasant show, whence came the name Princes Wood amongst our Cabinet-Makers, they using it very much...'.[8] However, at the time of writing no seventeenth century furniture made from *C. gerascanthus* has been identified. Microscopic analysis reveals that most 'princeswood' furniture was veneered with a type of rosewood, probably *Dalbergia cearensis* or a related species. This is now known as kingwood.

D. cearensis is indigenous to tropical America, and particularly Brazil. The tree is slender, producing narrow billets of timber rarely more than 4-8in. (10-20cm) wide with the sapwood removed. The wood is very hard and dense, with a fine, even texture. The wide creamy sapwood surrounds a heartwood of rich violet-brown streaked with strong striations of red, yellow and black.

In the late seventeenth century princeswood was imported in small quantities via France and Portugal, and the name almost certainly derived from its very high price of between £35 and £60 per ton. It was the most expensive of all cabinet woods and it is consequently found only on high quality furniture. Because of its small size, princeswood was used predominantly as a veneer, usually cut obliquely to emphasis the strong directional effect of the figure. The wood loses its colour quickly, but it is clear that in the seventeenth century the most sought-after veneers were predominantly red, rather than the more common violet-brown, and indeed princeswood was listed by John Evelyn among the natural red woods used by 'inlayers'.

Sycamore *(Acer pseudoplatanus)*
See Maple

Wainscot *(Quercus* spp.)

Wainscot was the name given to high-quality quarter-cut oak boards imported from the Baltic. The origin of the name is obscure, but the most plausible derivation is from the German *wandt-schott* or wall-board. Wall panelling was one of the principal uses for the boards and the modern term wainscot or wainscotting, for wall panelling, derives from this usage. By the seventeenth century the term had acquired a generic meaning, applied to furniture made from imported oak, as in 'a wainscot press'.

English cabinet-makers preferred wainscot to home-grown oak despite the fact that it was two or three times the price. It was cut from large, straight, slow-grown oaks. The timber was straight, free of knots, relatively light in weight, generally pale in colour and low in tannin. It was easy to work and there was little waste, so that the price difference between imported and home-grown varieties was smaller in practice than at first appears. Wainscot was also less liable to warp, an important consideration where veneered furniture is concerned. So consistent was the preference for wainscot among furniture makers in the south and east of England that it can almost be taken as a hallmark of quality. Conversely, the use of fast-grown native oak is often a sign of provincial manufacture.

Walnut (*Juglans* spp.)

Walnut was the most versatile wood employed by fashionable furniture makers during the period covered by this book. The timber has few vices, being strong, stable, moderately fine in texture and easily worked, although it is prone to rot and worm. In colour it ranges from a bland grey-brown to a rich purple-brown with black figuring. Most walnut is straight-grained, with some degree of the smoky grey pigmentation which is its most characteristic feature, but some cuts, especially burrs and root timber, are convoluted or tightly knotted, with dramatic contrasts between light and dark figure. As a general rule, plain, unfigured timber was used in the solid, for chair frames, etc., and figured timber was reserved for veneers.

Although the European walnut (*J. regia*) is now grown widely in England, it is not native and cannot be described as abundant. The tree grows best in the warmer climate of France, Italy and the Mediterranean littoral, and consequently a great deal, perhaps the majority, of walnut used in fashionable furniture at this period was imported. Unfortunately, Customs returns prior to 1698 do not survive, but contemporary commentators such as John Evelyn considered France to be the source of the best timber, and wood from Grenoble was particularly well regarded. From 1698 onwards the Customs returns show that walnut was also imported from Holland, Spain, Portugal, Italy, North Africa and Turkey. Almost 98 per cent went to London, which suggests not only that London dominated the fashionable furniture trade, but that provincial makers relied heavily on native timber.

North American black walnut (*J. nigra*) was also imported, though not in significant quantities until the 1720s. The main reason for this was the cost of shipping across the Atlantic, which meant that European walnut was both more widely available and usually cheaper. However, there are some notable examples of the use of American walnut, such as the staircase at Dyrham Park, made from wood imported from Virginia by William Blathwayt in the early 1690s. Blathwayt's connections in the Plantations Office and the Board of Trade were probably instrumental in obtaining this shipment.

American black walnut is generally darker than European and some authorities consider it to be more durable and resistant to worm. Some pundits claim to be able to distinguish between the two, but after three centuries of exposure, oxidization and patination this is mere guesswork. Indeed, the two woods are often inseparable even under a microscope, so it is usually impossible to make any meaningful observations about the origin of the timber used for individual items of furniture.

Yew (*Taxus baccata*)

The yew tree is one of our few native conifers and is distributed widely throughout the British Isles. Its timber belies the fact that it is technically a softwood, since yew is hard, heavy and tough. The colour is generally a warm orange-brown, sometimes with darker streaks or blotches, with finely-marked growth rings and a prominent white sapwood.

English yew tends to be fast grown, knotty and often blemished with inclusions of bark, so that it rarely has the properties of a fine cabinet wood and is most often found in vernacular or provincial furniture. It is also somewhat oily, which is a disadvantage when gluing veneers. However, some yew timber is highly decorative; good burrs were particularly prized and were sometimes employed on fashionable furniture. These are typically very tightly knotted, each knot being centred by a black pith or eye. Evelyn relates that 'inlayers and cabinet-makers (particularly for marquetry floors) most gladly employ it'.

SELECT BIBLIOGRAPHY

AGIUS, Pauline. 'Late Sixteenth- and Seventeenth-Century Furniture in Oxford', *Furniture History,* VII [1971], pp.72-86.

ANON. 'A true Relation of the Rise and Progress of the East-Indian Company', London [1697].

'England's Almanack, shewing how the East India Trade is Prejuditiall to this Kingdom', London [1700].

'The Case of the Japaners of England', London [n.d., c.1700/01].

'The Case of the Joyners Company, against the Importation of Manufactured Cabinet-work from the East-Indies', London [n.d., c.1700/01].

'For the Encouragement of the Woollen Manufacture of England, London [n.d., c.1678].

'For the Encouragement of the Consumption of the Woollen Manufacture of this Kingdom', London [n.d., c.1689].

'For the Encouragement of the Consumption of the Woollen Manufacture of this Kingdom', London [n.d., c.1698].

BAARSEN, Reinier. *Nederlandse Meubelen, 1600-1800,* Amsterdam [1993].

17th-century cabinets, Amsterdam [2000].

BEARD. Geoffrey. *Upholsterers and Interior Furnishing in England, 1530-1840,* New Haven and London [1997].

BEARD, Geoffrey, and GILBERT, Christopher (Eds.). *Dictionary of English Furniture Makers, 1660-1840,* Leeds [1986].

BEARD, Geoffrey, and WESTMAN, Annabel. 'A French Upholsterer in England, Francis Lapiere, 1653-1714', *The Burlington Magazine,* CXXXV [August 1993], pp.515-524.

BOSOMWORTH, Dorothy. 'The King's Metalwork', *Apollo,* CXL [August 1994], pp.65-68.

BOWETT, Adam. 'The Vigani Specimen Cabinet by John Austin, a Cambridge joiner', *Regional Furniture,* VIII [1994], pp.58-63.

'The Age of Snakewood', *Furniture History,* XXXIV [1998], pp.212-225.

'A new attribution for Bishop Compton's elbow chair', *Apollo,* CXLIX [January 1999], pp.22-24.

'The English 'horsebone' chair, 1685-1710', *The Burlington Magazine,* CXLI [May 1999], pp.263-270.

'The English cross-frame chair, 1694-1715', *The Burlington Magazine,* CXLII [June 2000], pp.344-352.

BOYNTON, Lindsay, and THORNTON, Peter. 'The Hardwick Hall Inventory of 1601', *Furniture History,* VII [1971], pp.1-40.

BREARS, Peter (Ed.). *Yorkshire Probate Inventories, 1542-1689,* Yorkshire Archaeological Society, Record Series, Vol. CXXXIV [1972].

BRISTOW, Ian. C. *Interior House Painting Colours and Technology, 1615-1840,* New Haven and London [1996].

BROOKE, Xanthe. *The Lady Lever Art Gallery, Catalogue of Embroideries,* Stroud [1992].

BUDDEN, S., and HALAHAN, F. (Eds.) *Lacquerwork and Japanning, postprints of the Conference held by UKIC at the Courtauld Institute of Art,* London [1994].

CAMDEN SOCIETY. *Lists of foreign Protestants and Aliens resident in England 1618-1688,* Old Series, 82 [1862], reprinted AMS Press, New York [1968].

CAMPBELL, Thomas. 'William III and The Triumph of Lust – The tapestries hung in the King's State Apartments in 1699', *Apollo,* Vol.CXL, No.390, (New Series) [August 1994], pp.22-31.

CARKESSE, Charles. *The Act of Tonnage and Poundage, and Rates of Merchandize,* London [1702],

CHILD, Graham. *World Mirrors, 1650-1900,* London [1990].

CLINTON, Lisa. 'The State Bed from Melville House', Masterpieces, Sheet 21, Victoria and Albert Museum.

COLERIDGE, Anthony. 'English Furniture Makers and Cabinet-Makers at Hatfield House – I: c.1600-1750', *The Burlington Magazine,* CIX [February 1967], pp.63-70.

COOKE, Edward S. (Ed.). *Upholstery in America and Europe from the Seventeenth Century to World War I,* New York and London [1987].

DAMPIER, William. *A Collection of Voyages,* 4 vols., London [1729].

DAVIS, Ralph. *The Rise of the English Shipping Industry in the Seventeenth and Eighteenth Centuries,* Newton Abbott [2nd ed., 1972].

DAWSON, P.G., DROVER, C.B., and PARKES, D.W., *Early English Clocks,* Woodbridge [1982].

DEFOE, Daniel. *A Tour thro' the Whole Island of Great Britain... by a gentleman,* 3 vols., London [1724-7].

DERRICK, M., DRUZIK, C. and PREUSSER, F. 'FTIR Analysis of Authentic and Simulated Black Lacquer Finishes on Eighteenth Century Furniture', in *'Urushi'* Conference Proceedings of the Urushi Study Group, Tokyo, June 10-27 1985, Getty Conservation Institute [1986], pp.227-233.

EARLE, Peter. *The Making of the Middle Class,* London [1989].

EDWARDS, Ralph (Ed.). *Dictionary of English Furniture,* 2nd ed., 3 vols., London [1954].

ESTERLY, David. *Grinling Gibbons and the Art of Carving,* London [1998].

EVELYN, John. *Silva, or a Discourse of Forest Trees and the Propagation of Timber in His Majesties Dominions,* London [eds. 1664, 1670, 1679 and 1706].
The Diary of Sir John Evelyn, ed. Wm. Bray, London [1818].

FINCH, Pearl. *The History of Burley-on-the-Hill, Rutland,* 2 vols., London [1901].

FORMAN, Benno. 'Continental Furniture Craftsmen in London: 1511-1625', *Furniture History,* VII [1971], pp.94-120.
American Seating Furniture, 1630-1730, New York and London [1988].

GARBETT, G. and SKELTON, I. *The Wreck of the Metta Catharina,* Truro [1987].

GILBERT, Christopher. *Marked London Furniture, 1700-1840,* Leeds [1996].
Furniture at Temple Newsam House and Lotherton Hall, 3 vols., Leeds [1978 and 1998].

GLOAG, John. *The Englishman's Chair,* London [1964].

GRAHAM, Clare. *Ceremonial and Commemorative Chairs,* London [1994].

HALL, Elizabeth (Ed.). *Michael Warton of Beverley: An Inventory of his Possessions,* Hull [1986].

HOLME, Randall. *Academie of Armory* [1688].

HOLMES, Geoffrey. *The Making of a Great Power: Late Stuart and early Georgian Britain, 1660-1722,* London and New York [1993].

HOUGHTON, John. *A Collection of Letters for the Improvement of Husbandry and Trade,* London [1683].

HUSSEY, Christopher. 'Walnut Furniture at Burley-on-the-Hill', *Country Life* [24 February 1923], pp.254-257.

HUGHES, Peter. 'The French Furniture' in Murdoch (Ed.) [1992], pp.119-127.

HUTH, Hans. *Lacquer of the West – The History of a Craft and an Industry, 1550-1950,* Chicago and London [1971].

JACKSON-STOPS, Gervase. 'William III and French Furniture', *Furniture History,* VII [1971], pp.121-126.

'English Baroque Ironwork – I, the sources of Tijou's designs', *Country Life* [28 January 1971], pp.182-183.

'A Courtier's Collection – The 6th Earl of Dorset's Furniture at Knole, I', *Country Life* [2 June 1977], pp.1495-1499.

'A Courtier's Collection – The 6th Earl of Dorset's Furniture at Knole, II', *Country Life* [9 June 1977], pp.1620-1622.

'Daniel Marot and the First Duke of Montagu', *Nederlands Kunsthistorisch Jaarboek,* 31 [1980], pp.244-262.

'Huguenot Upholsterers and Cabinet-Makers in the Circle of Daniel Marot', in Scouloudi, op. cit., pp.113-124.

'A Set of Furniture by Thomas Phill at Canons Ashby', *Furniture History,* XXI [1985], pp.217-219.

JACKSON-STOPS (Ed.). *Treasure Houses of Britain,* exhibition catalogue, New Haven and London [1985].

JAFFER, Amin. *Furniture from British India and Ceylon,* London [2001].

JENKINS, Susan. 'The Artistic Taste of William III', *Apollo,* CXL [August 1994], pp.4-9.

KENYON, J.P. *Stuart England,* London [1978, 2nd ed. 1985].

KIRKHAM, Pat. 'Inlay, marquetry and buhl workers in England, c.1660-1850', *The Burlington Magazine,* 122 [1980], pp.415-419.

The London Furniture Trade 1700-1870, Leeds [1988].

LANE, Arthur. 'Daniel Marot: Designer of Delft Vases and of Gardens at Hampton Court', *Connoisseur,* 123. [1949], pp.19-24.

LOUDON, John Claudius. *An Encyclopaedia of Cottage, Farm and Villa Architecture and Furniture,* London [1835].

LUNSINGH SCHEURLEER, T.H. 'Pierre Gole, ébéniste du roi Louis XIV', *The Burlington Magazine* [June 1980], pp.380-394.

MACAULAY, Thomas Babington. *The History of England from the Accession of James II,* 4 Vols. [1849-1855], Everyman ed. London and New York [1953].

MACCUBBIN, R.P. and HAMILTON-PHILLIPS, M. (Eds.). *The Age of William III and Mary II – Power, Politics and Patronage 1688-1702,* Williamsburg [1989].

MAROT, Daniel. *Oeuvres du Sr. D. Marot, Architecte de Guilliuame III, Roy de la Grande Bretagne,* Amsterdam [1712].

Das Ornamentwerk des Daniel Marot, P. Jessen (Ed.), Berlin [1892].

MOXON, Joseph. *Mechanick Exercises,* London [1678].

MURDOCH, Tessa. 'Huguenot Artists, Designers and Craftsmen in Great Britain and Ireland, 1680-1760', unpublished PhD thesis, University of London [1982].

(Ed.) *Boughton House – The English Versailles,* London [1992].

'The furniture for the King's Apartments: Wallnuttree, gilding, japanning and marble', *Apollo,* CXL [August 1994], pp.55-59.

'Jean, René and Thomas Pelletier, Huguenot family of carvers and gilders in England, 1682-1726, Part I', *The Burlington Magazine* [November 1997], pp.732-742.

'Jean, René and Thomas Pelletier, Huguenot family of carvers and gilders in England, 1682-1726, Part II', *The Burlington Magazine* [June 1998], pp.363-372.

OZINGA, M.D. *Daniel Marot, de schepper van den Hollandschen Lodewijk XIV-stil,* Amsterdam [1938].

PLUMIER, Charles. *L'Art de Tourner,* Lyon [1701].
POLLOXFEN, John. *A Discourse of trade, coyn & paper credit,* London [1697].
PRICKE, Robert. *The Ornaments of Architecture,* London [1674].

RAMOND, Pierre. *Marquetry,* Newtown, Connecticut [1989].
RICCARDI-CUBITT, Monique. *The Art of the Cabinet,* London [1992].
ROBINSON, Tom. *The Longcase Clock,* Woodbridge [1992, revised ed.].
ROSEVEARE, Henry G. 'Jacob David: A Huguenot London Merchant of the late Seventeenth Century and his Circle', in Scouloudi (Ed.), pp.72-88.

SALMON, William. *Polygraphice,* London [1672].
SCOULOUDI, Irene (Ed.). *Huguenots in Britain and their French Background, 1550-1800,* London [1987].
SHIXIANG, Wang. *Connoisseurship of Chinese Furniture,* Hong Kong [1990].
SLEEP, Janet. 'Patterns of Consumption Across an Urban Hierarchy, 1650-1725', unpublished PhD thesis, University of East Anglia [1996].
SMITH, Robert C. 'Five Furniture Drawings in Siena', *Furniture History,* III [1967], pp.1-15.
STALKER, John and PARKER, George. *A Treatise of Japanning and Varnishing,* London and Oxford [1688].
SWAIN, Margaret. 'The furnishing of Holyroodhouse in 1688', *Connoisseur,* 780 [February 1977], pp.122-130.
  'The State Beds at Holyroodhouse', *Furniture History* XIV [1978], pp.58-60.
  'The Turkey-work Chairs of Holyroodhouse' in Cooke (Ed.) [1987], pp.51-64.
SYMONDS. R.W. *English Furniture from Charles II to George II,* London [1929].
  'Charles II Couches, Chairs and Stools, 1660-1670', *Connoisseur,* 93 [January 1934], pp.15-23.
  'Charles II Couches, Chairs and Stools, Part II, 1670-1680', *Connoisseur* 93 [February 1934], pp.86-95.
  Cane Chairs of the late 17th and early 18th Centuries', *Connoisseur,* 93 [March 1934], pp.173-181.
  'Turkey work, Beech and Japanned Chairs', *Connoisseur,* 93 [April 1934] , pp 221-227.
  'Furniture from the Indies', *Connoisseur,* 93 [May 1934], pp.283-89.
  'Furniture from the Indies, Part II', *Connoisseur,* 93 [July-December 1934], pp.38-44.
  'The Craft of Japanning', *The Antique Collector* [September-October 1947], pp.149-154 and 172.
  'The Craft of Japanning – Part II', *The Antique Collector* [November-December 1947], pp.183-189.
  'English Cane Chairs – Part I', *Connoisseur* [March 1951], pp.8-15.
  'English Cane Chairs – Part II', *Connoisseur* [May 1951], pp.83-91.

TAIT, Hugh. 'London Huguenot Silver' in Scouloudi (Ed.) [1987], pp.89-112.
THORNTON, Peter. 'Back-stools and Chaises à Demoiselles', *Connoisseur,* 744 [February 1974], pp.98-105.
  'Some Neo-Carolean Armchairs at Ham House', *Furniture History,* X [1974], pp.7-11.
  'Upholstered evidence: or How the Members of the Furniture History Society came to assist in saving the remains of a Queen Anne Wing Chair', *Furniture History,* X [1974], pp.17-19.
  'The Parisian Fauteuil of 1680', *Apollo,* CI [February 1975], pp.102-107.
  'The Royal State Bed', *Connoisseur,* 195 [1997], pp.136-147.
  Seventeenth-Century Interior Decoration in England France and Holland, New Haven and London [1978].

Authentic Decor – The Domestic Interior, 1620-1920, London [1984].

Form and Decoration – Innovation in the Decorative Arts, 1470-1870, London [1998].

THORNTON, Peter and TOMLIN, Maurice. 'The Furnishing and Decoration of Ham House', *Furniture History,* XVI [1980].

THURLEY, Simon. 'The building of the King's Apartments', *Apollo,* CXL [August 1994], pp.10-21.

TRENT, Robert F. '17th-Century Upholstery in Massachusetts', in Cooke (Ed.) [1987], pp.39-50.

TURPIN, Adriana. 'Thomas Pistor, Father and Son, and Levens Hall', *Furniture History,* XXXVI (2000), pp.43-60.

WALTON, Karin-M. 'An Inventory of 1710 from Dyrham Park', *Furniture History,* XXII [1986], pp.25-80.

WANG SHIXIANG. *Connoisseurship of Chinese Furniture,* Hong Kong [1990].

WARD-JACKSON, Peter. *English furniture designs of the eighteenth century,* London [1958].

WELLS-COLE, Anthony. 'An architectural source for furniture decoration' *Furniture History,* XXI [1985], pp.16-18.

Art and Decoration in Elizabethan and Jacobean England, New Haven and London [1997].

WESTMAN, Annabel. 'Splendours of state: The textile furnishings of the King's Apartments', *Apollo,* CXL [August 1994], pp.39-45.

'Francis Lapiere's Household Inventory of 1715', *Furniture History* XXX (1994), pp.1-14.

WILLS, Geoffrey. *English Looking Glasses,* London [1965].

WILLS, Margaret and COUTTS, Howard. 'The Bowes Family of Streatlam Castle and Gibside and Its Collections', *Metropolitan Museum Journal,* 33 [1998], pp.231-243.

WILSON, Joan. 'A Phenomenon of Taste – The China Ware of Queen Mary II', *Apollo,* August [1972], pp.163-166.

WORSLEY, Giles. *Classical Architecture in Britain – The Heroic Age,* New Haven and London [1995].

YORKE, James. 'Archbishop Juxon's chair', *The Burlington Magazine,* CXLI [May 1999], pp.282-286.

INDEX